The Spiritual ROOT of the matter Is Found In me!

Cleansing Healing System

A type of spiritual anti-oxidant for those desiring to maintain their body, soul & spirit life in Christ

A reviving, renewing, restoring gift and teaching on spirit l fe activity to the body of Christ.

Acts 2.38 Eph 2.19–20 Ps 11.3

A Soul's Spiritual
Maintenance Study Guidance
Manual & Commentary to cleansing,
healing, wholeness, understanding for biblical
and spiritual soundness for the body, soul & spirit
life in Christ, in the midst of 2 spiritual kingdoms
operating among us

Job 19.28

Ps. 2.10, Eph 5.17
Eph 4.4–7 Corin 2.13,
Cor 12.6 Dt 4.9

Volume 1

All Rights Reserved By
Lord Ministry Services Staff

A practical, biblical and innovative way to guard & maintain one's soul spirit life from spirit impurities, defilement, violating and or undesired initiated spirit transfers – found in the cultures and communities of our society.

Copyright © 2012 by Pamela McKissack

The Spiritual Root of the matter Is Found In me!
by Pamela McKissack

Printed in the United States of America

ISBN 9781619967847

All rights reserved solely by the author. The author guarantees all contents are original and do not infringe upon the legal rights of any other person or work. No part of this book may be reproduced in any form without the permission of the author. The views expressed in this book are not necessarily those of the publisher.

Unless otherwise indicated, Bible quotations are taken from the King James version of the Bible.

www.xulonpress.com

Table of Contents

Part 1

Dedications and Thank you!	3
Introduction	13
Ancestral Stronghold Root Spirit Listings	15
Reasons for this precious gift from heaven	17
Root System Faith Method and Commands	22

Rejection	26	Haughtiness	64
Sorcery Grtoups Systems & Expressions	30	Jealousy	67
Anti-Christ	37	Lying	70
Fear	40	Heaviness	73
Infirmity	43	Deaf & Dumb	76
Whoredom	49	Slumber	78
Bondage	54	Death	80
Error	57	Opression	83
Perverse	60	Darkness	88

Part 2

Root System, Change the Strategy	95
Other Deliverance Methods	98
Evidence of Healing	101
Is Praise Underrated!	104
Glossary	106
Other dark spirit kingdom terminology	112
Other biblical solutions	122
Prophet in the heavenlies	00
Baal Brides	136
Nelson New Illustrated Dictionary	140
Spiritual History	143
Spirit molding	166
What's in a name	172
Suicide	176
Evil	179
Cities of Babylon	182
Ministry Sheet (all souls are mine)	186
Root of the Matter & Health Systems	187
Books/DVDs	191
Author	193
Roots Worksheet	192

For

Jesus

and

............the advancement of His extended Kingdom in the heaven and earth.

And the soundness of America's spiritual homeland security in Christ Jesus!

Then shall the end come when He shall have delivered up the Kingdom of God, even the Father, when He shall have put down all rule, authority and power.
Corin 15.24-28
Isa 33.10. Isa 42.8
Isa 42.1-4. Isa 52.8
Isa 62.10

Dedications & Thank you!

Neal thank you for your heartfelt commitment, prayers, strength and faithfulness to Christ and Him crucified (and to me also). Thank you also for the prayer support of others as well. Thank you for your encouragement for this work and service to the Lord! How could I have done it without you. Even the Lord said Himself, a faithful man <u>who</u> can find? Prov 20.6.

(Mt 25.21. Lk 16.10. Cor 4.2. Tim 1.12.2. Ps 31.23.)
Prov 28.20 says, A faithful man shall abound in blessings, so be prosperously blessed, in His name!

Naima and Niles I love you.

To our children, that you may understand and perceive by this writing that we are indeed spirit beings having daily human experiences with other (people) spirit beings that are continually expressing the position, personalities, characters and spirit natures of the spiritual kingdom they are choosing (willingly or by default-due to not learning how to guard, keep and protect their spirit life from dark spirit life activity that seeks, forces, violates and even will bring one into spirit domination to enlist others against their will to serve dark spirit operations) to represent a dark spirit kingdom here in the earth. Please remember and consider continually that even with all the spiritual confusion and vast opinions among the different religions with their "thinking/thought processes" and biblically questionable mindsets; that there are only 2 spiritual kingdoms operating in the earth, expressing itself through the cultures and communities of our society. All religions or non-religions will surely fit or will be spiritually forced into one or the other. The bible teaches and reveals that we shall judge spirits (and/or spirit activity). Corin 6.3 There are only 2 spiritual kingdoms by which all spirit life can be judged. Only 2. The majority of the angel spirits serve the operation of God's kingdom. The other angel spirits are fallen. Rev 12.7-9. 2 Pet 2.4. All religions, non-religious and spiritual belief systems will surely fit into one or the other. James 2.26. Corin 6.3.

To all mental health institutions and facilities of support, with the even-now continuing yearly rising statistics in case loads of intakes, especially in the areas of Bi-polar symptoms or conditions and growing depression among adults as well as our youth, considering that we are truly, foremost spirit beings (God is a Spirit and our Creator and source of all Spirit life), please consider, understand and perceive as you review this writing that you are dealing with mostly spiritual issues, conditions, symptoms and now another solution in Christ Jesus as it pertains to His complete work on the cross and Christ in us the hope of glory. Col 1.27 Spiritual symptoms and issues are resolved with spiritual solutions that only God himself can provide from His word and counsel can reveal in each generation. Eph 3.5 Eph 4.7. 1Tim 4.14. Acts 2.38. Pet 4.19. Isa 43.15. Ecc 12.1. Jere 10.10 Please consider this spiritual aide as a very possible, real solution and/or the possible breakthrough you've been looking for! Mt. 17.20. From much study and research, I too have found, like Kurt E. Koch, a Christian Counselor, that much of what you are dealing with seems to be foundationally spiritual and rightly so for all of life and living does, in fact, represent some level of and/or some area of spirit life and/or its activity. Kurt E. Koch is the author of, "Demonology Past & Present". Jn 6.53.

> Daniel answered and said, Blessed be the name of God forever
> and ever, for wisdom and might are His……
> He revealeth the deep and secret things. He knows what
> is in the darkness, and the light dwelleth with Him. Dan 2.20 & 22 & 28.

Once we can perceive the great need to gain the ability to learn how to process those more effectively with spiritual concerns because many tend to deal with spirit life:

• on the level they understand it or have learned it (whether right or wrong)

• some deal with spirit life based on personal interest (whether right or wrong)

• or based on spirit belief system acquired (perhaps due to any personal experiences and/or traditionally passed on family spirit beliefs-right or wrong)

And from many of these experiences, the concern is that many can be found sharing, their "spirit" life experiences however acquired not always gracefully (but in fact how they learned it). Some spirit belief systems were imposed upon them (due to the spirits operating in their life) and now (using them) to further impose (even traditionally) their spirit belief system on another even, at the expense of another person and/or generation bringing spiritual harm to many, until "truth" breaks questionable spirit life belief systems being passed on not based on truth but based on experiences, simply because there was not enough truth found in their experiences, evidently, perhaps until now to challenge unbiblical spirit life experiences and or traditions of men. May this writing speak to those areas also. Simply because, there are only 2 spiritual kingdom activities and operations among us. Only 2. And if our spirit belief experiences and/or family's traditional "spirit" belief system in not founded, foundationally on the truth of God's word and in line with the Spirit of truth then that only leaves the only other spiritual kingdom activity and spirit belief system that opposes biblical and spiritual truth. Hence, the reality of truth, found alone in Christ Jesus and Him crucified!

Even as a preventative maintenance, there is an extended need to be realized by reaching out with godly, biblical spiritual healing alternatives to the community and environment of those who are in your care to increase their awareness of the distinction of the 2 spiritual kingdom <u>agendas</u> operating among us and how it affects us whether we are in a religion or not. <u>Our society must begin to comprehend the extent to which spirit life is growing in its affect in our world and its inhabitants.</u> The bible reveals that demonic spirit activity can be recognized, measured and recovered from when the understanding and desire is there. Prov 3.15-26. Cor 12.7. Lk 9.1. One writer said of the darker spiritual kingdom that they are <u>trained to attack (directly or indirectly. Meaning, that depending on the level dark spirits are operating in a person's life (voluntarily, undetected or by force), spirit life can work with, through, around and/or in a persons life and/or through things to attack a person, realized or not)</u>. This is the spiritual dynamics of the operation of darkness, which will not go away just because we want it to but must be more effectively deal with; which can only come by a greater biblical understanding of spirit life activity.

Therefore, the different ways that dark spirits can and do attack can be on many spiritual and natural levels. Dark spirit life has the ability to transform its way into your body, soul and spirit life, situation and circumstances. Some attack directly from the spirit realm, independently or with help in the natural realm by those they have forced or cowered and made subject to their spiritual power abuse and/or among men who are in allegiance (hidden or revealed), or transmitting through men as conduits (through trance states) or as **gates** into our lives, whom they have literally trained to do their bidding by causing men to listen and take heed to their voice and/ or forced spirit power, obeying their (dark spirit initiatives/silent promptings) to move in the vicinity of the spirit lives of certain people by whose paths they have crossed or have been lured into so that the spirits can reveal themselves to their target are daily becoming real spiritual kingdom confrontations, challenges and concerns due to warring with seemingly, at first, with dark spirited friendly fire in and among cultures, families, churches and communities (expressions of society) and therefore make it needful and necessary to teach men how to guard and preserve their body, soul and spirit life or, if not continue to be victims of neglect/ innocence, ignorance, foolishness, spiritual bondage and captivity to these more common uprising **anti-social spirit** life occurrences in our day. Friendly fire in the sense that <u>dark angel spirits</u> have found, for the most part, seemingly (at first) in friendly (or personal) ways to attach themselves to those we know or whose path we cross, with hidden spirit agenda's that will eventually reflect the dark spirit's kingdom purposes in causing others to come under the same dark spirit allegiance they have been brought into. We are talking offensive (anti-social) outright-day-to-day open spiritual devastating intrusions and often hostile spirit take-over's of family, culture, church, community and all society at large by intelligent anti-Christ spirit beings representing a dark spirited (anti-social) government kingdom of fallen angels among us and in our world (and men in allegiance to it-voluntarily or involuntarily). One person at a time. Prov 16.17. Gen 22.1.7.

They (dark spirit life) through permission of the sins (ignorance, innocence and/or foolishness) of men; have broken into our society taking sin and wickedness of men to a new level, producing giants in the earth (and among us), where fallen angels union with men and/or are being spirit forced upon men. See Brother Swaggart's Expository Bible, Gen., Chpt 6.

Our bodies are not meant to house or union with "devil/demon spirit life". The condition or state of our spirit life; it's maintenance or non-maintenance is kept or not kept by our soul's efforts. Meaning simply that our like our bodies, our spirit and soul lives cannot maintain themselves especially in spiritually hostile environments. Neglect of maintaining one's soul and spirit life in Christ through daily scripture reading and biblical/spiritual disciplines of daily praise; prayer times and spiritual faithfulness to the Lord is proving detrimental to people's ability to hold on to the soundness and freedom of their soul and spirit life by faith in a risen Savior and allows those in Christ to be seen biblically as spiritually preyed upon by the only opposing spiritual kingdom and operation of darkness. This is the reality of living in the midst of 2 spiritual kingdoms operating in our midst. Prov 16.17. 1Jn 5.18. Acts 3.16. Dark spirit activity literally helps to create spirit impurities and diseases of the soul, body and spirit life. Continually unattended, ignored or neglect of these abilities and capabilities of dark spirit life activity is continually rising up against the people of our society (family, community, churches, etc) and nation as a whole and is helping to feed into the spirit operation of darkness.

Let us also understand and perceive that dark spiritual or spirited kingdom operations and activity is measurable and expressed by dark spirit abilities to keep cultures, families, communities and societies divided(disharmonious) and spiritually confused. Measured by corrupting the purist intentions and stealing the harmony out of what use to bring us comfort and peace. Measured by the broken hearts they plot in advance to destroy. They bring confusion to innocent tears and take away any mercy from wounded souls. Measured by sudden real (spirit) illusions (to the natural mind) by distractions, devastations and destruction that could not have been orchestrated and carried out, by no one but dark spirit activities, initiatives and agendas. Many now think that the spirit influences, activities and any sensed spirit presence among them, in many arenas, is God and therefore is being accepted as God. Many are seemingly being too spirit trained and conditioned by dark spirit life activity so that when the Lord tries to send in any truth by his spiritual kingdom protocol (the prophet, to help God's people get the understanding needed to get back on Kingdom course, Amos 3.5) it is quickly attacked, adding to the spiritual confusion. Even when I reveal by the Lord how to help any church (assigned by the Lord) how to regain God's spiritual dominion in their midst, from dark spirit training and conditioning (which is often attacked by folks and any belief system (truth or not) that does not fit in with the operation of darkness-or operation of men perceived as God, in their midst, but which biblically operates against God's Kingdom and biblical and spiritual system of God). Really, it doesn't seem like anyone has time to fight the good fight of faith because they are being too distracted by the operation of darkness in their midst with seemingly no clear biblical voice of truth because it's been removed by a dark spirited operation in their midst, yet God's Kingdom does not operate against itself.

These are some of the messes that the operation of darkness leave behind and make within and among families, cultures, churches, communities and lives they take and continual quiet noise they always seem to innocently instigate when everything was going well – <u>they are quiet storms</u> on a dark spirited mission to kill, steal & destroy <u>whenever</u> they come on the scene. <u>It's what they do</u>. This is another look, another perspective of the spiritual operation of the kingdom of darkness in our generation. Jn 10.10. So all we can do is our part, wherever the Lord leads us and then move on. Looking for faith in Jesus Christ & Him crucified, "just like Jesus". But, will He find faith when He returns?

Often, we find ourselves being given personal uninvited attention from seemingly just being there because dark spirit life are programmed to disturb by preying on men's souls, body and spirit lives. How to bring and keep another in dark spirit realm activity and devotions is their dark spirit quest and desire because those they use are in need of spiritual release and healing found only in Christ and Him crucified at the cross. Literally training men-often involuntarily, dark spirits use men to release their dark spirit natures through hard, channeled cold power stares or manifesting dark presence out of a captured and/or hounded through much transferring, trafficking and/or channeling dark spirit life powers and/or energies into the life of another as their method. Many seem to just let it happen, perhaps-too busy or tired to resist dark spirit life infiltrations, yet they are infiltrating to gain a dark spirit dominion in the life of a child of God, so that at the trumpet sound, when it is time to rise up with all the saints in the great day of battle, many will be overcome because they are not really (to the degree darkness has and is continuing to infiltrate) being trained to resist how dark spirit life is warring for their soul which only could leave one alternative, cooperating with it. What a seemingly "spiritual tragedy". Seemingly churches think they can affirm and confirm themselves, because when the Lord tries to come into their midst with a Holy Spirit protocol of God's Kingdom, they are again resisted by the spiritual infiltration of the kingdom of darkness. I wish this were an exaggeration. Dark spirit life activity includes releasing themselves whenever they get close enough to those with God's spirit nature and/or dormant souls (un-kept soul & spirit life) are some of the dark quiet **serpent ways** they attack among us, while you seem to be held in their presence by invisible, dark spirit sorcery pulls (a type of bewitchment – Acts 8.11) coming from bodies or souls or the environment or other's spirit lives that happen to be surrounding the situation at that particular time are some of the methods dark angel spirits are using to captivate, bewitch and eventually, spiritually connect or attach to, to begin to ensnare the soul and spirit lives of men in a dark attempt to secretly expand the operation of the kingdom of darkness happening among us. 2Cor 11.3 2 Pet 2.14. Isa 59. 7-8. Rev 16.10. Rev 18.2. Acts 8.11. Gal 3.1.

> They hatch cockatrice' eggs and weave the spider's web….
> Cockatrice is defined as a mythical serpent supposedly able to kill by a look. Isa 14.29-30.

These are some of the ways dark spirit activities are forcing their way into our lives, families, communities, societies; from nation to nation and our world among us. Part of their demonic system of processing and spiritually pressing those committed to Christ (even without their permission – they are being bewitched and/or are being pulled or drawn into dark spirit activity). A bewitchment is happening and going on in the midst of what people are calling church, daily drawing the church of the Lord Jesus into deeper and deeper depths of spiritual bondage. The church of the Lord Jesus, no longer knows – for the most part, how to receive Holy Ghost spiritual Kingdom protocol should the Lord send in a Kingdom prophet-yet the Kingdom of God **does not operate against itself**. Can we see the spiritual confusion getting and growing deeper and deeper? For the most part the churches of the Lord Jesus Christ have been too spiritually affected!). So I guess you could consider this writing a message and a method of Lord to once again, try to get biblical aide to His church but who "now" has a spiritual and biblically sound ear to hear! Souls of men, women and children alike are being more easily subject (without all of the gifts of God operating properly among us) to these <u>advanced ways</u> that darkness is using to take away the soul, body and spirit lives and destiny of men. Many lives have been so invaded that some can no longer enjoy one-on-one conversations with their loved ones or friends, because as soon as they do the spirits come down and interrupt and/or invade the simplest conversations and/or acts of kindness. By attempting to speak through the lives of those they thought they knew; only now voices are speaking through them, but it no longer sounds like those you've loved or known all your life. Now their behavior and voices and/or attitudes sound more cold, uncaring and often attacking (due to dark spirit initiatives trying to interrupt and invade a spirit and soul's (especially of those in Christ to bring disharmony and spiritual confusion against the true saints) life to press through, dark spirit kingdom initiatives, and instead of the saints stopping to resist the darkness, they allow themselves to be influenced for the sake of an illusion of spiritual harmony (feeding into dark spirited systems). Spiritual retraining is necessary, otherwise we will be found continuing to operate (and/or assist) in the wrong spiritual kingdom and lose by default. Yes. Does anyone understand the spiritual battle continually arising and intermingling among us. The only resisting I see (still) is the resisting of the Holy Ghost spiritual protocol of the prophet(s) of God's Kingdom due to the spiritual confusion being created among us! What is wrong with this picture? How can what we think is right and God be right at the same time if He is the one sending (trying to send) in the help we need? Do we need another century to figure out that maybe we are missing something, if God is trying to move among us, while we resist Him?

Sometimes, you simply have to come out of dark spirited environments that the dark spirits have attached themselves to in order to preserve your body, soul and spirit life in Christ because now our society is dealing more with daily dark spirit life operations-no longer as isolated or sometime incidences. And again, sometimes this is not readily possible, when you are dealing with those in dark spirited professions. Dark spirits can operate through spirit realms(created by them) using people, places and things. If we keep living, we find that those in dark spirit professions have the ability to pull many saints (one at a time) into dark spirit realm activities and spiritual battles that they are (presently) not seemingly being trained to withstand or stand and therefore, will be caught off guard. I say this by experience, that if it had not been for the Lord, I would be a casualty today, for this very reason. Mobile homes seem to be popular these days. But even then, people are simply taking the same dark spirits with them because <u>you have to spiritually release your body, soul and spirit life from them, cast them out and keep them out</u> in Jesus Name! Due to the lingering operation of dark spirit activity among us. I pray this writing find its way to you and bring you a new hope, peace, restoration and eternal recovery one day at a time. One soul at a time. In Jesus Name! Jn 10.10.

Often if we look closer, we can see and spiritually perceive (in a godly manner according to scripture) it is those in the environment and/or community from which patients are coming out of, that may also resemble the ones also needing spiritual healing and maintenance; that could have in fact helped (or have been unknowingly used spiritually) to bring the patient to the spiritual condition or present spiritual state of needing to be institutionalized or brought to the point of needing care. Simply because, people do not go crazy by themselves. Another dark spirit strategy, that helps to create and feed into the spiritual confusion. It is simply how spirits are operating among us. Lev 18.24-25:27-28. Mt 15.20: Mk 7.15. This is based on the thesis (proposition and truth to be biblically defended) that foremost; people are living in the midst of 2 (opposing) spiritual kingdoms. Both have 2 distinct and separate spiritual agenda's, which can no longer be hidden or ignored, both desire the souls of men. One lays claim by legal means because He is Savior, Lord and King. He commands us to have no other gods before Him. Dt 5.7. Ps 81.9. The other dark kingdom uses deceitful, deceiving and often spiritually violating, luring, bewitching and compelling, power-play (like tugs and/or sorcery pulls or manifestations through others in the spirit realm trying to steal your peace through spiritual mind transmissions, inceptions and/or continual disruption of your day, just to let you know that dark spirit activity is real) and other hidden quiet spirit ways to literally steal a man's soul, body and spirit life with NO warning. This is usually being done and/or initiated by those, mostly, in dark spirited professions, parading as ministers of light (in need of spiritual release and healing that has yet to be recognized among us) often to grab your interest and/or attention. 2Cor 11.15. A gradual behind the scene spirit degeneration (in allegiance with men) process among men that suddenly seems to reveal itself out of nowhere, the effects of which ultimately reflect, that dark angel spirits have been behind the scene spiritually operating all along. So lets take another biblical view. A closer look.

And when a soul refuses allegiance to dark spirited kingdom advances in their personal lives; dark angels can be assigned to press upon this soul and spirit life (even within the mind's thinking and thought processing system-though a process of spiritual mind harassment and spirit life invasion that can also come through men who never found out how to release themselves from spirit impurities and defilement) in a seemingly simultaneous manner to reveal and reflect their dark spirited intentions, strategy and agenda with men who are either in allegiance (usually of those who have been strangely elevated in dark spirited professions) to them or with men who seemingly may be losing their spiritual battles with dark principalic angel spirit assignments and are now being used by them. Help us Lord! <u>The best methods to stop dark spirited, spiritual kingdom conflicts, intentions and/or penetrating spirit attacks is to outright pray and praise God, like you mean it in their spirit face and/or behind closed doors if the enemy has found a way to attack you behind closed doors; the point is to resist at what point the spiritual kingdom conflict or opposition rises,</u> because spirits will always express their spiritual kingdom activities through available (dormant or suddenly spiritually hi-jacked captive) souls with or without their permission (especially those among us who are in dark spirited professions – who can gain the ability to hi-jack the souls of men (for sport), which I would not have believed unless I had witnessed this with my own eyes), with or without their knowledge to help satan's kingdom to operate among us. Many in dark spirited professions help to destroy the weak and literally take over the lives of the strong. This is why the bible tells us (and why we have got to gain the biblical and spiritual ability) to resist <u>them</u> because if you do not they will continue to spiritually impose (to gain spiritual inroads) into your body, soul and spirit life until you become spiritual captives <u>like them!</u> 2Pet.2.19 calls them servants of corruption. This is why I believe we will begin to see a lot of suddenly praises in our midst to invite and reveal that we serve a risen Savior who is able to come on the scene and preserve those that love Him! Amen! But, I have found that the praise must be initiated before the offense to bind arises. In this respect, timing is everything and practicing this tool of engagement makes perfect. Where we find that "timing is everything" when it comes to dark spirit life activity that seems to prize it-self in the many ways it uses to bind it's prey before their activity in a life can be discovered and/or recovered from. However, if we desire to remain spiritually free in Christ, we will sooner or later recognize and perceive our need to spontaneously praise as our Kingdom method to call upon Christ to intervene. Will it come to pass that the only <u>peace we will find, in the end times, is in our praise and hallelujahs!</u> Glory to God! James 4.7. Ps 22.3. Ps 46.1. Th 5.17. Th 5.23.

There is a difference in what appears and the truth that transforms us in Christ when the reality of the confrontational spiritual warfare and its adversarial affect among us (like those becoming mental because they do not know how to spiritually defend themselves in Christ when dark spirit life activity targets them or like the guy I heard that literally killed someone as a direct result of dark spirits influencing a person's life) really dawns on us, that NOW is the time to engage in spiritual warfare, with the weapons biblically given to us by Christ. We are in Christ as one and simply cannot lose from what Christ's finished work at Calvary has won! If we learn how to stand and how to not to give up resisting dark spirit advances in our lives and if we learn how to fight the good fight of faith in Christ and Him crucified and His complete work at the cross! In Jesus name. And even then, we are still at the mercies of the Lord because God gives grace to the humble. Lord, please strengthen us and teach us how to stand in the victories you have already for us, in Jesus name we pray! Tim 6.12. This is what this writing as an assignment from the Lord is designed to help us do. How to fight the good fight of faith and how to, having done all to stand therefore in Christ Jesus and His complete and finished work at Calvary! Amen.

Part of the concern that keeps presenting itself is that our society seems to want to continually over look, look the other way or find other solutions for the spiritual concerns among men by keeping spiritual issues in a natural pretense; **while hell works with this pretense,** to continue it's dark spirited intrusions, invasions, spiritual abuse that seems to disintegrate and transform into all levels of individual, family life and society at large through distractions and agenda among the minds, souls and spirit life and community of men and women to kill, steal and destroy the peace, love, strength and grace among families, churches and unity within and among cultures and communities, to find expressions in our society by not resisting it wherever it is actively found. In this sense are we not helping to empower dark spirit operations even against our society? The operation of the Kingdom of God helps to improve, strengthen our society and the souls of men individually and collectively, it seems however, there is a need to get a real grip in learning of spirit life activity and its significance in our world, that we do not be found continually to spiritually destroy that which we are continually trying to build, heal and strengthen in the natural.

God is a Holy Spirit. His Spirit brings rest, peace, hope, love, strength, soundness, wholeness and purity, etc.. He confirms and acknowledges those who are in His will and in line with His Kingdom operation and those who are not. He is the Lord. Founder of Zion! This is His work and this is what He does. Perhaps we can find comfort in remembering that darkness has an end but God's Kingdom is eternal and everlasting and is another reason to be encouraged in making sure that we are allowing the Holy Spirit to bring His spiritual Kingdom protocol (of the prophet) in our midst, when He sees fit that help us through the situations that arise in our journey and not get stuck in any areas along our (spirit life) journey.

Where does it teach in scripture that those whom the Lord decides to use to bring greater understanding in your midst, should only come from your inside church circle. What would be biblical about that? **What if the Lord needs to send someone with a greater understanding of the battle that you will be confronted with and seeing that your inner circle prophet(s) may not have that understanding, because often the Lord will allow them (whoever He trains) to first go through the particular battle coming your way and therefore will only send in those with the greater understanding, that can only come by walking through the battle itself with the Lord, Himself, leading the way into victory! Can we gain the spirit intelligence to allow the Lord to lead our**

way? This is a good place to shout church! Jesus is supposed to be head of the church. Where does it teach that the church (your church) is the head, leading its own way. The church must learn, re-learn God's spiritual, biblical protocol and operation so that dark spirit operations will no longer be able to continue to build dark spirit strongholds that we presently find resisting God's spiritual Kingdom operation, which does not oppose, nor operate against itself. Bless the name of the Lord. Cor 1.8&10. Cor 15.24. Gal 4.24.

> Can we pray as a nation for mercy, spiritual relief, reviving, recovery and restoration from this <u>apparent</u> plague of devil spirit invasion IN JESUS NAME! ……. www.<u>lordministries.org.</u>
> Ez 9.8. Isa 42.22. Rev 16.5. Ps 85.6

I pray this writing help those who have been trying to figure out how to work towards healing for their soul, body and spirit life from the contagious or assigned dark spirit transfers of trafficking, channeling and trance states of others so that they can willingly and effectively choose to serve God's Kingdom and not forced to serve hell's kingdom initiatives and agenda because they have not found out how to keep their spirit life free from the undesirable dark spirit transfers and trafficking into their body, soul and spirit life. Methods dark angel spirits are using among us to arrest, bewitch, control and take over the soul, body and spirit lives of men. Let us also consider that keeping one's body, soul and spirit life in Christ free in Christ is a part of our spiritual warfare.

Lord, we pray mightily for the recovery and release of any one ensnared by darkness , in Jesus mighty name!

Introduction:

A Great Ministry Concept in pruning, purging, and purifying the spiritual root tree of our lives to help sanctify and maintain the spirit fruit of our soul's life in Christ Jesus... Jn 15.2-Mt 3.8-Mk 11.20

I see men walking as trees.....as gardens by the river's side, as trees......which the Lord has planted besides the waters. Num 24.6. Mk 8.24.

> Blessed is the man that trusts the Lord
> And whose hope the Lord is, for he shall
> be like a tree planted by the water....Jere 17.7-8 2Kings 19.30

The fruit of the righteous is a tree of life...Prov 12.12. Prov 11.30

But in a great house there are not only vessels of gold and silver, but also of wood and of earth: and some to honor and some to dishonor.

If a man therefore purge himself from these, he shall be a vessel unto honor, sanctified and meet for the Master's use prepared unto every good work.

...A certain man had a fig tree planted in his vineyard and he came and sought fruit thereon, and <u>found</u> none. Lk 13. 6-9

And when the time of the fruit drew near, he sent his servants to the husbandman, that they might receive the fruit of it ... Mt 21. 34-43

The axe is laid at the root of the tree. Every tree which bring not forth good fruit is hewn down and cast out into the fire...Mt 3.10. What (spiritual) tree are you? Lk. 6.43-45.

....he was strong...yet I destroyed his fruit from above and his roots from beneath...Amos 2.9....Isa 14.29

Scripture, in a parable, reflect that men can be seen as trees; in which the man (Jesus) that plants the tree, returns sometimes at least three times to seek fruit, on any one tree ....Lk 13. 6-7

> Some will be plucked up. Some shall be cut off the tree of life, and some will be rooted out
> .... Prov 12.22 – Mt 15.13. Ps 129.4. Ps 54.5

The wicked shall be cut off and transgressors shall be rooted out ...Prov 2.22

The point is, is that no tree can maintain its body, soul or spirit life by neglect, ignorance or foolishness.... and must be guarded, cherished and protected, because there are:

2 Spiritual Kingdoms operating among us

He that is begotten of God keeps himself and the wicked one touches him not –
1Jn 5.18 Prov 25.4 Prov 16.17

Abide in me and I in you, as the branch *cannot bear fruit of itself*. Jn 15. 1-9….If a man therefore purge himself from these, he shall be a vessel unto honor, sanctified and meet for the master's use. 2Tim 2.21. Thess 5.23. Prov 16.6

We are to be rooted and grounded in love. Rooted and built up in him and established in the faith. Eph 3.17. Col 2.7

Yet many are hindered in their soul and spirit life by spirit impurities and therefore cannot or should I say are not able to express genuine love or kindness until they are first spiritually released to do so, perhaps from the spirit world activities that found ways to hinder another's soul and spirit life from its natural inborn instincts and abilities to love or express love unhindered

Let us learn together how to tend to the spiritual root of our souls and the spirit fruit lives of our character in Christ. Col.1.27.

Category of Ancestral Principalic Stronghold Root Spirits

1. Rejection (works in conjunction with its sister spirit "hate") Sam 10.19. Isa 53.3.
2. Sorcery Group Systems & Expressions: Baal, Wizard, Witchcraft, Divination, Necromancy, Familiar Spirits (spirit guides), Psychic/Occult i.e, things/works that are hidden, secret ,mysterious, which could include mystic arts, magic, gathering personal information for evil not good and such like=a work of idolatry and/or idols of devotion depending on where and/or who is the object of your faith. These things can operate through hypnosis – bewitchment, trafficking/channeling, trance states, conjuring and seducing spirit violations to cause another to be spiritually impure, defiled and/or violated. Mediums. Prophets of Darkness or False Prophets can and do work through any of the above expressions. Cor 10.14&21-23. Gal 5.19-21.
3. Anti-Christ
4. Fear
5. Infirmity
6. Whoredom
7. Bondage
8. Error
9. Perverse
10. Haughtiness
11. Jealousy
12. Lying
13. Heaviness
14. Deaf & Dumb
15. Slumber
16. Death/Destruction
17. Oppression
18. Darkness

These bear record....... Rom 10.2 & 4. Rom 11.17-22. Rom 12.1-2. Act 26.20. Mt 3.8.

This is the spirit flesh fruit and roots grounded in the operation of darkness that is dividing and producing spirit fruits of division and devastation in individuals, families, churches, communities, cultures, cities, nations and society at large. A spirit work, according to the word of God, which will be cut off and rooted out. Prov. 2.22. Lk 11.17. Lk 11.2. Rom 16.17-18. Mt 6.10.

The bible also reveals we are to speak the same thing.... that every tree which brings not forth good fruit ...... the axe (judgment) is laid to the tree, because the root of the righteous is supposed to yield fruit (good fruit). Prov.12.12. Mt 3.10. 2Cor 10.3 1Cor 1.8-10. Mt 8.12. Jn 12.31. Mt 6.10. Ecc 12.14.

Pruned   Purged   A Place of Grace

These are the root spirit strongholds and spirit flesh fruits that are constantly trying to rule our lives, souls, situations and even destiny. Eph 2.2. The spirit root and fruit activity can also be seen as spiritual conditions of one's soul and spirit life and even a deeper condition or place found coming from any family root spirit strongholds that has passed into one's spiritual "state", meaning not everything that everyone is dealing with is by their choice, but by choices (whether good or not) that we make and/or that we have allowed others to make concerning us the accumulation of choices, which encompasses the choices that were made from previous and ancestral generations. Sometimes discovery must be made.

The root of the matter can be seen as a godly (biblical) method **to make room** for the healing presence of the Lord; to help spiritually inoculate oneself from the effects of growing dark operations among us (the transfer and trafficking of spirits – "which is a present day fetish of dark spirit activity") and a way to spiritually off-set the effects of having to be around dark environments and the up-close and personal psychic soulish seizes of Sorcery Group activities and professions of darkness. There is a process in keeping one's soul and spirit free, cleansed and healed from dark angel spirit activity. Yes, Jesus Christ and Him, crucified paid the price for sins and released blessings. Yet, like many others, I wondered why certain people were not able to hold to certain healings (seemingly on any level). I was puzzled for a long time then the Lord finally told me that you can't cast out an operation you must be healed from it. Just as there is a process that the operation of darkness does or uses in its approach and desire to spiritually violate, and defile the soul and spirit lives of men through trafficking, channeling and transferring dark angel spirits into the lives of men as a method to draw and enlist a soul to serve and by-which to increase the operation of darkness or leave a soul in a psychotic and/or mental states that resist their process or cause to become to spiritually weak to guard their soul's spirit life....are only some of the things happening among us that one must be healed from.

The root strongholds listed can be found in the King James Bible or corresponding translations. The spirit fruit listed for each root spirit was compiled from deliverance ministers, ministry or based from scriptural situations in context relevant to the root stronghold, and present revelation received from the Holy Spirit. Efforts were made to find scripture for each spirit fruit to reveal scripturally that there is nothing new under the sun and a new consideration to what Jesus meant when He said, the words that I speak are spirit and life. Due to the time constraints spirit fruit not yet listed with scripture, will need to be released under a separate writing and/or a Volume II of this book, as it becomes available considering that revelation is ongoing, forthcoming and key to spiritual maturity, growth, authority and breakthrough. Mt 16.18. Corin. 10.4. Ecc 1.9. Jn 6.63.

Acts 2.38

Biblical reasons for this precious gift from Heaven

Sound reasons to incorporate this soul/spirit system into your prayer time
The Root System bears witness to Truth. Jn 8.32 & 36

Scripture reveals that the time will come when they will not endure sound doctrine. This can readily and fore see-ably occur when you consider that we are spirit beings and that (many have been collecting spirits) without knowing how to release themselves. Some still may not think it necessary seemingly due to a limited biblical knowledge and the need for personal spiritual release. In this respect and for this reason <u>The Spiritual Root of the Matter is Found in Me</u>, can help us to uncover the Excellency of the treasure of Christ in each one of us from dross or spirit impurities transferred, channeled or perhaps traditionally inherited and because of this many are in need of soul, body and spirit cleansing, release, healing, reviving and recovery. Seemingly, we tend to view and process things differently, when we are at rest, rather than restless. Many have yet to consider that once they learn how to find healing for their soul's spirit lives, many other areas or perspectives of their lives will come into focus (a right or biblical focus). Ps 138.7 Cor 5.7-8. Isa1.26. Jere 15.19.

Often we find we struggle to reflect a pattern of good works regarding the body, soul (mind: thought & thinking processes, will, memory, emotion/desires, imagination, etc.) and spirit until we receive the healing we need. Titus 2.7. Some may struggle with etiquette concerning their tongue and therefore, can be rash with their words because their tongue is in need of healing and somewhere in their spirit lives they need a release. James 1.19.

<u>The Spiritual Root of the Matter is Found in Me</u> can help you to know and/or discover the level of your soul and spiritual state, condition and necessary healings realized and needed from a biblical and spiritual standpoint (through the eyes of the Lord). Because this system has the ability to teach us how to make room for the Lord in our lives, some have found that He has a way of calming what we thought were storms, naturally and spiritually so, when we make room for Him. This system also has the ability to help us find a place of rest in Him. Really! Simply put. <u>We still need the Lord!</u> This system seems to almost put us back into the sheep of His fold. Bless the Lord. Phil 2.19-20. Ps 138.8. Cor 11.31. Mt 12.45 Mt 15. 18-19. Lk 11.26. Ez 34.31.

It reflects an up-to-date and effective way of demonstrating how the principles of binding and loosing can help release the wounded and un-surrender parts of the body, soul and spirit life, relationships, circumstances and situations in life that one might find themselves. Ps 102.20. Mt 16.19. Isa 52.2. <u>The Root of the Matter is Found in Me</u> can also help cleanse, release and heal one from secret (hidden) and or presumptuous sins; even the area that the Lord may be desiring for us to deal with. At last help is here. We believe it is possible to reverse any negative spirit DNA activity, if the desire, determination and will is there with the Lord's help. Can we say thank you Lord! Ps 19.12. Sam 23.9

<u>The Spiritual Root of the Matter is Found in Me</u> has the God given ability and potential through faith and consistent commitment and determination to stop unfavorable Ancestral Stronghold Root Hereditary, cultural, community or group spirits from continuing to travel generational-y and contagiously within and through family, community, culture or any size people group ultimately affecting society

at large in a spiritually healing and positive way (Pet 4.11). This system can help strengthen your spirit abilities and discernment in God to resist dark invading spirits that greatly desire to find any expression in one's body, soul and spirit life of men. It is possible to overcome stronghold spirit obstacles, in Jesus Name. 1Jn5.4. Mt9.22. Prov 18.14. Lk 1.37.

The conscious is the faculty by which one should enable us to discern right and wrong. Often our unbiblical and/or unspiritual belief systems, friends, fellowships, community, family traditions, cultures or society itself (through media) will have a louder (spirit) voice and effect than the word of God. 2Ki 19.22. The knowledge of God's word, in many areas and arenas of life, must be engaged, rediscovered, revisited, recovered, studied and mediated upon and its rightful place found, to bring our body, soul and spirit life, even the spirit of our nation back into realignment with the will and purposes of God.

It's been said that the word of God works from the inside out and then reaches out to help renew our body, soul and spirit life according to His will, purpose and destiny. This manual and guidance tool will help us to see how some can be born again of God's spirit, filled with the Holy Spirit (or baptized) and still be gripped by bondages in either of the body, soul, spirit realm and/or environments. As commanded by the Lord, this system helps us teach the people of God how to more clearly distinguish between holy and profane…..clean and unclean things. Ez 44.23. Scripture reveals that we are bought with a price, yet the need to learn how to effectively protect, preserve and glorify our body, soul and spirit life in Christ is ever present. This system, along with our Advance Prayer Root System Method of praying, can also help to biblically and spiritually position you in a place to make room for the Lord to perfect that which concerns us. This system also helps us to learn how to find the "rest" of the Lord; thereby calm the things that need to be calmed in your life. **He is able**.
Mt 11.28&29. Mt5.45. Cor 6.13&20. Ez18.4. Ps 107.29. Heb 7.25. Ecc. 12. Dan 3.17.

So the issues still to be considered is that once one is born again and baptized by the Holy Spirit; how can one love, if a person is still troubled in their soul and spirit life by spirits and spirit life activity that push people to hate? How can one stop feeling hurt or always feeling wounded except they are first released in their soul and spirit life from dark principalic angel spirits and their activity, unclean and or familiar spirits that continually play back daily reruns of the pains and painful incidents; or how can one stop killing, or stop having the desire to kill except they are first set free or released in their soul and spirit lives from spirits that are programmed or emotionally designed to cause, by producing in you, the desire to kill.

How can people stop outright racial and prejudice without being first released from radical racial and prejudice spirits? Spirit life can live without a body but the body needs the Spirit breath of life to live. However, biblically we understand that Spirit life in Christ is not in allegiance to every spirit (even though all spirit life come from God, however some angel spirits are fallen). 2Pet 2.4. There are different levels and functions of spirit life that can and do profoundly affect out world and its inhabitants, Therefore, the reality of 2 spiritual kingdoms operating among us should be taught due to the unveiling impact in our world realized by all or not, does not seem to be the issue. Simply because spirit life whatever level it is operating within your life will always express the will and desire of the spiritual kingdom to which it is designed through allegiance to serve. Again stressing the importance, for one to gain the ability to release oneself from spirit impurities, defilement and/or spiritual violations. This truth causes us to take more seriously the spiritual meaning of the Christ crucified life, death, resurrection and our authority in Christ in maintaining, protecting, preserving and even holding onto our spirit life liberties in Christ from dark spirit advances and the pursuits of the operation of darkness against a soul. God created us in His (Spirit) image. There are no racial or prejudice spirit images in Christ's Spiritual Kingdom or image. However, there are radical racial and prejudice spirits that reflect the fallen spirit images and idols of darkness. Therefore, those <u>still</u> openly expressing racial and prejudice issues <u>are really revealing</u> their need for spiritual release, cleansing (or deliverance) and spiritual healing from radical racial and prejudice demon spirit impurities and the defilement they cause to oneself and society. James 2.4. This could also be a good example of an ancestral stronghold spirit that could have spiritually and behaviorally reproduced, transferred and traveled generationally working division through family or within and among cultures, communities or any size people groups. This also works behaviorally where dark spirit angel life and activity desire to express their dark spirit life and dark spiritual kingdom governing agendas among men and through men. Their process to spiritually reproduce themselves among us can be gentle, or what I call palatable (or subtly transforming) to taking or using very aggressive (channeling/trafficking) violent spiritual means, including spirit trance states and other ways like transmittal meditation, deceitful tactics and methods to gain entry (and/or inflict as much influence as they can) into any body, soul or spirit life that they are desiring, pursuing, hunting and/or have targeted. The latter found more so among those in dark spirited professions and from the way things are going, would it be wise to assume that people can figure out how to resist dark spirit pursuits and ever increasing soul and spirit hunts that are happening now among us, especially by those in dark spirited professions who do not have a problem drawing and keeping the people of God in dark spirit realms (by constantly warring against them with penetrating spirit attacks). This is happening now. Present day, biblical spirit life activity must be taught in light of 2 spiritual kingdom activities operating among us. No matter the religion. Not doing so continually (as history continues to repeat itself in this area) has helped to cause satanism to be one of the fastest growing religions in our world. Rom 14.12. Dt 5.7. Ecc 12.14. Prov 28.5. Malachi 3.18. Prov 15.16. Prov 3.7. Ps 60.4. Rom 8.10. Gen 37.4. Mt 28.18. Ps 24.1. James 2.26. Job 33.4.

Spirit life in Christ must be maintained and guarded internally and externally; whereby when spirits can't get you internally, then they will so try to spiritually penetrate your outer spirit realm (within your environment) so that they (dark spirit life) can gain the ability to come down and influence your behavior at will. The next writing "The Advanced Prayer Root System", will deal more with the more spiritually aggressive ways dark spirit life will pursued a life to cause spiritual bondage and thereby creating servants of corruption. 2 Pet 2.19.

Scripture reveals that maintaining one's spirit life (through a biblical/spiritual cleansing process – which now must be related, relational and translated into new testament times, as the Lord would reveal the need), by sending in His Kingdom apostolic protocol into needed areas, as a present truth; instead of cleansing through the killing and sacrifice of animals, since the sacrifice of Christ at Calvary has been satisfied and accomplished, cleansing now comes through the word and blood of Christ and Him crucified. 2 Pet 1.12. Corin. 2.2.

Brother Jimmy Swaggart's, **<u>Expository Study Bible</u>**, reveals to us in Exodus 40.7:

> And you shall set the Laver between the tent of the congregation and the Altar and shall put water therein. (The revelation: the Priests, upon entering the Holy Place, which they did constantly

had to wash their hands and feet in this water each time they went in, signifying the cleansing by the Word, which is needed by all Believers and constantly). Eph 5.26.

> Wherewithal shall a young man cleanse his way, by taking heed thereto according to Your Words. (The revelation: The applied Word alone can cleanse). Ps.119.9. Jn 1.1.

His words are spirit and life. His life is in the blood. Jn 6.63. Jn6.54. Lev 17.11. The ministry of the apostolic prophet is sent and comes in the season needed to communicate the will and purposes of the Lord and the desires of the King, Christ and Him crucified, to keep us on track and spiritual course. Heb 6.20. In these days and times, it is crucial that we learn to receive this gift, that is sent to help us stand in battle and win the war that continues to wage against us. Amos 3.6-7. Hosea 12.10. Eph 3.5. Hosea 4.6. Ecc. Thus Sayeth the Lord God:

> The Lord is still "Holy"! Isa 42.8

Whatever, the situation the root of the matter soul's spirit maintenance system, along with the "The Advanced Prayer Root System" will help you to understand:

1. How to get <u>out of agreement</u> with the operations of darkness and resist dark angel or evil spirit activity that may be desiring your attention.

2. How the principles of binding and loosing can help you get pass those sensitive or personal hard to surrender (causing one to live in a spiritual rut or stuck place) or wounded areas and why certain spirit fruit need pruning, which should and can affect your healing process. A soul's spirit maintenance system that will help strengthen and preserve your soul and spirit life and help to create the glory of God in a life which will be needed in these last days as our defense against the operations of darkness… A spiritual system that you will be able to pass on in an effort to help preserve and spiritually strengthen the next generation. All you basically need is mustard seed faith, continual hope in God, coupled with daily bible study, prayer & devotion of praise and desire to stay with the Lord (revealed and reflected in one's lifestyle the attitudes of the heart) Mt. 13.31. Isa 40.5. Mt 12.34. Heb 11.6.

These ideas listed above were more on a personal and/or, individual level and the need to learn of spirit life activity. However, on a spiritual warfare level we could seriously consider that keeping one's body, soul and spirit life free from spirit impurities, defilement and violations (that can secretly come anytime and from anywhere at unaware) **is key to maintaining our strength and position of authority in Christ and His complete work in the cross, through and during any level of spiritual warfare.** The enemy is secretly using his powers (or the power of his presence in these last days (concentrated, penetrated powers, trafficking, channeling powers and trance state released powers) strategically and in strange ways, to war against the saints, hoping to spiritually disable them, before they realize they have been spiritually weakened by the enemy through these various avenues, just listed. This means, in a nut-shell, <u>that we can no longer ignore the slightest impression of any secret types of spirit manifestations upon our body, soul and/or spirit life and relationships because ultimately, it will be the sum total of its affect that will have the ability to disable us at a time,</u> when all of us are needed. And often, because of this, the enemy is able to use the saints of Christ to literally war against themselves. The enemy is secretly using spirit penetrations to attack the saints while asleep or awake! <u>The Spiritual Root of the Matter is Found in Me and The Advanced Prayer Root System</u> will prove to be a spiritual safeguard (discovered on the front line while battling with the operation of darkness) from the quiet or subtle attacks of the enemy that many are not yet able to discern, seemingly due to a lack of understanding of the spirit activity operating among us (<u>and therefore are not being trained to resist the reality of how darkness is warring against us</u>) because of the quiet spirit and aggressive spirit attacks the enemy has been releasing among us, much of which, seemingly are being ignored and/or overlooked.

This writing then, along with <u>The Advanced Prayer Root System</u> among other things, is to help equip the saints to resist various levels of spiritual warfare. To help you resist personal strongholds and/or grips of darkness. To help you resist ideological, philosophical and/or territorial levels of spiritual warfare. 2 Tim 15-17.

A personal stronghold could be considered anything that would hinder you (this would include spoken word and/or actions of others or of oneself) from doing and/or being what God has called, designed and equipped you to be.

Territorial strongholds can work through the mindsets of people in any particular territory……
to keep out truth and fortify the lie (being exalted) over truth. Jn 8.32. Jn 14.6. Jn 18.37.

There can be philosophical doctrines (or teachings using bewitchment) that satan can impose on a people (this is happening now behind most secret society type of organization, yoga systems, lodges and societies, etc., to keep people under deception. Currently, the enemy is using and imposing his presence (through dark spirit life activity) manifesting and/or infesting people individually, through groups, cultures, customs, organization, religion, etc., that are silently moving people into dark spirit belief systems, initiatives, agenda and/or ideologies, etc., and not a word is being spoken for/or against it but the spirit activity is operating on a level above and below most spiritual and biblical intellects, proven by the growing spiritual deception happening before our eyes in many secular and religious arenas. A secret and/or quiet work of spiritual bewitchment (or dark spirit manifestations or infestations) that are individually and/or collectively moving people into position(s) and/or higher levels within the operation of darkness that is silently (or so it seems) yet literally, opposing the operation God's Kingdom. A type of dark spirit life molding being intertwined within various secret societies, religious and non-religious activity, dark spirit belief systems are still being taught, and where Jesus Christ nor the cross is not being acknowledged (even spiritual networking to accomplish this) is happening and operating among us. Just to stay spiritually un-tangled and free from it in Christ Jesus, is proving to be a great source of warfare for many ideologically, philosophically, territorially, biblically (and spiritually). A great fight of faith that works much patience! Lk 21.19. Heb 6.12. James 1.3&4. There seems to be a real need for people to revisit the condition or state of their spirit life activity in light of the truth of God's word and spirit life in Christ in line with His word as a witness. Simply because, the Kingdom of God's system never operates against itself.

<u>It is written:</u>

If they listen not to Moses and the prophet, neither will they be persuaded, if one rose from the dead, is still a present truth today. 2 Pet. 1.12.

Root System Method

(We are to overthrow the works of darkness and break down their (spirit) image. This root system helps to do just that. Ex.23.24. He that keeps (maintains) his way preserves his soul). Prov. 16.17. 2Chr 25.8.

The following list can be used generically after reading each root stronghold category to help with the ministry process of spiritual cleansing, deliverance, release and healing for each category.

(Also, you are free to take pauses as the Lord leads, when you go through each root and fruit spirit listing. If other spirit fruit comes to mind you are free in Christ Jesus to add to the list and you may remove what you may sense is no longer needed, to personalize it). Also, you can supplement the faith commands below with our "WASH" Flow Chart.

Also, I have found this page and the page following of faith commands a great tool to copy and carry with you to help those around you in community and marketplaces, etc. when spirits may try to rise just because you(or any particular one) come on the scene to cause others to begin to crowd you and or pull you into a dark spirit realm and is the purpose dark spirit life are using others as their spirit method among men (with unmaintained or captured spirit lives) to pull others into dark spirit realms. Confessing faith commands could also help to bind the dark spirit life and realms from trying to bind you. This would also work along with breaking forth in praise to help keep you from being over powered by dark spirit raids in the environment and or through men, as our method in Christ Jesus to make room for the Lord to come into your experience. Ps.46.1.

Jesus said, these words I speak are spirit and life. As you notice others around you being affected by dark spirit life simply begin to read these faith confessions, appropriately (when needed is considered appropriate) as you go about your business, perhaps in a way revealing that you are more concerned with reading your confessions (that will shortly affect any spirit life trying to rise in the area), begin these confessions unto the Lord right on the scene and you will begin to notice people literally being released from hindering spirit raids on the scene. Thereby revealing that, all spirit life are affected by the words of Jesus spoken in faith it becomes our protection, guard and shield. Because His words are spirit and life! Eph 6.6. Jn 6.63. Bless the name of the Lord.

It would be a good idea to receive Jesus as your Lord and Savior, if you have not done so, according to Rom 10.9. This may also be a good time to repent from allowing (knowingly or not) any root and spirit fruit activity room to develop in your life without resisting it. Lk. 13.5. And, forgive anyone who helped to produce any questionable root and spirit fruit activity into your life and ask the Lord to set them free, for His mercy endures forever. And may the Lord bless their area of need, for there is not one alive that does not need the Lord. Col 2.13. Col 3.13. Hosea 13.4.

Please Note: During the process of binding and loosing of any ancestral and/or spirit fruit or principalic root strongholds, cause any mild and/or strong reactions to arise and where it appears the person being ministered to could be struggling to get a release or if the person being ministered to suddenly begins to manifest by a stiffening of any body part, or by vigorously shaking their head side to side, giving the impression that the spirit does not desire to leave. This could be a spirit response to hinder release. Therefore, it may be helpful to express the following or similar faith commands with authority and faith in the name of Jesus. Persistently, repetitiously, until release and/or peace occurs. Mt 16.19. Lk 9.1. 2Tim 2.26. Jn 11.44. I bind, loose and release hidden, secret or dormant spirits to go in Jesus name.

Faith Commands Begin

I sever and divide any connected principalities, wicked, evil and unclean spirits in Jesus name. Mt 12.26. I bind and break by the blood and name of Jesus any holds, defiance... resistance... grips...hardness...etc., of any demonic principalic spirit wills....and any demonic desires to hinder release in Jesus name. I bind, break by the blood of Jesus and cast out hidden, secret or dormant spirits in Jesus name. Phil 2.10. Lk 9.1. Mk 3.25-27.

I bind and break the power of any, stubborn hateful spirits by the blood of Jesus that do not want to let go. In Jesus name. I cut off any principalic sorcery and/or bewitching powers trying to work through witchcraft, divination, necromancy, psychic, occult, magic, familiar spirits, rulers of the darkness, evil angels, etc. or dark trinities from the powers of the air. I bind and cast you out in Jesus name. Mt 16.19. Ps 54.5. I drive you out of the body, soul, spirit life, relationships and environment in Jesus name. I resist you in Jesus name! Jesus is the head of all principalities and powers and I am complete in Him who is the head of all principalities and powers. And an ever present help in time of need, in Jesus name. Ps.46.1 Col 2.10. Pet 5.8. Pet 5 8-9. Rev 18.2. Sam 15.23. Jn 2.15. Ps27.22. James 4.7. Dt Chpt. 18.

(Also, whatever spirit nature is being revealed or arises you can call out that name or just be led by the Holy Spirit)

If resistance continues, simply begin to speak out any of the scriptures of authority (listed below) and then go back to using the resistance statements above until hell backs off and peace is restored. In Jesus name. The following consistent truths applied skillfully with understanding in a repetitious manner can cause a hammering effect and help bring our confessions into our healing experiences. You can be as determined as you need or desire to be. Jere. 23.29. Pet 5 8. James 4.7. Mt 8.8. We have power and authority in Christ Jesus to resist dark angel spirit powers (DAS) in Jesus name. Lk 9.1. However it is very necessary to gain the ability to apply ourselves in these biblical truths and faith principles, in Jesus name. Corin. 12.7. James 4.7. Jude 20. Rom 15.13. Angels, dominions, principalities and powers were created by and for Him therefore subject to Him. In Jesus name. Col 1.16. Pet 3.22.

Have faith in God! Mk 11.22. Let us remember to also worship Him in the gates of our lives (and/ or where dark spirit life tries to rise, either in the spirit realm or through men that have yet to learn how to maintain their spirit lives in Christ Jesus) as another method of having done all to stand, in these last days! Ez 46.3. Ps 100.4. Rev 14.7. Isa 61.3. Ps 9.3. 2Chr 20.21.

****

Other Faith Commands

Signs follow those who believe. Mk 16.16 & 20. Eph 6.16. Tim 2.8

It is written:

Submit to God, resist devil (spirits) and they will flee. James 4.7. Eph 4.27. Greater is He that is in me than he that is in the world. 1Jn 4.4. Thou shall have no other gods before Him. Dt. 5.7. Exo. 20.

Lord, you said you would cut off my enemies in truth. Ps 54.5. That you would cut off the spirit of princes. Ps. 76.123. Ps 37.22. That you would cut off the remnant of baal. Zeph. 1.4. Now is the judgment, now shall the prince be cast out. Jn 12.31. Phil 2.11.

Faith Commands

I have been delivered from the powers of darkness and translated into the kingdom of God's dear Son. Col 1.13. We are to give no place (room, time, spirit space, thought, voice, position, etc.) to devil (spirits). Eph 4.27. It is written to have no fellowship with devil spirits. Eph 5.11. Cor 10.20. Greater is he that is in me than he that is in the world. 1Jn 4.4.

Jesus said, be holy for I am Holy. Pet 1.16. I have the keys to the kingdom....Mt 16.19. God anointed Jesus, who went about healing all that were oppressed of the devil, for God was with him. Acts 10.38. Jesus came to destroy the works of the enemy....1Jn 3.8. Lev 20.7. Jesus said, the body is for the Lord and the Lord for the body. Cor 6.13. Heb 12.9. Jesus said, all souls are mine. Ez 18.4. That even the captive of the mighty would be set free. Isa 49.25. The Lord has promised to cut off my enemies in truth. Ps 54.5. The Lord has promised to subdue those who rise up against me. Ps 18.39. He is Lord of all! Acts 10.36.

I break any principalic root and command the spirit fruit to come out in the name of Jesus. I cast you out of the breath of the mouth, nostrils and body pores. Mk 16.17. Lk 9.1 decree that I have power and authority over all devil (spirits) in Jesus name. Jesus broke the staff of the wicked in Isa 14.5. Lk 9.1. Our weapons are mighty through God to the pulling down of strongholds. 2 Corin 10.4-5. Where the word of the King is there is power. Ecc. 8.4. Rom 8.17. Ps 46.1. Prov 14.19. It is written: He upholds all things by the power of His word. Heb 1.3. Through the greatness of His power shall the enemy submit. Ps. 66.3. Jude 20. Corin 12.7. No weapon formed against us shall prosper. In Jesus name. Isa 54.17. Feel free to add and insert your own favorite scriptures of authority.

I release the anointing of God to search our environment, the inward parts of our body, soul and spirit to bring release. In Jesus name. Mt 28.18. Faith is our victory. 1Jn5.14. Mt 9.29. Cor1.24. We overcome by the blood of the lamb and word of our testimony. Rev 12.11. Acts 19.17. Cor 12.7. Isa 10.27. Mk 6.7. Mt 8.16. Lk 9.1.Mk 16.16 & 20. Mt 12.29. Jesus rose from the grave in all power and authority. Mt 28.18.

I bind divide, break any holds, defiance, resistance, rebellion, dark covenants, grips, desires and forbid any communicating and help between (ancestral) principalities, spiritual wickedness, rulers of darkness or any demon will to hinder release and I cut off their work from the power of the air and cast it out in Jesus name. Lk 9.1. 2Tim 2.26. I loose (.....)from any deception, delusion, illusion, magnification or obsession of darkness, wrong stronghold principalic patterns of thinking and every wicked and evil spirited imagination, memory, inclination, spirit vision, wrong desires, will, attitudes and belief systems produced by any (ancestral and/or) principalic root and spirit fruit activity. In Jesus name. Mt 16.19. Isa. 52.2. Jere 48.42.

Feel free and encouraged to repeat the commands ……as often as necessary until release and/or peace occurs. Mt 22.21. Or, from here you can go to our individually marketed "Wash" Flow Chart, to continue plowing through the darkness, until release and/or peace occurs, in Jesus name.

Holy Spirit come with your healing power and might. Purge, wash and cleanse us as we make room for you. Isa 1.16. Eph 5.26. 2Cor 7.1. Heb 9.22. We make room for you to come restore and make us whole. Rom 13.14. Free us completely in our body, soul, spirit life and relationships. In Jesus name. That we may serve you without reproach……without defilement, breach, interruption, transgression or presumption. IJN. Then shall we be upright, for we are the redeemed of the Lord. Lord we thank you for power and authority over all devil (spirits). IJN. We thank you for power to tread upon serpents and scorpions and over all the power of the enemy and nothing by any means shall harm us. IJN. Lk 9.1. Lk 10.19. Ps 107.2. Ps 86.4. Ps 62.1. Ps 143.6&8. Jere. 23.29. Pet 5.8. James 4.7. Mt 8.8 Ps 19.13. Corin. 5.7-12. Corin. 6.11. Eph 5.26. Jere 17.14. Ps 147.3. Ps 65.3. Isa 27.9.

****

*Fallen angels, biblically, are considered cursed spirits and must be commanded to leave (allowing them to stay in your life can cause a curse to come into your life). Mt 25.41. 2Pet 2.4.

Fallen dark spirit angel spirits will try to become, spirit gods or idols, through a process and series of mind (and/or psychic realm) invasions and forced spirit intrusions by certain ones in dark spirit professions. Let us remember to thank the Lord for any and all releases. Col 4.2. Ps 136.1-2&26. Phil 4.6.

Confidence in faith commands should grow (through daily meditations, scripture readings, praise and prayer times) with the Lord. A biblical, godly system of maintenance for the body, soul, spirit life and relationships in Christ Jesus. Eph 3.12. Gal 5.10. Heb 10.35. 2Tim 2.15. Corin 1.8. Corin 14.2&4. Jn 7.38. Let us remind each other to release the blessings of the Lord after each ministry session. We honor the Lord when we honor each other. Ps 129.8. Note: Godly angels do not desire to be idolized. Rev 19.10. They point to truth and refer to scripture. Dan 10.21:9.22.Heb 1.6.

Hate is a work of the flesh. Gal 5.20. Exo 20.5. 1Jn 2.11. 1Jn 4.20-21. Without spiritual release the symptoms of hate grow into perpetual hate issues and concerns when there are no consistent releases especially when a perpetrator is consistently releasing spirits into someone's life and/or if spirits could be using anyone or someone to transfer or traffic hate spirits into a life. Having a multiplying affect. Ps 38.19. Sometimes this type of spirit activity must be discovered before there can be a release otherwise, it will transcend into a reality in any life from there filtering into our world. Likewise some homosexual spirits also have this ability to reproduce itself when there are no consistent releases from spirit impurities and/or defilement in Jesus name. Gen 1.21. Jn 1.3. Dark spirit life activity can work independently, depending on how much they can accumulate into one's soul and/or spirit life of any subject being used or targeted. That's the nature or another aspect of spirit life activity and reason spirit lives of people must be maintained in Christ Jesus, due to opposing spirit life intrusions and invasions. Lam 2.14. Gen 1.

I Renounce the Ancestral Principalic Stronghold Root Spirit of Rejection 1

He that rejects you rejects me. Lk 17.25...Jn 8.4-7....Rom 15.17

Hating another without a cause works through rejection Hate is a spirit work of the flesh. Lk 23.25. Gal. 5.20. Jn 15.24-25. Prov 26.28. Est. 5.9. Gen 37.4 & 18. Jn 16.2-8.

I decree I am not the victim, vessel or carrier Rom 9.21
We plead the blood and name of Jesus 1Jn 1.7-9. Exo 12.23. Eph 1.7. Rom 8.29. Rev 1.5.
To resist It. IJN. *(in Jesus name)* James 4.7

I Take Authority I Bind, Break & Divide it's work & false authority. IJN. 2Tim 2.26. Exo 12.23. Eph 1.7. Cor 11.25

I loose Rejection from the bloodline, (body, soul, spirit life & relationships) to cut it off at the root. I cast out... In Jesus name. Mk 16. 17. Jn 12.31. Ps 54.5.

To make room for the Holy Spirit in the up-rooting process of purging, cleansing and healing of spirit impurities and defilement. Acts 2.38. Mk 4.17.Isa 11.1. Mt 12.28. Eph 5.26. Cor 6.11. Heb 4.16. Zec 4.6. Eph 2.18-22. Jn 13-15. Thess 5.23.

I Bind, Break and Divide the spirit fruit and principalic root of Rejection trying to work in our lives through:

A spirit and spiritual work against the mind, thought & thinking process until the spirit fruit is produced. Col 1.21.

Self – Character spirit fruit   **Personality-Relationships / Environment**

Chaff personalities. Mt 3.12. **Defined as anything worthless. To annoy or be Annoyed. Also includes work of flesh & thorn personality or sin spirit natures.** Heb 6.8. Prov 22.5. Ps 1.4. Jn 17.2. Rom 8.3 & 8. James 4.7.

Abusive (behavior) or being Abused. 2 Sam 21.1. Mt 27.30-41.

Betrayal Lk 22.6. (An unclean spirit – Jn 13.11. Mt.24.10.)

Confusion James 3.16. Ps 35.26

Control Issues (some use rejection to control). Heb 12.14.

Distress (body, soul & /or spirit) 2 Sam Chpt 22. 1 Sam 22.2. PS 25.17 Sam22.

Defilement Eze 36.17

Discontent Tim 6.8

Eye Gates Mk 7.22. Mt 20.15. Mt 6.23. Prov 28.22. Lk 11.34-35. Gen 39.7

Doubtful reasoning Mk 12.24. Heb 3.12-19

Heart Issues Ps55.21. Ps 21.11. Mt 22.37. Hosea 10.2. Heb13.9

Accuser (of the brethren) Rev 12.10-11

Accusing/to find fault (unproved) Acts25.7

(seeking to accuse) Lk 11.54.

Angry Eph4.31. Prov14.17.

Condemnation Rom 8.1

Conspiracy Gen3.18. Acts23.13-21

Counsels of the heart Cor4.5.

Covetousness Eph5.3. Rom1.29.

Deception Gal 6.3. Ja 1.22.

Deceit Jere9.6. Mk7.21-23. Prov. 26.26.

Deceiver (can bring a curse) Gen27.12.

Distress/worry 2Sam 22.7

Division (differences) A fruit of rejection Cor 1.10. Lk12.52.

Arrogance Prov8.13.

Adversary Ps38.20

Affliction Gen29.31-32.Job10.15. Ps25.18. Lam 1.9.

Argumentative Tim 6.5.

Strive Prov 3.30 Gen 27.4. Gen 26.10, 20 & 27

Bitterness (defiles spirit life) Heb 12.15.

Carnal (envy,strife,division) Corin.3.3. Corin 3.1

Complain Ps144.14. PS 77.3. Lam 3.39.

Contrary Acts26.9 Rom 16.17.

Critical (with no grace, unbiblical) Mt 12.36.

Dishonoring (dishonoring others can affect family) Lk18.11.2 Sam6.20,22. Sam23.9

Lying lips (hide hatred) Prov 10.18

Self-importance Self-love (idolatry) 2Tim3.2. Prov 24.28

Selfish (self-centered) Prov 21.2

Low self-esteem, Inferiority

Unstable emotions, emotional insecurity or sense of inadequacy. 2 Pet 2.14. James 1.8

Over sensitive (even with godly biblical consoling) James1.8. Prov24.28. Jn7.24. Lk4.18.2. 2Tim 3.16.

Un-forgiveness Lk23.34. Mt18.35

Un-fair Gen 31.41

Ungodly aloneness (some are set apart or severed by will of the Lord) Jn14.18. Jn16.32. Lev 20.24 & 26.

Ungodly perfection Eph 4.3. James 4.6.

Ungodly Competition Eph 4.30. Mt 23.12

Ungodly Achievement Eph 4.30. Mt 23.12

Ungodly Aggressiveness (form of pride) Ps123.4.Ps140.5

Worry Rom2.16. Mt12.37. Mt6.34. 2 Sam 22.7

False Witness: Prov 21.28

Evil doing 2Sam3.39.

Evildoer Prov.24.1. Pet 4.15

Fear Rom8.15. Lk8.37. Lk21.26.

Feeling offended (offended feelings) Mt24.10.

Foolish heart Rom1.21

Foolishness Ps 5.5. Ps 69.5.

Fouls Eph 5.16

Foolish Talking Job 5.3

Grief Gen26.35   Guilt Dt 21.9

Hate issues (a sign or form of walking in darkness) – 2Sam13.22. Ps69.4 & 14. Ps97.10.2. Sam13.15. Mt24.10. Ez35.11. Gen37.4 & 5. Ps106.1).

Hate (without a cause): Ps 35.19

Cruel Hatred: Ps25.19. Gen37.4

Hate (for wrong reasons-release is needed) Ps38.19

Hate (Some hate the evil and love the good- release is needed from the spirit operating behind the spirit nature behavior) 1Jn2.11.2 Sam13.22.

Hardness-Harshness Hypocrisy Lk12.1Mk7.6

Iniquity/Iniquitous family patterns Jere11.18. Jere30.15.2 Sam7.14. Ez36.31 Isa31.2. Ps14.4.2 Tim2.19 Hosea 14.1. Zeph 3.5.

Impatience-Intolerance James 1.3

Lying (can be caused by jealousy) Prov17.4. Ps35.28.

Malice Cor5.8. Eph4.31.

Murder (a spirit of rejection can lead to murder). Including murderous intent. Ps 10.8.

Possessiveness Heb 12.14. Lk 1.51.

Proud (reasoning) Exo18.11.

Presumptuous sins Ps19.12.

Prejudice Gen37.4

Racism/ist

Refusing Comfort-a form of hurt (fruit of rejection) Gen37.35.

Secret Faults Ps19.12.

Secret Sins: Ps 90.8. Ps19.13.Lk19.1

Seeks Mischief Prov 11.27

Shame Isa61.7. Ez36.15. Ps4.2. Job8.22. Ps35.26

Sin (iniquity) Ps38.3 Mt 12.31. Prov 14.35

Temptation Lk 22.26, 28, 40, 46

Treason Judges 2.11. Joshua 23.16

Treacherous Malachi 2.10.

Transgression (causes you to fall) Hos 14.1. Joshua 23.16.

Unreasonable Acts 24.25:25.27

Usury Eze 22.12. Jere 15.10

Vanity Rom8.20. Acts14.15.

Ill-treatment Ps69.9 & 19.

Discredit Jn19.21.

Envy Gen37.11. Titus3.3. Eze35.11 Job5.2

Failure

Fighting Ps140.2. Ps 56.1

Frustration

Grudge Lev19.18. James 5.9

Haughty Ps123.4.2 Sam22.28. Prov 21.24

Insurrection Ps64.2. Acts18.

Jealousy Gen37.4. 1 Corin 10.22

Mean Isa5.15.Acts21.39.

Partiality Prov24.23 Cor12.25. James 3.17.

Pointing Finger Isa58.9.

Provocations Kings 21.22. King 15.30

Provoking Ps106.43. Gal 5.26
(some provoke yr. by yr.) Sam1.7.

Rejection   Jn 12.48. Sam 8.7

Retaliation Revenge 2Sam 13. 2. Cor 10.6

Sows Discord Prov 6.14

Superstitious (belief inconsistent with known facts or rational think- ing or biblical truth) Acts17.22.

Stander Prov 10.18

Unnatural Affection Col3.5

Unthankful 2Tim3.2. Ps26.7

Vex (to vex or be vexed) or mock / bullying another Exo22.21. Gen 27.46

Weary Dan 7.25

Whisperer Ps. 41.7.

Other Dark

Spirit Realm Influences (of darkness) Eph4.23. Heb9.14. Acts24.16. Rom12.2. Jere48.42. Dan8.11

Affects mind, conscience, will desire, memory, vision, sight, eyes, voice/vocal cords, imagination, inclination, thinking & thought processes (mindset-through dark effigies/engraftment) and magnification until it turns into obsession.
Mt3.8-10.1 Jn2.16. Heb5.14. Ez18.4. Corin 2.13.

Idol spirits: defiles the natural mind/conscious (subconscious) and spirit life. Cor8.1. Titus1.15.

Evil patterns of thinking/thoughts (bombarding the mind re: rejection) Ps56.5:55.3. Prov 30.32

Images of men: (like a playback) Ez 16.17

Vanity of Mind (There is a need to think more biblically) Phil4.4. Eph4.17. Prov 12.11

Self-Delusion: (re; rejection due in part to dark spirit thought activity) Titus1.15. Gal 6.3

Un-steadfast: fellowship w/God. 2 Pet 3.17.1

Evil desires. Ps 40.14.

Err… in spirit (shall come to understanding). Isa 29.24.

Rebellion: Also starts in the spirit realm of one's Imagination – with/or without awareness.
Sam 12.14-15. Ez 20.38. Jere 29.32. Isa 1.2. Isa 30.1 & 9.

Compulsive or hasty: Driving spirit urges and/or cravings to: shop, eat, sugar fits, lie. Num 11.34. Isa8.22. Mk1.12. Prov 21.5

Prov 21.5.

Wounded Spirit: Prov18.14

Vain fellowships. relationships
Can be initiated or developed by dark spirit activity or assignment. Eph5.11. Eph4.27. Prov2.13 & 17. Cor1.29. Prov12.11.

(Some in dark spirit professions have the ability to draw you into a dark course and/or spirit force you onto a dark course by marshalling evil spirits into a soul or spirit life or realm. If this would occur consistent spirit release would become necessary for the protection and preservation of one's body, soul and/or spirit life or realm)

Confused noise: Often to extreme negative spirit image & vision recall. Isa 9.5. Ps 91.6.

Discernment/Vision: Can be affected by dark angel spirit seizes, intrusions or assignments. Mt 3.8,10. Heb 5.14. 2Ki 18.19. Neh 4.1. Ez 44.23.Ez44.

Voice of the enemy: (Must be biblically and spiritually discerned) Ps. 55.3

Unbelief: First begins in the spirit realm. Rom 11.20. Titus 1.15. Heb 4.6. Mk 6.6

Lust/Desire: Lk 22.31

__Multiple spirit personalities:__ Mk, Chpt.5.
Schizophrenic (and/or spirit types behind the spirit symptoms)

Eye gate: Gen 39.7. Mk 7.22

Deception/Deceived: (Can also first form in the spirit realm before it manifests in the natural). This literally means it is a spirit activity happening first. 2 Coren 11.3. Gal 6.3

Betrayal: Starts in the spirit realm. Mt 26.16. Rev 12.9

Dark counsel & encouragement: Using dark secret influences, opinions & persuasions. Mt 27.23-43. Isa30.10. Jere18.23. Ps64.5. Prov21.3. Prov12.11. Isa29.15.

Dark paths course: Isa 30.11
Some in dark professions have the ability to draw you on to a dark course or spirit force you on to one, by marshalling evil spirits into your life. Pet1.16. This is why it is good to learn to release yourself from spirit impurities and or defilement.

Destroyer Evil – (sometimes persecuting/warring principalic angel spirits) Jn10.10. Ps78.49. Exo12.23. Ps17.4. We drive you out and mirror any attacks back to its habitation. Rev 18.2.

All of the above dark spirit activities and influences try to

Create chambers of rejection by working through mindsets, images, imaginations and memory recalls of rejection thoughts & thinking patterns — Ez 8.12. Zec 7.10

Herein lies the need to learn the biblical and spiritual ability to distinguish spirit voices, to be able to cast down the wrong spirit thoughts that affect our individuality in Christ and with one another. Cast out spirits affecting the thinking/thought processes and any spirit image recalls flashing before you, revealing rejection….or the enemy will continue to send vessels (some call them henchmen) used by darkness to continue the (spirit) rejection process of developing a mindset of rejection. Consistent release is needed IJN (in Jesus name).

Familiar wicked, unclean, and evil spirits of Rejection working infectiously or contagiously through culture, community, business, marketplaces, families, any size people groups and/or those in dark spirit professions to defile the soul and spirit lives of men (who do not know or realize how to maintain, guard and protect their soul from ancestral spirit impurities and defilement or that of others). These are other ways spirits desire to travel among us to affect us.

Break any mindsets, curses (dark angel spirit come with curses, because they are fallen or cursed spirits – 2Pet2.4) and reverse and mirror any spirit transfers back to its kind. Habitation in the name of Jesus. Mk 16 & 20. Jn1.11. Acts19.16. Acts17.5-7. Acts14.2. Acts13.50. Acts8.7. Lk6.18. Mk6.7. Mt13.19 & 49. Jude1.13. Job1.7. Rev 18.2. Gen 1.

We break dark trinities of principalities, rulers of the darkness (working individually and/or through dark spirited territorial assignments). Break the assignment by the blood of Jesus and bind their demonic agreement by cutting them off from the power of the air and cast it out of your life. In Jesus name. Burn the assignment at the root. In Jesus name (using the "Wash" flowchart) if necessary. Is14.5. Dt6.19. Mk3.12.

Cut Cords: Pride, Vanity, wickedness, affliction & sin, that connects or could cause you to reject others or visa versa. Isa 5.18. Job 36.8. Prov 5.22.

Loose from: Pride of life, lust of flesh & lust of eyes, that would produce the spirit fruit of rejection. 1Jn 2.16

I loose the Holy Spirit to uproot, cleanse, release, restore, mend and heal in this area. I release the blessings and peace of God to replace the curse. In Jesus name. Prov . 26.2. Mt.16.19.

Keep Mercy & Judgment

Hosea12.6. Amos5.15.

I Renounce the Ancestral Principalic Stronghold Root Spirit of Sorcery

Group activities, systems and expressions of Dark spirit Kingdom governing systems of operations. And his kingdom was full of darkness or dark spirit activity. Rev16.10. Mal 3.5. Isa47.9 & 15.Isa48.11.

By Sorcery were all nations deceived Jere25.6. Jere7.24-28. Dt30.17   **2**

I decree I am not the victim, vessel or carrier of sorcery. Rom9.21

We plead the blood and name of Jesus to . 1Jn1.7-9 Exodus12.23. Eph1.7. Cor 11.25. Rev1.5

To resist it. IJN. James 4.7

I Take Authority   I Bind, Break & Divide this root work & false authority that it can no longer operate (past present future) by the power of Your blood. IJN. Lk11.18. Mt16.19. Lk9.1.

I Break the power, curse, passion, assignment, will of any sorcery activity. In Jesus name. 2Tim2.26. Isa14.5.

I loose sorcery and it's expressions from our bloodline, and cast it out of (body, soul, spirit life , relationships and environments in Jesus name. Mk16.17. Jn12.31. Lev17.11. Ps54.5. Ps37.22. Ps76.12. Dt6.19.

To make room for the Holy Spirit in the up-rooting process of purging, cleansing and healing of spirit impurities and defilement & spirit violations of others. Acts2.38. Mk4.17. Isa11.1 Mt12.28 Cor12.7. Zec4.6. Thes5.23.

Some sense the need to call up 10, 30 or beyond generations for any ancestral sorcery group activities. Scripture does refer to such things as iniquitous family patterns. Therefore, some dark spirit activity can be passed on as a tradition. Some sense the need to break all known or unknown spirit contracts and illegal contacts, deals and/or agreements on one's mother and/or father's side of the family heritage or heritage of others affecting them, in Jesus name). There are signs for biblical basis for all these ideas. The decision will be between you and the Lord. Phil 2.12.

I Bind, Break, Divide, Cut-Off and Cast-Out the spirit fruit and principalic root of Sorcery & governing systems & expressions *of darkness* **that are trying to work/operate in our lives through:** (A spirit and spiritual work that first begins in the mind, thought/thinking patterns until the (spirit fruit or personality) is produced or formed. Col1.21.Isa14.5.

Personality   Relationships   Environment

Self (The spirit fruit character Satan seemingly tries initially to destroy life on 3 different levels (body, soul & spirit life/or realm) and then spreads to community (individually or collectively to reproduce itself). Gen 1. Thess. 5.23.

Stages-Breakdown of the Soul (A bound state). It's personal, then proceeds to immoral spiritual **Degeneration** by *spiritual* **Corruption** (defilement and/or violating spirit activity)

2Pet2.12 & 19. Tim6.5. Rom 8.21.

(Next level of dark spirit fruit influence, intrusion or violation with in family, environment/community territories, or any size people group) Rom 1.23. These try to change the spirit image of man. *Warning in advance: It is noted that some dark spirit professions are definitely into <u>hi-jacking</u> soul and spirit lives of men, working illegally in the lives of others above and below our human right laws, biblical or spiritual laws. Rom 8.2. Aren't the laws of the land to be by the people and for the people? What good are laws that are not meeting nor reflecting the needs of the people? Yet, there is a high percentage of those who die of satanic sacrifices and ritual abuses each year and our laws seem to grant them protection of the freedom of religion laws. Some ritual abuses were done by those who could not find spiritual healing and so then became part of problem and learn how to perpetuate the same sin, sickness and spiritual disease into the lives of others. Lord, please help us do better.

Chaff personalities: Mt3.12. Judges16.16. Prov10.23. Cor1.29. ...also considered flesh and thorns. Corin1.29. Heb 6.8. Prov22.5. Thorns (as people) can keep you from finding your path and/or course in Christ with constant distractions, dark spirit assignments and hidden agendas. Hosea2.6. Jere 2.21. What is the chaff to the wheat?

Adultery (natural adultery can be symbolic) Dt 5.7 Isa 57. 3.Prov30.20. Isa53.3. Prov6.26 & 32.Job24.15. Ez23.37

Adversary Ps 38.20   Bigotry

Low self-esteem Job 12.3

Respect of persons James 2.1 James 2.9

Selfish (self-centered) Prov21.2
Self-willed 2Pet2.10

Deceitful Prov 101.7 Deception Jere9.6. Gal6.3

Deceitfully Jere 48.10

Entangled (ment) 2Pet 2.20.

False witness Mt 26.59. Insecurity

False accusers Titus2.3 (seeking to accuse-a heart issue) 2 Ti 3.3

Passivity   Self-love 2Tim3.2

Back slider Jer 3.21-22. Prov14.14

Boasting 2Cor 9.4.2 Cor10.15

Bitter Eph 4.31   Brutish Counsel
Isa19.11. Prov 12.1

Envy Prov 27.4   Jealousy Corin 10.22

Eye (evil) Mt 6.23

Evil inventions Rom 1.30

Servants of Corruption (A foundational dark spirit truth for those in dark spirited professions; spiritually programmed to defile and/or spiritually violate others on any level. 2) Pet 2.19. Ez24.13.

Treacherous Jer 9.2. Lewdness
Eze24.13. Jer 13.27

Tempt (Tempting...to provoke)
Lk 8.6. James1.13. Jn 8.6. Acts 5.9

Trouble Job 5.6 (where spirit activity interrupts natl' expressions with expressions of affliction, usually there is a evil spirit behind it. Any man being used for evil is revealing

Betrayal Lk 22.6

Condemnation Jn3.19. Contrary
Tim 1.10. Prov 16.28. Acts 26.7

Discontent Tim 6.8   Discord Prov 6.14

Degenerate

Error (from sorcery) Isa29.24. Jere23.13

Evil doing 2Sam3.39. MK7.21-23. sa5.20.
Exo 23.2. Pet 4.15

Fault finding-accusation Acts 25.7

Hate Prov 14.21. Haters of God and His Spirit
Rom 1.30. Ps 81.15 Hate: Some love those who hate God

Haughty (naturally &/or spiritually so)
Zeph 3.11

Hypocrisy Lk 12.1   Idols Ez22.4. Ez 23.37

Being Rejected Lk 17.25. Jn8.4-7. Rom15.17 (some allow darkness to work through them to resist others-realized or not) Sam 15.23

Iniquity Ez 33.15

Iniquitous/idolatrous family patterns Jere11.10. 2 Pet2.16

Liar (s) Jn8.44. Jere23.14. Ps52.3. Prov17.4. Eph4.29. (Some walk in lies)

Lead astray Prov28.10   Pursue evil Prov11.19

Profane Mal 2.10-11 (Until it affects the land)
Jere23.15

Pride (ful) Proud purposes) Ex 18.11
Prov 16.5.

Prejudice/Racism Gen 37.4. Self-will 2Pet 2.10

Revenge Ps 18.47   Retaliation Ez 35.15

Strife Gal 1.9. Rom7.5   Stubborn Sam 15.23

Sin Jere 30.11-15 (presumptuous sins)
Ps 19.13

Stumbling Block Eze 13.3 (a person or iniquity can be one) Rom 14.13

Abomination Ez43.8:44.7. Dt20.10 & 18

Confusion Job 10.15. Ps35.26. (can be caused by consist dark spirit affliction transforming into a soul)

Despise Prov 14.21. Despiteful
Rom1.30

Division (divisive-disharmony)
Mt 12.25-26. Mk 13.8. Corin 1.10. Acts 15.9.
Lk 11.17-18. Lk 12.51

Dishonoring others (ill-attitudes-release needed. 2Sam 6.20)

Fools/Foolishness   Eph 5.15

Forceful behavior Jere 23.10. Sam 2.16

Hard heart Mk6.52.Mk7.21-23

Heart Issues (hidden intentions)
Jere7.24. Acts8.21. Mt9.4. Hosea10.2.
Heb13.9. Acts10.29.

Intrusive, Interrupter, INVADER
(type of vexing)

Malice Corin 5.8

Manipulation (naturally and/or spiritually) 2 Tim 3.13

Perverted ways Jer 3.21

Provoke Sam1.6. Ki21.22.

Attitudes/personalities (that seem to over throw judgment of the righteous) Ps140.4.

Reputation Phil2.7

Rebellious Ps 66.7

Spirit of the world 1Jn1.15-16.
Corin 2.12

Unsoundness (biblically) in soul and spirit life. Tim 1.10. Tit 1.9

the need for spiritual release, cleansing and healing on some level. Ez36.

Vain glory Phil 2.3. Jere23.16. Phil 12.3

Vanity Habb2.14. Ez13.6. Acts14.15. These allure through flesh and wantonness. 2Pet 2.18. King 16.26.

Victimization (or object of spirit led territorial assignments dark spirits working through men or women needing to learn How to maintain their spirit lives in Christ). Victimization can occur in the natural or/and spiritual through dark spirits trying to govern your soul, spirit life and/or body. It's the process of it.

Unforgiveness Mt18.35

Transgressions Ps119.158.

Vile Affection Rom 1.26. Sam3.13

Wages of unrighteousness 2Pet2.15.

We continue to bind, break, divide, cut-off and cast out the spirit of sorcery trying to work in our lives through:

Unnatural affection Rom 1.31

Adulterer (spiritually) Isa 57.3 Ez23.37

(for those in dark spirit professions', this can also be a type of hunting spirits for souls and brings a work of the occult and witchcraft spirit powers, etc. on the scene to traffic spirits into the life of another to bring others into dark spirit captivity. Sam 24.11

Defiant (Contrary/Froward) Tim 1.10. Prov 16.28

Hinder or block another (naturally and/or spiritually so or that distract from the things of the will of God) Gal 5.7. Thess 2.18. Lk11.52. Ps140.4

Meddlesome/Snoop/Busybody Tim5.13. Prov26.17. Prov20.3

Foul/Evil spirits (unclean) Mt 10.1. Mt12.43. Mk1.23,26 & 27. Mk3.30. Mk5.2 &8. Lk11.24

Religious examining/sifting Sam1.12-15. 2 Cor11.3.

Love of power & control (close to obsessed due to "spirit domination" driving them to control others) Ki 18.4. 2 Ki21.5-7

Deceitful workers of Christ Ps17.4. Prov 11.18. 2. Corin11.13

Grievous Acts 16.18. Eph 4.30

Dark spirit watches (some watch with no reason seemingly or real purpose-just spirit led not for good, more of a nuisance because spiritual release and healing is needed). Lk 20.20.

Evil spirits Sam16.14:18.10

Strivings seemingly due to a dark spirit nature (or seize in the environment) some in dark spirit professions will even strive to Spiritually defile and/or spiritually violate others. Prov 3.30. Prov 25.8

Principalities, familiar, unclean, seducing, bewitching fallen angel or demon spirit activity will work individually or together consistently, depending on who is perpetuating, in the following areas…..always to reveal and reflect dark spirit kingdom initiatives and agenda.

Bewitchment Acts8.11. Gal3.1

Hypnosis, trance like states (some induce these states and are keenly developed for spirit activity.) Acts 8.9.

Zombie states

Spiritualism/Spiritism/Spiritist 2Ki23.24 Isa 8.19. (could also be considered a work of familiar spirits)

Consulting or allegiance with dark fallen spirit images, demons or principalities for direction, etc. Eph4.27. Eze 21.21. Dt 18.11

Astral Projection – works through power of air. Eph 2

Prognosticators – /foretell. Isa 47.13

Poltergeist type spirit activity noisy…mischievous spirit type behavior (within or out of a person) Sam 23.9. Ps 7.14

Peepers Sitting in time & space just to snoop should be avoided to protect one's spirit life & soul. Isa 8.19.

Charmers Ps58.5. Isa19.3

Ghost spirit activity Isa 29.4. (We believe can also be men in trance states causing people to believe they are ghosts, but are really spiritual perpetrators (working through their human spirit) with nothing better to do and must be discovered)

Dreamers Jude 1.8 (vs. dreams. Sam 28.6)

False divination Ez 21.23

False vision Jere 14.14

Mutterer Isa 59.3-NKJV Isa 8.19.

Shaman (ism)

Enchanter/Whisperer Lev 19.26. Ex 7.11. Num 23.23

Hex/Vex/Jinx.Chant/Spell/ Curses/Magic vexing another is a work of unclean spirit activity and reveals that release and healing are needed. Lk6.18. Amos 6.5. Dan 2.10. Dt 30.7

Ventriloquism/False Voices of God (can be a work of familiar spirits or perpetrated by those in some dark spirit professions, those in need of healing) Isa59.3.2. Isa 29.4. Dt 18.11.

Unrest states of being 2Ki9.22. Prov27.23. Phil4.11

Weary counsel (can come from constant psychic realm Activity and/or spirits being trafficked or marshaled into a person's spirit realm or soul) Isa47.13. Isa8.19. Judges16.16-17. Acts 16.16-17. Dan 7.26

Hunting spirit/activity One who has a need to pursue men and/or women for the operation of darkness to spiritually and naturally; defile and violate them, usually a dehumanizing process being done by those in need of spiritual release from the "dominating spirit" activity causing them to behave in this questionable manner. Sam 23.14:23.25:Sam24.11. Prov 6.26. Pet 5.8. Gel 1. (spirits like to find a way to reproduce themselves in lives of others, and in the process cause wounds in the lives of others)

Spirit (or spiritual) bondage
Pet2.19. Prov25.26. Mt12.33. Pet5.8. Jn12.35.2 Cor11.14

Spirit Guides or false spirits of light trying to find place in a soul. Dt 18. Isa 23.4. (also, some in dark prof. are able to work thru their human spirits to operate in lives of others)

False Christ spirit activity/Anti-Christ spirits Mt 24.24. Jn4.3.

False Apostles 2Corin 11.13-15

Corrupt Springs There is a need to find where or how and the spirit actually causing the spiritual corruption and the spiritual perpetrator (or person) initiating this spirit activity. Prov 25.2. Job 5.6. Prov 25.26

Transidental Meditation (or trance state vs. trance states of hypnosis caused by witchcraft or spirit damnation that seeks to dominate the spirit lives of others.) Pet 5.8. Prov 25.26

Wizard Sam 28.3

Mediums Sam 28 & 9

Spirit illusions/fantasies can be caused by evil spirit assignments. Sam19.9. Sam, Chpt.22.

Spirit natures of unrest

Spirit healers (can also be a type of spiritism)

Spirit of jealousy Num 5.14:5.30

Anti-Christ (spirit activity can also include any combination of root spirit activities) 2Jn7.1. 1Jn4.3.

Astrologer Isa 47.13

Other Dark

Spirit Realm Influences

We resist, bind, break, cut-off and cast out principalic witchcraft (sorcery) governing spirit activity & influences – trying to :

Create dark fellowships (or even point out to others if you do not join with other groups-dark spirits way of finding a place in your life – a spirit type of networking through ignorant/innocent or spiritually blind people as victims and/or vessels of darkness. Isa19. Eph5.11. Eph4.27. Jere8.6. Our pursuits should be centered around Christ and then from these relationships we learn that it's ok to love people. Not a low hell to use us for dark governing purposes. Everyone must spiritually locate themselves. Prov 27.23

Idol spirit activity: Ez 14.4-7. (helps to create a spirit life of idolatry in the lives of others because spirits like to reproduce themselves). Gen 1. Idols can be created or developed by images placed in the imagination of the conscious, subconscious, unconscious.

Create a desire or drawing in you to be around evil men or cause them to come around you (or cause a spirit drawing in the environment in or upon you to others). It's a part of their dark demented spirit nature. It's what they do. Prov24.1 & 8. Lk22.31-32.

Draw and or keep you on a dark course/path. (Using seducing spirits and bewitchment to accomplish this) Prov5.3-6. Ez16.57. Jere23.10. Job8.13. Acts8.9 & 11. 2 Sam 13.12.

Wicked counsel (sent by them working thru ignorant, innocent and or spiritually blind) vessels and/or victims. Those who will help darkness bring you into their will and purposes. Ps71.10. Ez11.2. 2 Tim 2.26.

Evil angel activity, marshaled assignments and/or familiar witch craft spirits that try to stick with you in spirit realm only, especially when they find it difficult to stay or attach to your body, your soul life. Ps78.49. Jn10.10. Exo12.23. Ps17.4. (this is when it becomes imperative for you to understand the ways of the Lord prayer, authority confession, praise and tread methods to spirit activity in the faith until they flee) James 4.7. These are serious dark spirit offenses to contend with!

Spirit Realm Defilement: Is realized when, especially prophets, see only vanity and lying divination. It can also reflect a spiritually defiled spirit realm that can be initiated by oneself (or ancestrally) or spiritually defiled or violated by someone in dark spirited professions (and/or sons and daughters of baal) who have the ability to force evil spirits into a life until the subject/victim can only see what theses spirits trafficked and channeled are imposing and/or by them being directed to impose upon the person. Either way this dark spirit life intrusion need to be resisted continually until the Lord brings complete healing and deliverance. Not to ignore that the person behind this demented, demonic assignment also need release and healing from spirit domination and must be discovered and also resisted in Jesus name. These dark spirit professionals have the ability to observe spiritual territories and saints that make progress for the Lord and then find a way into their life to stop them. Time to fast and pray and stay close to the Lord for the battle is the Lords. He is a man of war and you'll need His strategy. Seriously, do what you can to stay out of being drawn into dark spirit realms (and the fantasies and the spirit illusions that go with it). Too many spirits trafficked into a person's life can begin to operate in a person's life above and/or below the persons discernment. Mk 5.8-13

Spirits in prison: This could also be a mindset, as well as a physical place. Pet 3.19

Spirit seizes: where principalic spirits (or those in dark spirit professions working behind the scene can assist principalic activity against you) can cause sudden spirit attacks in ones environment or the environments of others that you walk into. Some false prophet/sorcerers have gained the spirit ability to literally descend upon you in a trance state to spiritually war against those in higher level s of those operating in the kingdom of God, which is not much, if any, realized in our church world. Remember hell also has a purpose for your life. You must learn to resist the dark transforming presence of darkness however it reveals itself (as an assignment from hell) off your life. James 4.7

Betrayal: Is first created in the spirit realm and is a part of their demonic arsenal. Jesus did say, blessed are they not offended in Him. Mt26.16. Some are betrayed at every turn, perhaps revealing an assignment that must be discovered and resisted, in Jesus name.

Treachery: 2Ki 9.22-23.

Creating chambers of Sorcery/Witchcraft dark mindsets, imagination and memory recall until it becomes a magnification and/or obsession in one's life.

This could come from principalic spirits trying to continually transfer spirits to bring you to the point to cause you manifest their dark spirit powers without using another vessel and/or victim even by transmittal descending spiritually into your life. Consistent resisting is needed until the Lord brings deliverance into your situation and/or experience. Sometimes this will also produce spirit voices of the enemy to defile the mind, conscience, thinking & thought processes, hearing, sight, memory, spirit vision, impression and spirit magnification, etc.,) Mt 20.15. Release is needed in the soul and/or the spirit realm.

Any new "spirit" experiences in the above areas can also be viewed as dark spirit seeking to find a place in your life. They must be resisted. One way of resisting is going through the appropriate root system or the advanced root system method of release using a flow chart. You cannot continually ignore spirit life activity seeking to find a place in your life. They must be effectively resisted until spiritual peace is restored again. If not, the repercussions can be devastating! No matter the religion, there is a present-day need to learn how to maintain their spirit life, among 2 spiritual kingdoms operating among us desiring the souls of man. Jn16.33. Rom3.17.

The Kingdom of God does not operate against itself. Roman 8.16. Each has their own way and method of operation. There is no spiritual confusion in heaven as to who serves who. Roman 14.17-19. Revelation 16.10-14. Dt.13.1-8. Mt.23.34. Both spiritual kingdoms operating in the earth have their own system of operations. Mt.23.34. Jere 2.26-28.

We continue to renounce, resist, bind, break, divide, cut-off and cast-out the spirit fruit & principalic root of sorcery trying to work in our lives through:

Spirit of baal (also called lord, master, husband). Also, a warring spirit that works through various spirit activities and manifestations to hunt souls for the operation of his spirit" kingdom activity. He works through the sorcery group "spirit activity" of trafficking, channeling and trance state spirit penetration, transformation, bewitchment, seducing spirits with various levels of hunting programs of harassment, mischief, fear tactics, intimidation, spiritual and/or natural abuse (consistently) to wear out the saints. Some would consider it more of process of demonization. Overall, it's a spirit type of defilement and series of spirit violations that transcends often into a process of anti-social, dehumanization and/or committed crimes against humanity. Dan 7.25-27. When the spirit of baal is able to influence people enough to impact a society, those usually influenced come out as extremist (whether in the lime light or behind the scene) which is usually just another form of "spirit domination" when it doesn't recognize, acknowledge or focus exclusively on Jesus Christ and His complete work at Calvary. Some that would biblically need healing and release and a greater understanding on spirit life activity would be:

KKK	Radical Islam/ Muslims/Jihad	Satanism/Lucifer an
spirit belief system	spirit belief system	spirit belief system wherever found

Islam/Muslims & Jihad seems to call their spirit domination "jennies'. See the www.majorreligion website. There is a process not only of breaking this spirit domination off one's life but one must also get out of agreement with "spirit and/ or natural" activity that would keep you connected. Dt 18. 10-13. Isa 8.19-20. Rev 16.10. 2 Corin 6.16. 2 Corin 7.1.

It is said that many of the animals in the bible can represent and/or reveal higher occult powers. Be it according to your level of faith, biblical knowledge & spiritual warfare. **We take our authority to bind, break, cast out and drive out any occult activity working through......the following animal spirit natures (in Jesus name):** Lk 9.1. Eph. 6.12. Phil 2.10.

Lion Job 10.16. Ps7.12. **Fowl (er)** Ps 91.3.Job 35.11. **Horses** Jere 12.5
(the spirit nature of the attack and/or warring can reveal the type of animal spirit being used or influenced). Some in ancestral dark spirit professions have the ability to work through animal spirits as well as human spirits. See; "The Prophet's Dictionary" and Rebecca Brown books.

Prophets of baal spirits 2Ki 10.18-28 **Sons or daughters of baal** Sam 1.16.Sam2.12

Dark Trinities: Can be compromised of; but not limited to the following spiritual variables:

Powers of the air: Eph 6.12. Eph 2.2   **Dark angelic hosts:** Isa 24.21.Isa34.4. Acts.7.42-43. Judges 5.20.

Sea: Isa27.1 Ps104.24-25. Ps74.13-14.

Principalities: Col 2.10 **Rulers of the Darkness:** Eph 6.12

Sorcerers are also called or can be described as false prophets (witches and/or warlocks). In a nutshell, sorcerers can use divination, witchcraft, the occult, magic and they can work through the false prophet's gift (using any of the dark arts). Ecc 12.14. Mt.12.33. Jere 23.32. Acts Chpt. 13. The works of sorcery can spiral you into the spirit work of dark arts/ activity, including any of the above and wizardry. Isa 8.19. Lev 19.31.

Witchcraft: Sam 15.23. Dt 18.10-12. Micah 5.12. Witchcraft seems to govern the operation of darkness. It is said that witchcraft has the ability to mobilize spirit activity and the dynamics of the operation of darkness and/or the false prophet can direct any level of operation of darkness from the heaven-lies because of a higher authority working with the spirit of baal to manipulate (using deceit), control to dominate man's will. 2Tim2.23.

Whoredom: Harlots are called the mistress of witchcrafts due to the multitude of their whoredom. Nahum 3.4. Eze 23.14, 17.

Divination: Acts 16.16. Isa44.25. Lying divination. Ez13.7, 23. Uses magic. sorcery, fortune telling and witchcraft with occultic practices. Forbidden by the Law of Moses. Dt18. It is said that these also have found ways to steal the word of the Lord. Jere 23.30. The good news is that there is no divination against Israel that will prosper. Num 23.23.

Necromancer: Sam 28.13. conjuring. Medium. Also practices of wizardry. Dt.18.11. Ez13.6. A practice of calling up the dead is what the OT witch did. Mt 7.15-16. Mk 13.22.

False prophets/Dark prophets: These could be any church prophet and/or those with the prophet's call needing spiritual healing and release (realized or not). True prophets of God (even apostolic sent prophets) are often spiritually and/ or naturally warred against (by dark spirited prophets and/ or false prophets-and/or those in dark spirited professions until they (spiritually conform) and/or yield to what dark spirit operations are desiring within and/or without the church. Though it is needed, there doesn't seem to be much, if any teaching the prophets of God how to protect, maintain and guard their spirit life from dark spirit intrusions and invasions specifically because they can be prophets of either kingdom, depending on who they yield or lose their vessel to (in battle). They are definitely warred at on higher levels than the church can seemingly handle and/or are aware of, because darkness is desiring to spirit force them into serving the operation of darkness. This spiritual warring often seems to confuse the body of Christ (and local churches) but there is no spiritual confusion in heaven who is spiritually serving in God's spiritual kingdom operation. James 3.16.Eze13.9-12. Jere 23.13-14. Jere 2.21. Jere 2.21-23. Corin 14.12. 2 Jim 2.20.

Foolish prophets: Ez13.3-4 & 67. (Ez 13.3-4, 6). **Prophets of deceit:** Ki 13.18.Jere 23.18. Jere7.24.

It seems continual release would be necessary (as outlined) in this writing to maintain ones spirit life & gift in Christ – as long as we live in communities & family etc...that can be

Spiritual wickedness in high places: Eph 6.12. Isa 58.6. These also can build dark spirit networks in the heaven-lies and in the earth. Isa 19.9 2 Hm 3.13.

These also can work with or through trafficking, channeling, bewitchment, seducing spirits, demons, evil and/or unclean spirits, etc., to help keep you connected to them. Their spiritual penetrating can also cause physical, mental and/or spiritual ailments (or degeneration). Jere 23.14.

affected by dark spirit activity. Aware or not doesn't seem to be the issue.

Occult: Micah 3.6,7. Mk 4.22. Lk 12.2. Mk 12.33. Isa 29.15. These also like to use a demonic (silent) language of communicating. Kurt E.Koch, A Christian Counselor, states that starring is actually an occult activity.

Familiar wicked, unclean, evil sorcery group spirit activity: Working infectiously through cultures, communities, business/market places, families or any size people groups to defile & violate the body, soul & spirit lives of those in need of learning how to maintain their spirit lives in Christ.

Break any curses (dark angel spirits come with curses because they are fallen or cursed spirits. 2Pet2.4) and reverse and mirror any spirit transfers back to its kind. In the name of Jesus. Mt27.20. Acts19.16. Acts17.5-7. Acts14.2. Acts13.50. Lk6.7. Mt13.19 & 49. Jude1.13. Jon1.7. Rev 18.2.

Bind and break dark trinities or principalities, rulers or darkness & spiritual wickedness in high places (working individually and/or through dark spirited territorial assignments) in Jesus name. Bind and break demonic agreements and assignments by cutting them off from power of the air and cast it out. In Jesus name. Burn demonic yokes: assignments and agreements at the root by confessions of faith. Dt6.19. Isa14.5. Mk3.27. Acts 8.7.

Cut Cords: Pride, Vanity, Wickedness, Affliction & Sin that would connect one to sorcery activity and/or its witchcraft governing influences. Isa5.18. Job36.8. Ps129.4. Prov5.22.

Loose from: Pride of life, lust of flesh and lust of eyes that would keep one connected to any sorcery group influences or activities. 1Jn2.16. Mt16.19.

> I loose the Holy Spirit to up-root, release, deliver, cleanse and heal in the areas needed. I release the blessings, goodness, mercy and peace of God to replace the curse and ill-works of darkness and sorcery group activity and/or any specific assignments against the child of God. In Jesus name. Mt 16.19.

> For those needing witchcraft protective prayers: You could also pray a perimeter boundary of the blood (of Jesus) and annoint with oil to protect against any and everything that could be witchcraft affected or initiated by them. Exo 40.9. 1 Jn 1.7. Be conscious of any trauma used by them to install curses, claims, demons, spirits, etc. Renounce and/or refuse everything of witchcraft claims, curses, false blessings, covenants, spirits, demons, portals, ...then rescue (deliver, free and/or save from danger any parts....affected from the spiritual trauma). For Satanism, the same idea would apply. See: www.witchcraft/satanismdifferences.

---

before the gods will I

Eze44.10-13. Eze44.23 **Sing Praise to Thee** Ps138.1.

I Renounce the Ancestral Principalic Stronghold Root Spirit of Anti-Christ

2Jn7, 1Jn4.3.   **3**

I decree I am not the victim, vessel or carrier of Anti-Christ. Rom9.21. Rom 10:9-10.

We plead the power of the blood and name of Jesus. 1Jn1.7-9 Exodus12.23.Eph1.7.Cor 11.25.Rev1.5
To resist it. IJN. James 4.7

I Take Authority

I Bind, Break & Divide it's work and false authority that it no longer stands (past, present, future). IJN. Lk11.18 Mk16.17. Lk 9.1.

I Break the power, curse, passion, assignment and will of Anti-Christ. 2Tim2.26. Isa 14.5.

I loose Anti-Christ from the bloodline, (body, soul, spirit life, relationships and present environment) to cut off at the root. I cast it out. In Jesus name. Mk16.17. Jn12.31. Lev17.11. Lk19.31. Lord, we repent...we forgive...

To make room for the Holy Spirit in the up-rooting process of purging, cleansing and healing of the spirit impurities and defilement. In Jesus name. Acts2.38. Mk4.17. Isa11.1. Mt12.28. Eph5.26. Cor6.11. Heb4.16. Zec4.6. Eph2.18-22. Thess5.23.

I Bind, Break, Divide and Cut-Off this spirit fruit and principalic root of Anti-Christ trying to work in our lives through:

A spirit and spiritual work against the mind, thought and thinking patterns, desires, will and emotions until the desired spirit fruit is produced. Col 1.21

Self spirit fruit character

Personality-Relationships / Environment

Chaff personalities: Mt.3.12. Chaff is defined as anything worthless. To annoy or be annoyed. Also included works (attitudes, desires, thoughts/thinking & work of the hands) and thorn personality spirit natures.
Heb6.8. Prov.22.5. Ps1.4. Rom3.3 & 8. James4.7. Ps49.3. Isa33.12.2 Sam23.6-7. Ez44.7-10.

Abuse (spiritual or nat'l) Mt27.30-41.2 Sam21.1	Affliction or to afflict	Accusation (unapproved)
Arrogance Sam2.3	Accuser	(Religious accusation)
Belittling (make seem less important) Mk9.12.	Corrupt minds (defiled minds resist the truth naturally/spiritually so)	Apostasy: Denial of one's faith can also be caused by being under severe dark spirit trafficking &/or and channeling of spirits into a "targeted soul's life" w/no consistent releases.
Boast (ing) 2Cor9.4.2 Cor10.15	Covetousness	
Cold Love Mt. 24.10-12. (hate, betrayal)		
Confusion James3.16. Ps35.26.	Division/Disharmony	
Deceived 2Jn7.Titus Deception Gal 6.7. Prov12.20	Evil eye (light of body is the eye)	Betrayal
	Hate (despise)	Dishonest gain Evil doers

Defilement Cor3.17.Mk.7.15 & 23.Heb12.15. Ez44.23-24. (including being around dead not of immediate family.)

Disrespect (dishonor)

Doubt/Unbelief-vocalized

Discontent Tim6.8. Lk12.29. Mk12.24.

Fears Rom8.15. 2Sam1.7. Sam18.15.

Lies Jere 23.14

Manipulation

Offenses (offended) Mt.24.10. Mt.13.57. easily offended Jn5.18) (or over sensitive)

Rejection Mk8.31

Self-Importance Titus1.7.

Willfully Contrary Heart Prov11.20. Acts26.9 2Sam6.16. Prov28.14.

Hypocrisy Mt23.23-24 & 28

Lawlessness

Iniquity Ez36.31. (Break any iniquitous/Idolatrous family patterns

Murmur   Mock (would include bullying).

Provoke

Pride/Proud purposes

Religious sifting

Seeks Mischief

Stubborn

Sin (spirit nature)

Treason

Transgression

Vanity

Vain

Error....

Hindering (other's from truth)

Lukewarm (or indifferent)

Ill-Treating (of others)

Mean

Profane

Prejudice/Racism

Respect of Persons

Strive

Un-forgiveness

Un-godliness

Un-holy/Un-clean (body, soul and/or spirit)

Vexation or to be vexed daily.

Wrestle with truth (is a type of striving)

Other Dark

Spirit Realm Influences – and/or experiences

Eph2.2-3. Eph4.23. Heb9.14.2

That try to affect the memory, desire, will, impressions, imagination, inclination, spirit vision, sight and discernment until the darkness is magnified. Mt.3.8-10 Mk7.21-23

Eye gate Prov27.20. Isa1.16. Ez20.7-8. Ez33.25

Ear gate 1Jn4.6. Ps 55.3

Spirit voice realm of darkness (can influence men. Must be Biblically and spiritually discerned) Ps50.16-17.

Religious error can encourage or produce Anti-Christ expressions

Abominations Ez43.8. Ez44.7.   **Covenant Breakers** Lev 26.15, 24, 25

Lack of a life of praise   Ps47.7. Acts17.23

Mixing holy with profane (without acknowledging the Lord, they could be negatively affecting their spirit life in Christ.) Jn 15.26. Jn 16.13. Lev5.15. Lev10.10.

Neglect Commands (instruction) and/or commandments Ps119.21 Num15.22-23

Religious Observations, tradition & policy contrary to the word & Spirit of His Kingdom of God. Lk6.7. Religious erformance Mk7.9 Reject the word of the Lord &/or counsel: Prov. 28.9. Rev22.14.

Dark spirit life can create the following spirit life activity:

Spiritual blindness Lk 19.42 Spirit of religion (can produce indifference)

Seducing spirits (briefly defined also as alluring, defiling, to lead astray &/or through bewitchment, spiritual hypnosis violations (channeling/trafficking) Tim4.1

Unstable/Un-steadfast (in script and biblical principles) 2Pet3.17.

Evil thinking and thought patterns and influences (can come from listening consistently to wrong spirit voices-even unaware-so to be safe cast out/drive out any un-scriptural spirit thought voices) Col.2.18. Eph2.3. Ps56.5. Acts 19.12 & 16.

Corrupt minds 2Tim3.8. Tim6.5. Titus1.15.   **Confused noise** Isa 9.5

Doubtful mind Lk12.39   **Another spirit** (from Christ) 2Cor11.4

Spirit of the world Cor2.12   **God hating spirit** Rom 1.30

Demonic watches Ps 37.32.

Idol spirits (defile the conscious) Cor8.7. Titus1.15.

Noise-some pestilence Ps91.6

Torment (can come from unclean spirits, being in wrong spirit environments and channeling and trafficking of spirits) Lk6.18.

Desire Eph2.3. Isa1.16. Lk22.31. Prov.21.10.   Discernment (seared) Tim4.2.

Rebellion (starts in the spirit realm) Ez20.38 Sam2.14 Rev18.23)

Unbelief Titus1.15. Acts28.24 **Deception** (starts in spirit realm) Gal6.3 Sam23.

Allegiance (any collaboration with fallen angels) This activity knowingly, grieves the Holy Spirit) Eph5.11. Eph4.27. Prov2.13 & 17

Dark spirited initiated course/path (the above activity can put you on this course). However, the caution is that those in dark spirited professions have the ability to pull you into dark spirit realms, professions & spiral you onto a dark path or course without resistance. Prov3.6. Eph 2.2.

Destruction/Destroyer (evil angel spirit activity) Ps78.49. Jn10.10.Exo12.23. Ps17.4

Persecuting Principalities Ps 119.161.

Create chambers of principalic Anti-Christ mindsets & imaginations. Must be broken off one's mind and imagination and one must do their best to come out of agreement with how hell is trying to spirit train the mind and imagination through demonic mind repetition. Daily sometimes continual release is needed until the assignment is broken. IJN. Ez8.12.2 Cor10.5. Phil2.5.

Disregard/Disrespect for the work of the Lord on any level. Ps28.5

Insurrection (against biblical authority) Exo16.2. Sam24.6-7. Sam26.9

Unfaithful to God (including His word and/or counsel) Jere17.13

Unreasonable Acts25.27. Sam 25.17

Shamanism

Superstitious Acts17.22	Lucifer an	Satanism
Mormonism	Catholicism	Phariseeism	Unitarism
Hinduism	Nazism	Atheist	New Age
Communism	Buddhist	Yoga	and such like Tim1.10

*Anything influenced, initiated and/or operated by another spirit life activity. Rev 18.23. Exo 23.24 & 33. Acts 17.23.

Any religion, organization, denomination, expressing or teaching spiritual belief systems (individually or collectively) that causes spiritual confusion, strife and/or anything that is contrary to truth and faith in Jesus Christ and Him crucified. Tim 1.10. This would include any areas of Freemasonry, Eastern star, Secret societies, any Lodges, Muslim &/or Islam teaching, etc; much of which seem to teach & enforce their type of spirit life activity which often seems to oppose scripture &/or not acknowledge or exalt Jesus Christ. .Ps38.3. Jn8.32. 2 Pet3.16-17. Dt 5.7,. Exo. 23.24 & 33.

Familiar wicked, unclean & evil Anti-Christ spirits

Working infectiously or contagiously through culture, community, business/marketplaces, families and any size people groups to defile the soul and spirit lives of men (who may be in need to learn how to maintain, guard and protect their spirit lives from spirit from spirit impurities). Ps38.19. Lev19.33. Acts19.16. Acts17.5-7.3 Jn18.3-9. Acts 14.2. Acts 13.50.

Bind and break any curses, dark grips, agreements or holds and reverse & mirror any transfers back to its kind(or habitation in cases of spiritual warfare) In the name of Jesus. Keeping in mind that some spirits can be cast out however, some must be driven out! Mk3.27. Mk16.17. Jn2.15. For more information and insight on driving out spirits that seem to have more of a grip (or that has been assigned), please refer to "The Wash" Flow chart.

Scrip Ref: Mk15.13-14 & 16,20 & 31.3 Jn1.11. Acts17.5-7. Acts8.7. Lk6.18. Mk6.7. Rev 18.2. Gen 1.

Cut Cords: Pride, Vanity, Wickedness, Affliction & Sin that connect you to works of Anti-Christ. Isa 5.18. Job36.8. Prov5.22

Loose from: Pride of life, lust of flesh & lust of eyes that helped to produce the spirit fruit and root of Anti-Christ. 1Jn2.16.

I loose the Holy Spirit to up-root, cleanse, release, and heal in this area. I release the blessings and peace of God to replace the curse. In the name of Jesus. Prov. 26.2. Rom 8.26.

HONOR THE KING

Peter 2.17
Dt 5.7
Tim 3.16. Jn 3.36. Malachi 1.6
Sam 12.20 & 24. Eze 44.23

I Renounce the Ancestral Principalic Stronghold Root Spirit of Fear

<u>Fear can cause men's hearts to fail</u>   Tim1.7.   **4**

I decree I am not the victim, vessel or carrier. Rom9.21. Rom 10.9-10.

We plead the power of the blood and name of Jesus. 1Jn1.7-9 Exodus12.23. Eph1.7. Cor 11.25. Rev1.5

To resist it. IJN. James 4.7.

I Take Authority
I Bind, Break & Divide this root work and it's false authority. In Jesus name. Lk11.18 Mk16.19. Lk 9.1

I Break the power, curse, passion, assignment and will. 2Tim2.26. Exo12.23. Isa 14.5.

I loose Fear from the bloodline, (body, soul, spirit life, relationships and environments) to cut off at the root. I cast it out. In Jesus name. Mk16.17. Jn12.31. Lev17.11. Lk19.31. Lord, we repent...we forgive...

To make room for the Holy Spirit in the up-rooting process of purging, cleansing and healing of the spirit impurities and defilement. Acts2.38. Mk4.17. Isa11.1. Mt12.28. Eph5.26. Cor6.11. Heb4.16. Zec4.6. Eph2.18-22. Thess5.23.

I Bind, Break, Divide, Cut-off and Cast-out this spirit fruit & principalic root of Fear trying to work in our lives through:

A spirit and spiritual work against the mind, thought and thinking process until the spirit fruit is produced. Col 1.21

Self **Personality-Relationships / Environment**

Chaff personalities: Mt.3.12. Chaff is defined as anything worthless.
To annoy or be annoyed. Heb6.8. Prov.22.5. Ps1.4. Rom8.3 & 8. James4.7. Ps49.3. Isa33.12.2 Sam23.6-7. Ez44.7-10.

Fright (ful-fear tactics) Job15.24. Rev21.8.2 Sam17.2. (fear is a snare Prov29.25. Ps124.7). In spirit or natural realms.

Abused or Abusive 2Sam21.1. (naturally or spiritually)

Accuse/accuser of the brethren Rev.12.10.

Bondage (can cause fear) Rom 8.15

Condemnation Rom 8.1

Doubtful Reasoning (can be caused by fear) Mt14.31

Embarrassment

Fetish (can also come from fears)

Fearful heart Isa35.4. Lk21.26.

Procrastination (could be a type of indifferent or)

Indecision

Insomnia (can be caused by fear)

Affliction and/or oppression can produce fear. Gen29.31-32/Job36.8. (naturally or spiritually so)

<u>Anxiety</u> Lk12.22. Gen37.4.

Anguish   Job 15.24. Jer 49.24. Jere 9.5.

Betrayal (can cause a person to fear) Jn13.11 Lk22.2-4 Lk22.6

Distress Ps 107.28

Deceit (can be caused by fear)

<u>Fatigue</u>   Grief   Ps31.9 & 10

Critical spirit (can be a by-product of fear)

<u>Fearful situations</u> Jn6.18. Mt8.26. Job15.24. Lk21.26

Heaviness (can also be a by-produce or fruit of fear)

Iniquitous family patterns Jere11.10.

Iniquity Exo 36.31. 2 Tim 1.7.

Insecurities James 1.8

Inferiority (can be a fruit or bi-product of fear)

Introvert (can also be a fruit of fear)

Migraines (can be produced by fears)

Mischief: (being the subject, vessel or carrier of) Ps119.150. Ps94.20. Ps62.3. Prov.6.18. Eze 11.2.

Paranoia (can be caused by fear)

Panic Attacks Jere49.24 & 29

Shyness

Timid…Timidity Lk8.37. Rom8.15

Unbelief/ vocalized Mt17.20

Wounded spirit can produce fears Prov18.14

Worry (also a spirit fruit of fear) Mt6.34

Intent (unbiblical in nature. desire or action) Acts10.29. Ps21.11. (unkind intent revealed can cause fear)

Intimidation (can cause intentional fear, bullying or vexing….naturally or spiritually

Sorrow Ps 3.2&4.

Suspicions/Suspicious (can be a by-product of fear)

Stress (fruit of fear) Acts 18.5

Self-willed (when exalting over the Lord's will) Titus 1.7.

Terror (or terrorizing, begins with spirit flesh works of mischief & harassment) Job 18.11.

Troubles Job15.24. Mt14.26. (trouble can make one afraid)

Traumas (can affect you from the natural and/or spirit realm)

Un-forgiveness (can also arise from fears) Mt18.34-35.

Victimization (can come from by dark spirit led territorial kingdom assignments). And from any of the following areas or levels of dark spirit operations. Principalities. Rulers of Darkness. Spiritual Wickedness in high places, wicked, evil and or unclean spirits, working through the powers of the air, & human spirits etc, as distracting and invading forces.

Witchcraft: activity can cause fear. Kings, Chpt.19.2.

Other Dark

Spirit Real Influences &/or experiences
Eph 2.2-3. Eph 4.23. Heb 9.14.

This spirit activity tries to affects the mind, conscience, memory, will, desires, spirit visions, imaginations and inclinations, along with impressions, thought/thinking processes, obsessions to the point of magnifications to cause fear. Jere 48.42.

Idol spirits defile the conscious or subconscious. Corin 8.7. Titus 1.15

Spirit voice (s) of the enemy (can also cause fear). Ps 55.3. Neh 4.1

Noise-some pestilence (can emulate fear) Ps 91.6

Confused noise Isa 9.5 Doubtful mind Lk 12.39

Evil patterns (of fear thoughts and thinking) Ps 56.5

Vanity of mind Eph 4.17. Eph 4.23

Compulsive, hasty behavior can be triggered by fear Prov 21.5

Bondages to fear (any level) Rom 8.15

Often Offended 2Tim 1.7

Fear of people Is usually created in the natural &/or spiritual realm. Sam 15.24. Isa 51.12. Sam 30.6.

Relationships. Some can create &/ or Gen 37.4.

Rejection can produce &/or create fear

Commitments can produce fear(s)

Abandonment can cause fear

Retaliation can be a fruit of fear

Could actually be a cover-up for fear. Jn 16.1.Gen37.4 & 5. Deeper study and meditation of God's word to the level needed to off-set the fear Is needed. Mk4.6 & 17.

Fears of certain foods

Fear of speaking one's heart

Fear of failure

Unreasonable fears Acts 25.27

Fear of death Corin 15.26

Fear Seizes Principalic stronghold spirits of fear can cause an unusual or unnatural fear….. Also, someone who has experienced channeling, trafficking and/ or transferring fear spirits into one's life could also begin to sense or suddenly feel un-natural fearfulness seemingly arising from no-where. Whether or not a person realizes this could be happening to them or not is not really the issue in our present day and time. Especially where fear was never present before. Fear can also arise from spiritual and/or natural trauma experiences. Some in dark spirit professions have the ability to pull others into their dark spirit realm(s) causing a spiritual and/ or natural trauma which can also produce fear. 2 Tim 1.7.

<u>Desires</u> can feed into fear in the spirit realm.
Gal 5.26

<u>Unbelief</u> (in thought and thinking processes can be initiated in one's spirit realm. Spiritual release, cleansing & healing is needed. Rom 11.23. Titus 1.15.

<u>Sorrowful spirit</u> Sam 1.15.

<u>Torment</u> (can be caused or by provoked by fear or... 1 Jn 4.18. Lk 6.18.
<u>Unclean spirits</u> 1Lk 6 *(NKJV). Lk 4.36.

Familiar wicked, unclean & evil spirits of fear

Working infectiously through family, culture, relationships, community, business/marketplaces, security/police services, legal/local government systems and any size people group (s) and things to defile and/or violate. Lev 19.33. Acts 19.16. Acts 17.5-7. 3Jn 1.11. Jn 18.3. Break any curse and/or behavior that feed into fear systems and reverse or mirror any spirit transfers back to its kind. In Jesus name. Acts 13.50. Acts 14.2.

Bind and break any possible trinities assignments of principalities, fallen angels, rulers of darkness and spiritual wickedness or any demon wills (working individually and/or through dark spirited territorial plots and plans) trying to develop fear, by the blood and name of Jesus. Cut off the agreement and cast it out. In Jesus name. Please note: Some spirit assignments need to be driven out. If so, please refer to our "Wash" flow chart, for further instruction as an aide to this root system. Isa 14.5. Dt.6.19. Mk 3.12. Mk 3.27.

Cut cords: Of pride, vanity, wickedness, affliction & sin that help connect to fear. Isa 5.18. Job 36.8. Ps 128.4. Prov 5.22.

Loose from: Pride of life, lust of flesh & lust of eyes that help to feed into fear. 1Jn 2.16.

I loose the Holy Spirit to up-root, cleanse, release and heal in this area as we apply our authority in Jesus name. I loose the blessings and peace of God to replace the curse symptoms in Jesus name. Prov 26.2. Mt 16.19. Isa 26.12. Lk 1.79. Rom 8.26.

Fear is a smoke screen: You must do what works for you in faith and agreement with God's word to resist it in Jesus name! 2 tim 1.7. 1 Jn 4.18.

Lord, we pray for victory over fear in our lives, in Jesus name.

You who fear the Lord

Praise Him!

#4

Not the fear.
What time I am afraid, I will trust in Thee
Ps 56.3. Ps 22.23. Isa 51.12. Ps 16.1. Ps 64.1

I Renounce the Ancestral Principalic Stronghold Root Spirit of Infirmity

5

Some learn how to loose themselves. Isa52.2 Some need others to help them get loose before they can gain the ability to stay loose in Jesus name. Lk13.12-16. Lk19.31. Lk8.35. Heb4.15. Mt16.19.

I decree I am not the victim, vessel and/or carrier. Rom9.21 Jn8.32 & 36

We plead the power of the blood and name of Jesus to resist it . 1Jn1.7-9 Exo12.23 Eph1.7.Cor 11.25. James 4.7.

I Take Authority

I Bind, Break & Divide its root work and false authority that can no longer operate (past, present & future). In Jesus name. Lk11.18 Mk16.17.

I Break the power, curse, passion, assignment and will of Infirmity. In Jesus name. 2Tim2.26. Isa 14.5.

I loose Infirmity from the bloodline, (body, soul, spirit life & relationships) to cut it off at the root. I cast it out. In Jesus name. Mk16.17. Jn12.31. Lev17.11. Lk19.31. Exo 12.23. Lord, we repent...we forgive...

To make room for the Holy Spirit in the up-rooting process of purging, cleansing and healing of the spirit impurities and defilement. In Jesus name. Acts2.38. Mk4.17. Isa11.1. Mt12.28. Eph5.26. Cor6.11. Heb4.16. Zec4.6. Eph2.18-22. Thess5.23.

I Bind, Break, Divide, Cut it-off and Cast out this spirit fruit & principalic root of Infirmity trying to work in our lives through:

(A spirit and spiritual work against the mind and thought/ thinking patters until the desired spirit fruit is produced). Col 1.21

Self Thess 5.23 — Personality/Relationships/Environment

I continue to bind, break, divide, cut off and cast out of the body, soul, spirit life/realm and environment any of the dark spirit activities and/or influences,...

Abandonment (concerns),
Anxiety
Anguish/Agony (in natural or spiritual realm)
Attacking/Attacking to war: (spiritually and/or naturally so)
Boast
Bitterness
Broken Hearted
Brokenness
Disquieted Heart
Faint Hearted

Bribes (initiated or to tempt)
Busybody
Bullying others is a type of harassing/vexing-release is needed.
Bitter Words
Deceitful Tongue (hypocrites mouth)
Evil Tongue (unruly tongue)
Grudge
Lying Lips
Mouth of the Wicked
Murmuring, complaining

Amnesia
Confusion consistent ambiguity
Distracting or interrupting another, or being imposed upon with unnecessary distractions:
Envy
Division/Disharmony
Drugs/medicine: (symptoms or side effects)
Deceit (in the heart)
Hiding (any prison type spirit)
Nausea

- **Offended Heart**
- **Offended Soul**
- **Emotional wounds or spiritual Immaturity**
- **Feeble** (feebleness)
- **Fear** (can be a fruit of infirmity)
- **Depression, Desperation, Despair, Distress.**
- **Frustration**
- **Humiliation**
- **Infirmity of flesh**
- **Insecurity/Insomnia**
- **In-content**
- **Lust**
- **Misery/Pain** (worry)
- **Mourn(ing)**
- **Rejection** (see Root #1)
- **Sorrow**
- **Slumber**   **Self-will**
- **Strife**   **Sarcasm**
- **Sin** spirit nature (can be the cause of infirmity)
- **Transgression**
- **Unbelief**
- **Un-thankful**
- **Un-soundness** (body, soul or spirit life)
- **Un-soundness in flesh**

- **Loneliness** (all spirits of separation and it's links)
- **Perverse Lips**
- <u>**Pride**</u>
- **Tale bearing**
- **Tongue Tied**
- **Slow of Speech** (stutter)
- **Illegitimate** (issues)
- **Corruption Linked to Infirmity**
- **Control** (control concerns/issues)

- **Distress in the gate** (any gate)
- **Doubt**
- **Double Minded**
- **Fatigue**   **Numbness**
- **Lethargy – Stupor**
- **Grief**
- **Hate**
- **Iniquity**
- **Presumptuous sins**
- **Shame** (scrip. reveals it is the promotion of fools)
- **Soul unrest** (reaction to spirits trying to operate in a life)
- <u>Thorn type personality (ies)</u>. Perplexing, bothersome or just plain hard to get along with...
- **Un-cleanness**
- **Weak** (tiredness)

- **Inflammation**
- **Distractions** (naturally or spiritually)
- **Jealousy**
- <u>Perverse</u>
- <u>Panic attacks</u>
- **Stress**
- **Vexed**   (a state of being)
- <u>**Victimization**</u> **(natural/spiritual) (this can reveal oppressive spirits manifesting in the natural through men that need healing and/or release. In Jesus name.)**
- <u>Weariness</u>
- <u>**Witchcraft:**</u> Anyone working sorcery, magic and/or occult activity can work with ancestry, sun/moon deities and animal sacrifices to increase their spirit power. Spiritual abuse causing wounds can transcend negatively into the natural, affecting the body, soul & spirit. Consistent spiritual releases using the Root System help off-set any dark spirit assignment against ones body & soul, in Jesus name.
- **Worldly** dance

Cords of Affliction

Affecting the soul (mind, will, emotion) spiritually or naturally so. Any form of affliction that is continual and/or comes in a series.

Affliction from abuse

Affliction from calamity

Body parts

Nose	Eye (area)		
Neck	Face	Female and/or Male (private parts or concerns)	Breasts
Jaw	Ears	Lungs / Chest	
Tongue	Hands	Stomach/Belly	Bladder
(Incl. any tongue impediment	Shoulders	Intestine	
Affecting speech).	Arms	Kidneys	
Tonsil /	Legs	Organs	
Vocal cords			
(voice symptoms)	Bones	Heart (condition/symptoms)	
Esophagus	Knees	Back	
Pharynx	Bone joints	Spinal Cord	
Head	Bone marrow	Bowel System	
Blood			

Leukocyte cells (whether deficient or abnormal, call out any imbalances, to help off-set Leukemia blood disease or aids daily if this is your area of spiritual battle, in Jesus name).

*Other conditions or symptoms list here

Conditions and/or Symptoms

	Fibromyalgia(a type of pain/discomfort)		
Headaches	Emphysema	Impotent	Chemical Imbalance
Nasal congestion	Nausea	Cancer	Off-balance (during times of standing can be spirit activity)
Asthma	Fever	Ulcers	Cist
Colds	Gluttony	Heart condition(s)	Bruises (nat'l or spiritual)
Allergies	Hernia	Infection	Diabetes, release blood and urine from sugar excess
Sinus	Osteoporosis (bones)	Glaucoma (eye disease)	restore insulin balance in Jesus name
Germ life	Premature Aging	Anorexic	Bulimia (call out the symptoms) in Jesus name.
Cramps	Skin conditions/rashes/ itchy/infection	Breath	
Blood conditions/impurities	Body Orders	Arthritis (bitterness)	
Scars/Scar tissues		Meningitis: Inflammation-pain, heat and/or swelling in body to injury or disease, etc.	
Deformities	Cripple symptoms		

Nerve conditions and/or symptoms (usually caused by spirit activity)   Cerebrum(upper part of brain)
Nerve Center (a control center)   Cerebellum (sec. of brain behind /below the cerebrum)

Central nervous systems   **Ruling paralysis spirit activity** can cause:
<u>Neurotic</u> Anxiety, compulsions, phobias/Various mental disorder   Cerebral palsy (*muscular disorder* resulting from damage to nervous system)
<u>Hyper-active</u>   <u>Extreme mood swings</u>
<u>Nervousness</u>   <u>Nervous Disorder</u>

Nervous System: all nerve cells/nervous tissues in an organism/ vertebrate/brain/spinal cord/nerves.

*Call out any degenerative brain activities (or spirit symptoms) causing Alzheimer's. *In Jesus name.*

*Call out any *neurodegenerative disorder & movement disorder symptoms <u>daily</u>* (and/or spirit activity) that can help to produce Parkinson.

<u>Call out</u> the chronic and progressive symptoms and/or product of these symptoms causing secondary concerns, such as pneumonia or falling related incidences. They say there is no cure for it, but not all symptoms come from the senses. And therefore may take a bit more faith (in the name of Jesus and belief in the complete work of the cross). Like ingredients in a cake sometimes you have to call out (or leave out) what should not be there. *In Jesus name.*

<u>Mania:</u> A wild or violent mental disorder. A type of mental disorder. An intense enthusiasm.

<u>Bi-Polar:</u> Having alternating periods of mania. A type of mental depression. See index

<u>Epilepsy:</u> A recurrent disorder of the nervous system characterized by seizures that cause convulsions &/or unconsciousness.

<u>Autism:</u> Developmental Disorder

<u>Balance off/Stumbling</u>

<blockquote>
<u>Creeping things</u> (nat'l or spiritual)

<u>Sick</u> (sickness)

<u>Mute/Dumb</u>
</blockquote>

(Palsy can be accompanied with paralysis of a muscle sometimes with tremors). Call out the symptoms (or any spirit activity causing or behind the).

<u>Spastic:</u> A type of spastic paralysis

<u>Muscular Dystrophy:</u> A progressive wasting away of the muscles…call out/cast out symptoms. IJN.

<u>Multiple Sclerosis:</u> A loss of muscular coordination.

<u>Muscle Spasms:</u> Any sudden, temporary activity, muscular contraction. Spasmodic; fitful.

<u>Stroke:</u> A interruption to normal blood flow to blood flow to brain, from hemorrhage…causing paralysis.

<u>Stiffness</u>

<u>Polio</u>

Leper (is one that has leprosy caused by unclean spirits) **Leprosy**
Leprosy is a progressive, infectious disease of the skin, flesh, nerves, etc. Characterized by ulcers, white scaly scabs, deformities. (Disease of unclean spirits are spiritually and biblically treatable) Dark spirit life can and do attack the body, soul and/or spirit life.

<u>Atrophy</u> (a wasting away or failure to grow) (wasting away can also be a spirit fruit or by-product of iniquity)

<u>Pining away</u> (can also be caused by or be a spirit symptom or reaction to sin, transgression or iniquity)

Mental Concerns (usually brought on and/or stirred up by spirit activity-release is needed in the area being spiritually influenced)

Oppressed: State of being or the Oppressor). Release is needed.

Possessed (with evil spirits) (also possession can occur from not resisting evil spirits until there is need to deal with the accumulation)

<u>Agony:</u> Principalic assignments can literally try to take over it's subjects mind with constant/consistent spirit affliction that can lead to a type of spiritual trauma which can adversely affect the soul, mind, will, emotions and spirit life, up to controlling and/or manipulating the subjects spiritual environment. To off-set this type of spiritual traumatic spirit attack one must become immersed in meditations, daily confessions of authority, prayers and complete trust in Jesus Christ and His complete work in the cross even as a daily confession of faith bring Jesus into your experience until the Lord brings complete healing.

<u>Sorrowful spirit:</u>

<u>Mad:</u>   <u>Fierce Spirits:</u>

<u>Unclean spirits:</u> Can produce a violent nature and betrayal.

Evil spirits: Operating in a person's body, soul and spirit life, cause a person to jump on you. Release is needed in Jesus name.

Perverse: Can also create unsoundness and can provoke the Lord. Release and healing.

Lunatic: Irrational, idiotic, senseless, psychotic, deranged, insane).

Legion: Many or collection of unclean spirits due to no release can cause a problem naturally and spiritually so.

Schizophrenia: Can be a plague affecting the body, soul, spirit life, relationships and/or environment.

*Please note: That witchcraft/occultic/sorcery and/or false prophet assignments can also provoke some of the above ailments. See section 2.

Other Dark **Spirit realm influences** & experiences. Eph 4.23. Eph 2.2-3. Heb 9.14.

That would affect the soul's chambers which include the mind (thinking/thought) processes, memory, will, seeing vision, sight, hearing, imagination, inclinations, impressions and magnificat on until it becomes an obsessions.

Desires. Some spirits will rise through your desires, to make them contrary to God's desires revealed in His word, present truth and/or counsel.

Will. Some spirits will war against a person's will through consistent patterns of affliction and/or constant spirit impurity release through channeling, trafficking and/or manifestations and/or infesting processes to literally break you away from God to serve the operation of darkness. People are literally being used for this. It appears that constant spirit abuse and deception could also force a change in one's will and is a reason to learn how to resist it.

Idol spirits defile the conscious

Vanity/Vain thinking/thought patterns

Evil patterns of thinking

Confused noise	Noise-some pestilence
Doubtful Mind.	Unbelief
Betrayal	Corrupt spirit life.
Foul Spirit	Vision (can be spiritual defiled by constant unnatural spirit intrusions)
Spirit of infirmity Lk13.11	Spirit Illusion: (spiritual interference can cause unsound judgment).
Discernment	

Magnification (of any dark spirit life activity can form); when consistent release is not found (IJN).

Dark course or path (some will help to create, find, keep or spirt force you on a dark spirit course/path into the will and assignment of dark operations instead of the will and on course/path within your assignment in operation of God. Please understand And recognize the spiritual distinction.

Allegiance or alliance with dark angel spirits must be broken. Principalic spirits have the ability to force you into allegiance with them working through community and/or any size spirit group (in the spirit realm if not in the natural).

Wrong spirit covering (even unaware) Can keep you connected to dark angel spirit activity and/or demonic environments. This is another reason why "out of the blue" anyone could be "spirit" targeted by principalities to constantly traffic, channel and transfer dark spirit life into a person's life. A dark spirit method of keeping a unwilling person connected to dark spirit life activity and realms to serve the operation of darkness. This is also a dark spirit method to weaken a spirit life and will in Christ. Constant trafficking, channeling and transferring of dark spirits into a life can also produce a fearful conscious and/or mindset, if there are no consistent spirit releases. Therefore, it is necessary to come out from among them to preserve and/or regain one's spirit life and soul in Christ.

<u>Familiar wicked, evil & unclean spirits of Infirmity</u> can work seemingly, infectiously through culture, community, environments, things, family, any people group to defile one's body, soul & spirit for dark operations. James 4.7. Lev 19.33. 3Jn 11.11. Jn 18.3. Acts23.20-21. Acts25.7. Jn 18.3. Acts 14.2.

Bind and break any dark trinities, agreements and/or assignments of principalities, fallen angels, rulers of darkness, spiritual wickedness, fallen angels or demons in high places (working individually and/or through dark spirited territorial assignments) by the blood and name of Jesus. Cut them off from the power of the air and cast them out. In Jesus name. Isa14.5. Dt6.19. Mk3.12. Mk3.27. If it is a spiritual assignment it will tak a process of time spent with the Lord in resisting hell's will for your life. 2Tim 2.26.

Cut Cords: Pride, Vanity, Wickedness, Affliction & Sin, that would connect one to infirmity. Isa 5.18. Job 36.8. Ps 128.4. Prov 5.22

Loose from: Pride of life, lust of flesh, lust of eyes bands of wickedness and affliction that would keep one connected to infirmity. 1Jn2.16.

Scrip Ref: Pride: Prov8.13. Prov13.10. Prov16.18.
  Ps36.11. Ps10.2. 1 Jn 4.18. 2 Tim 1.7
  Vanity: Isa5.18. Acts14.15. Ps24.4. Ps62.9. Prov22.8.
  Wicked: Exo23.7.

I loose the Holy Spirit to uproot, cleanse, release and heal in the needed areas. I release the blessings and peace of God to replace any curse or ill symptoms of infirmity. In Jesus name. Isa 26.12. Rom 8.26.

I will take sickness away Exo 23.25   Thou are loosed from you infirmity. Lk13.12   I am the Lord that healeth thee. Exo15.26.
Himself took our   #5

Infirmities

Likewise the Holy Spirit helps our infirmities.....and makes intercession for the saints according to the will of God. Prov18.14. Rom8.26-27. And in the same   hour, He cured many of their infirmities, plagues and evil spirits and unto many that were blind He gave sight. Lk7.21-23. The spirit of a man will sustain his infirmity, but a wounded spirit who can bear? Prov.18.14. A man was healed after 38 years of infirmity. Jn5.5-6. To who Jesus asked, will though be made whole? And to him that is near, I will heal.....Isa57.19. Mt8.17. Prov16.14. Lk8.2.Lk13.11. Rom15.1. Lk7.21. Isa10.27. Lk 9.11.

I Renounce the Ancestral Principalic Stronghold Root Spirit of Whoredom   6

Whoredom, along with idols can cause a land to fret. Ez16.41. Lev19.29. Lev18.25. Hosea1.2. Idolatry: Rev21.8.

Whoredom is the mistress of witchcraft. Nahum3.14. Mistress can be defined as: one who is the head of something. Whoredom can cause the land to be full of wickedness. Lev19.29. Do not define the land. Num 35.34.

I decree I am not the victim, vessel and/or carrier. Rom9.21.

We plead the blood and the name of Jesus. 1Jn1.7-9 Exodus12.23. Eph1.7. Cor 11.25.
To Resist it. James 4 7

I Take Authority
I Bind, Break & Divide it's work & false authority that is no longer stand, operate or influence. In Jesus name. Lk11.18 Mk16.19.

I Break the power, curse, passion, assignment, obsession and will of Whoredom. 2Tim2.26. Isa14.5.

I loose Whoredom from the bloodline, (body, soul, spirit life & relationships). I cut it off and cast it out. In Jesus name. Mk16.17. Jn12.31. Lev17.11. Lk19.31. Exo 12.23.

To make room for the Holy Spirit to help with the up-rooting process of purging, cleansing and healing from spirit impurities, defilement & spirit violations. In Jesus name. Mk 4.17. Isa11.1. Mt 12.28. Zec4.6. Eph 2.18-22. Thess 5.23. Acts 2.38. Corin 6.11.

I Bind, Break, Divide and Cut Off this spirit fruit principalic root of Whoredom trying to work in our lives through:

A spirit and spiritual work against the mind, thought and thinking patterns until the spirit fruit is produced. Col 1.21

Self (Spirit fruit Character)   **Personality-Relationships / Environment**
Chaff personalities: Ps1.4. Mt.3.12. Heb6.8. Judges16.16. Flesh Gal 5.13. Job21.18-19

Adultery	Abominations	Abuse
Idolatry	Angry	Bitter
Confusion	Affliction or being afflicted	Defilement
Contrary	Covetousness	Flattery
Deceitful lusts Deceit		Greed
Filthy (Uncleanness, spoiled, polluted, defiled, dirty, daubed activity can affect the land).	False accusers	Idols
	Fear	Lies
Heart Intent (Wrong or quest. Heart belief system)	Fool (foolish)	Lust of flesh/eyes
Harlot behavior	Filthiness	Manipulation Provok
Exhibition of the body	Haughty	
Harlot clothing	Lusts for money	
Lewdness Iniquity/Iniquitous family patterns Prostitution/Fornication	Love of position	

Self-Centered

Selfish

Self-exaltation

Whorish eyes (never satisfied)

Whoredom (break curse off & release children from like spirit (along with spirit images)

Homosexuality (a spirit type of whoredom and therefore an expression of the witchcraft religion)

Eyes of vanity

Weak Heart (describes the whorish women

Whorish heart (that departs from the Lord)

Whoring inventions

Whoremonger

Pollutes (whoredom & wickedness)

Pride

Riotous behavior

Seek mischief, daily vexing

Shame

Sows (seeds of strife)

Strive

Unnatural affection

Wickedness Can produce whoredom

<u>Rape</u> concerns (any sex sins or rape experience flash back & hurts. This flashback would a dark spirit activity as consistent mind flesh)

Spendthrift

Scorn/mock/bullying

Transgression

Vain

Vanity

Witchcraft

Worldly lusts

Spirit realm influences &/or experiences. Rom 5.4.
Eph4.23. Eph2.2-3. Heb9.14. Jere16.12.

Affects mind/conscience (thinking/thought) process, desire, inclinations, memory, will, imagination, voice, sight, spirit vision, eye gate to produce magnification and obsessions of dark spirit activity.

Create flesh mind   Idol spirits activity that affect the conscience mind, thinking
                                        & thought processes.

Spiritual confusion (brought on by dark spirit provoking negative and/or constant confused noise and noise-some pestilence with no release) Ps91.6. Isa9.5 or destroying evil angel spirits

Create evil patterns of thinking
Voice (vocal cords/throat area)
Evil communications (verbal or non-verbal)

Create vanity of mind

Self-delusion.

Un-steadfast spirit life with God

Unbelief   (always begins in the spirit realm first, then manifest verbally).

Evil eye (eye gate)   Unless there is release, I have even seen the enemy flow his power through the eye gate to restrain or delay a person long enough to connect them in the spirit realm with another person nearby or for nonsense reasons spirits are forever trying to network people and/or spirit activity together (for natural reasons) in the spirit realm in an effort to establish Satan's governing influence in earth realm over everyone.

Corrupt springs (spirit life affected) Possibly through a succession of spirit trafficking or marshaling spirits into one's body, soul and/or spirit life.

Seeds of sorcery.

Spirit of whoredom.   Seeds of whoredom

Spirit of the world

Wrong "spirit" life coverings.

Create rebellion.

Allegiance, alliance of those in collaboration with dark angel spirits that birth or keep you (through others or directly in spirit realm) connected to principalities and powers of the air.

Dark course/path Those with dark spirit initiatives have the ability working in and/ or through others to direct ones activity towards a path – which must be spiritually and biblically discerned. In short, some in dark spirit professions have the ability to draw others into their dark spirit realms. Whether, a person realizes that they were doing it or not (actually drawing another soul into a dark path), should be aware, realize and understand that there are only 2 spiritual kingdom activities. Without this awareness, spiritual and biblical aptitude (these days) would be seen as the blind leading the blind.

Desire to be around evil (spirited) men. (lust = overwhelming desires, intense desire, etc…)

Create chambers of whoredom mindsets, imagination, (spirit) images and memory. Ez8.12.2. Cor10.5.

Familiar wicked, unclean & evil spirits of Whoredom working infectiously through culture/community/business-marketplace, family or any size people groups to spiritually defile the body, soul, spirit life and relationships Jn18.3. Ja. 4.7. Acts 14.2.

Bind and break any dark trinities, agreements and/or assignments of principalities, rulers of darkness, spiritual wickedness in high places or demons (working individually and/or through dark spirited territorial assignments) In Jesus name. Cut off their activity from the power of the air and the earth. In Jesus name. Isa14.5. Dt6.19. Mk3.12. Mk3.27.

Cut Cords: Pride, Vanity, Wickedness, Affliction & Sin, that would connect you to the spirit activity of whoredom. Isa5,18. Job36.8. Ps128.4. Prov5.22

Loose yourself from: Pride of life, lust of flesh, lust of eyes that would keep you connected to the spirit of whoredom. 1Jn2.16.

I loose the Holy Spirit to up-root, cleanse, release and heal in this area. I release the blessings and the peace of God to replace the curse and/or ill symptoms of whoredom, in Jesus name. Isa 26.12. Rom 8.26

...AND I WILL BETROTH THEE TO ME IN RIGHTEOUSNESS, JUDGMENT, LOVING-KINDNESS MERCIES.......FAITHFULNESS & YE SHALL KNOW THE LORD

Hosea 2.19-20. Hosea 3.5

Binding afflictions (until spiritual or natural bondage occurs)

Bitterness

Blocking/Hindering (attitudes, relationships or prayers, etc.)

Busy-Body

Continual Sorrow. (whether caused by you or someone else, release is needed, IJN).

Fears (or intimidation can produce and/or be the spirit fruit of bondage)

Heart Issues (that are contrary to truth)

Hurt (bruised) emotions

Ignorance

Infirmities (body, soul, spirit, relationships) that produce bondage. See stronghold root spirit #5

Intent (questionable/unbiblical)

Insecurity can be a spirit fruit of bondage

Rebellion

Self righteous (ness)

Shame

Sin (spirit nature), can produce bondage

Twist words

Perversion

Un-forgiveness

Anger

Arrogant Pride

Driving Compulsions/Inclinations leading to bondage like urges to: overeat, over-shop or suddenly display un-usually or un-rational emotions, habits of striving, or the love pleasures more than God, etc.

Bondages to: condemnation

Corruption/corrupt communications (any type)

Foolishness

Hate (various levels of hate until it becomes perpetual, because "hate" is a spirit and spirit life never dies, it only finds ways to reproduce itself)

Lovers of this present world.

Mourning

Suffer / Suffering some use suffering to force relations.

Some are bound in the suffering. Either way release is needed.

Tale bearing   Stubborn

Vexing others: Either the vexed or can be bound to dark spirit powers (that are actually using the person causing the vexation) and the vexing can be done by spirits territorially through people can bring bondage in the life
of the person being vexed. For those being spiritually warred against in public places and/or arenas could use our flow chart to confess the authority of Christ wherever one is being warred against. Until, peace is restored.

Anguish

Atheism-Anti-Christ (naturally or spiritually expressed)

Deceit

Distress

Division (creating any divisive tactics to work against harmony)

Fault-Finding

Envy

Error

Hypocrisy

Intellectualism (unharmonious with truth)

Jealousy

Lawlessness

Lack

Rationalism (over the truth of God's word)

Scorn, Bullying, Belittling

Transgression

Un-stable/Un-steadfast time with God. (could also be caused by distracting spiritual warfare).

Unbelief (vocalized)   Vile

Other Dark

Spirit Realm Influences (that can transcend into experience)

Affects mind, memory, desire, will, imagination, sight, spirit vision, voice & hearing; mind/conscious, thinking/thought processes into a spirit type of magnification until it becomes an obsession.

Unbelief (can also be created and/or initiated first in the spirit realm and them manifest in the thinking/thought processes by releasing consistent negative thoughts, causing the constant negative thoughts being sent to become your thought pattern, when it's not really the person but the principalic spirit itself trying to mind force itself into the person's personality in effort of permanently becoming the person's personality. Release from the principalic spirit reveals, the developed spirit mindset was an assignment and not actually the person.

Vain thoughts   Can help create a flesh mind.

Confused noise

Noise-some pestilence

Financial Bondage Concerns/Issues

Concerns can be broken down in the following areas:

Generational symptoms of poverty (Python characteristics) could come from individual or family iniquity, or:

From holding first fruit

From withholding tithe/offering

Symptoms from unpaid vows

Symptoms of Haggai. (an attitude more concerned with ones own house than the house of the Lord).

Symptoms of stolen inheritance.

Symptoms for spirit of failure   Symptoms (or spirit of need)

Symptoms (or spirit of lack)   Mammon (servant more than God)

*Sometimes the enemy will so spirit attack a person through people needing spiritual release, cleansing and healing as a assignment to keep a person from working and/or in a constant state of lack and need. It is not always the person per se.

I Renounce the Ancestral Principalic Stronghold Root Spirit of Bondage

2Cor11.20 **7**

(or spirit invasion, intrusion and/or spirit domination of oneself or another person's spirit life activity – under spirit domination (and/or individual spirit belief system) trying to break through into your life). You must rise up to resist it on any level! In Jesus name. Until one gains the spiritual ability and knowledge to release themselves from spirit impurities, defilement and/or violations that can occur without consistent release. In Jesus name. Domination is defined by Webster's Dictionary as: a person or thing that rules, controls, masters, command or power over a situation, person or thing. Therefore, as concerning the only 2 spiritual kingdoms operating among us either we can allow Jesus to be our Lord, Savior and King and learn to resist dark spirit life intrusions, invasions and activity or be overcome, overpowered and forced by spirit domination into dark spirit servitude always using you to affect society, to pull others into dark spirit realms, until you rise up in the authority of Jesus Christ and exclusive faith in complete work of the cross. Keeping one's body, soul and spirit life free in Christ Jesus is a part of our spiritual warfare.

Some have bondages rooted in the mind/thinking-thought processes, desires, will & emotions. Some are in the areas of health, relationships, finances, etc…

And God remembered His covenant. Exo2.24.2. Pet2.19. Jn8.36.

> **I decree I am not the victim, vessel and/or carrier.** Rom9.21. Col 2.10. Jn 8.36.
>
> **We plead the power of the blood and name of Jesus.** 1Jn1.7-9. Exodus12.23. Eph1.7. Cor 11.25. Rev 1.5.
>
> To Resist it. IJN. James 4.7.

I Take Authority

I Bind, Break & Divide it's work & false authority that is no longer operates. Lk 11.18. Mt. 16.19. Jn 8.32. Lk 9.1.

I Break the power, curse, passion, will, assignment, purpose of bondage in Jesus name. 2Tim2.26. Isa14.5.

I loose Bondage from the bloodline, (body, soul, spirit life & relationships & environment). I cut it off at the root. I cast it out. In Jesus name. Mk16.17. Jn12.31. Lk19.31. Ps 54.5.

To make room for the Holy Spirit in the up-rooting process of purging, cleansing and healing from spirit impurities, defilement and/or spirit violations that can cause spirit domination (or another level of spiritual bondage). In Jesus name. Mk4.17. Isa11.1. Mt12.28. Zec4.6. Eph2.18. Thess5.23.Acts2.38. Eph 1.7.

I Bind, Break, Divide and Cut-off the spirit fruit and principalic root of Bondage trying to work/operate in our lives through

(You can pencil in below whatever is not listed here to personalize this list):

A spirit and spiritual work against the mind, thought & thinking process until the principalic spirit fruit is produced.

Self (Spirit fruit Character)   **Personality-Relationships / Environment**

Chaff personalities: Heb 6.8. Ps 1.4. Mt. 3.12. 2Corin 10.3.

Desires wrong desires created to draw others to you, producing wrong relationships/fellowships.

Evil spirited patterns thoughts & negative spirit image recall or visions

A bound spirit   Sons of baal

Spiritual Bondage   Spirits in Prison (due to disobedience)

Destroying evil angel spirit

Will

Unclean spirits (can produce symptoms (if not resisted) of bondage by trying to affect or overcome the following areas). Therefore, resist and/or cast out an of the following spirit reactions and/or spirit symptoms in Jesus name.

Your voice

Your mind and will try to bring your mind to a tormented state (without consistent release of spirit impurities & defilement).

Can physically seize a person's body (sometimes causing convulsions-violent, involuntary spasm of the muscles)

Can open the way (or door) for other spirits to enter your body, soul, spirit life, relationships and/or experiences without release of spirit impurities.

Can cause or produce lust desires (intense and overwhelming desire and flesh states of wantonness)

Can cause crying to the point of excessive.

Can cause people to scoff, scorn, stalk or cause mocking (spiritually and/or naturally so) expressions, selfishness, hate of others and have zero tolerance for other races, cultures and other or any noticeable differences or distinctions one could mock or scorn at.

Can cause or produce a violent spirit nature *if there are(no) consistent releases of spirit impurities and/or defilement.*

Can cause one to cut oneself.

Can cause bruises (can also be caused by spirit penetration; they almost feel like a spirit burn sensation, and sometimes the bruise is more underneath the skin).

Can try to return with other (wicked) spirits, therefore unclean spirits can also be considered wicked spirit nature.

Can attach from things or from places found in community, bus/mktpl., recreation/park areas, even churches, etc. IJN.

Chamber thoughts & thinking patterns that can cause &/or create a bound mindset (to include imaginations, memory, thinking & thought processes and/or visions)

Need to be broken through and by applying consistent faith principles to resist and stop the dark spirit life invasion and apparent assignment against one's mind, thought/thinking processes and eventually the takeover of one's body, soul and spirit life in Christ and relationships.

Familiar wicked, unclean and evil spirits of Bondage working infectiously through culture, community, family, any size people group to defile or violate the soul and spirit life in Christ Jesus. Some may need to resist consistently, due to some being more susceptible to spirit transfers than others. Some need to resist only if confronted by dark spirit intentions, not to resist will and would eventually cause increases of spirit activity in one's life (body, soul and/or spirit life until bondage occurs).

Bind and break dark spirit assignments and agreements or principalic trinities, fallen angels, rulers of darkness, spiritual wickedness in high places (working individually and/or through dark spirited territorial assignments). Cut it off and cast it out. In Jesus name.

Cut Cords: Pride, Vanity, Wickedness, Affliction & Sin that would keep you connected to spiritual Bondage.

Loose yourself from: Pride of life, lust of flesh & lust of eyes and affliction being used to keep one or bring one into spiritual bondage or domination.

I loose the Holy Spirit to up-root, cleanse, release and heal in this area. I release the blessings to replace the curse or symptoms of the curse that spiritual bondage or domination can cause, in Jesus name.

*Please note: that often affliction of/or if coming from any level of dark spirited operations are designed also, among other things, to keep you connected to dark spirited ways, activity or some will try to control through the affliction process until spiritual and/or natural bondage occurs, therefore a spirit type of witchcraft control activity to govern one's soul, spirit life and/ or environment. *Pray for any houses of bondage to be released in Jesus name.

***Please note:** The various levels of spirit magnification and obsessions that exists in a life will determine the depth, level and intensity of the "spirit domination" operating. Therefore, it is easier to maintain one's spirit liberties in Christ Jesus and exclusive faith in His complete work at the cross when releasing oneself with consistent spiritual releases of spirit impurities, defilement and seducing, bewitching spirit violations or presence of the enemy. The enemy can't operate fully or fully manifest in your life until he can gain position of either the body, soul, spirit life and/or spirit realm.

"Stand Fast in the Liberty Christ has made us"

Free

He brings out those which are bound with chains
Gal 5.1 & 13. PS 68.6. Ps 9.9.
Pet 2.19. Jn 8.36.

I Renounce the Ancestral Principalic Stronghold Root Spirit of Error 8

(Isa 29.24. 2Sam 6.7. James 5.20. 1Jn 4.6. Ez 45.20)

I decree I am not the victim, vessel or carrier. Rom 9.21.

We plead the blood and name of Jesus. 1Jn7-9. Exo12.23. Eph1.7. Cor11.25.

To resist it. James 4.7.

I Take Authority

Bind, Break & Divide it's work & false authority that is no longer operates. Lk11.18. Mt.16.19. Lk 9.1.

I Break the power, curse, passion, assignment and will. 2Tim2.27. Isa 14.3.

I loose Error from the bloodline (body, soul, spirit life & relationships). I cut it off at the root. I cast it out. In Jesus name. Mk16.17. Jn12.31. Lk 19.31.

To make room for the Holy Spirit in the up-rooting process of purging, cleansing and healing of spirit impurities and/or defilement. Mk 4.17. Isa11.1. Mt 8.16. Mt 12.28. Zec 4.6. Eph 2.18. Acts 2.38.

I Bind, Break, Divide and Cut-off the spirit fruit and principalic root of Error trying to operate in our lives through:

A spirit and spiritual work against the mind, thought & patterns until the spirit fruit is produced.

Self (Spirit fruit Character)   **Personality-Relationships / Environment**

Chaff personalities: Mt. 3.12. Ps 1.4. Job 21.18-19. Heb 6.8.

Confusion (is envy, strive = evil work)
Error (to plan evil)
Error of wicked (Fall from steadfastness)
Vanity (work of errors & flesh)
Heart issues (contrary to scripture –
Selfish
Self will
Un-forgiveness

Over-sensitivities Can reveal that release is needed from either spirit impurities, defilement or spirit violations of others.
2. Over-sensitivities could also cause one to get an attitude and a attitude could make it easier for one to cause and/or get into sin. For whatsoever is not of faith, is sin.

Accuser
Accuse falsely (seeking to accuse)
Anger
Arrogance
Argumentative/Unreasonable
Avenger R
Corrupt Sacrifice or service
Deceit – Deception
Deceitful workers of Christ
Err from truth
False submission
Fears can produce err
Form of godliness, denying the power
Gossip
Hate
Hypocrites
Ill-Treating others

Abomination
Annoying (spiritual &/or natural behavior)
Abuse from perpetrators or self abuse Mt27.30-41 Attitude(s)
Contentious
Digs up evil (one who looks for evil or trouble)
Devilish wisdom
False prophecies (words spoken to me, by me or over me)
False matter/way
Envy
Fools mouth
Foolishness
Greed
Hypocritical Comfort
Iniquity
Iniquitous family patterns

Insurrection (rising against biblical authority)

Lies

Murmur to complain

Mix profane with holy (without biblically and spiritually acknowledging the Lord).

Neglecting the commandments & commands (form of disobedience)

Nosey. Snoop. Meddlesome

Profane (dishonor) God's name

Possession issues: trying to control what belongs to the Lord

Provoked to jealousy

Provoking – Provocations

Lawlessness

Mischief

Offended/offensive

Punishing the just

Pride/Pride of Life

Perversion

Proud purposes E

Provoke (ed) to jealousy

Prejudice   Racism

Double Minded

Refuse godly correction or instruction

Rebel against will of Lord
(sometimes in ignorance or confusion)

Spirit realm Influence

Affects mind/conscious (thinking/thought) patterns, desires, memory, will, voice, imagination, inclination, sight, seeing, spirit vision and magnification until the error becomes an obsession.

Idol spirits defile the conscious

Spiritual confusion through noise-some pestilence and negative spirit image recall or can also come from spiritual persecution (naturally &/or spiritually so.

Evil thinking thought pattern.

Unbelief (unbelief start in the spirit realm)

Destroying evil angels spirits and, or warring spirit of baal.

Spiritual blindness innocence/ignorance or foolishness.

Corrupt spring or Spiritual corruption (defiled spirit life-can also come from someone &/or something consistently channeling &/or trafficking dark spirits into one's spirit, soul &/or body life and, or a unmaintained spirit life)

Sin spirit nature: Has a desire for sin and must be ruled over.

Spirit of Whoredom: causes err. Hosea 4.12.Hosea 5.4

Allegiance & collaboration with fallen/dark angel that will birth and/or keep you connected to them-the error of the group (and their dark spirit life activity).

Desire (to be around evil men, places and/or things can be initiated by dark spirit angel life activity.

Dark fellowships can also be initiated &/or plotted by dark spirit life activity for the purposes of birthing or keeping you connected to them and their error (their dark spirit will, plans and purposes).

Dark courses/paths can also be swayed, initiated, created, birth, manipulated and maneuvered by those with dark spirit personalities.

Spendthrifts

Slanderous

Shame

Strife Prov

Superstitious reasoning

Swearing

Self-preeminence
(spirits of self-importance)

Transgression

Un-steadfast in the Lord

Unbelief (vocalized)

Wasteful

Vain Comforting

Work of errors

Wearisome (can weary you with vanity).

Sorcery: working through witchcraft, whoredom, divination, magic, occult and/or any type of dark spirit profession.

*Hopefully, we can begin to perceive and see that spirits can house personality traits and/or can even create a belief system without consistent release. In Jesus name.

Familiar wicked, unclean & evil spirits of Error coming through family, culture, community, business/marketplaces, any size people group.

Bind and break any dark trinities, assignment and agreements of principalities, rulers of darkness, fallen angels, spiritual wickedness in high places (working individually and/or through dark spirited territorial assignments). We resist you from the North. South. East and West. We cut you off from the power of the air and earth. In Jesus name. GO!

Cut Cords: Pride, Vanity, Wickedness, Affliction & Sin that would connect or bring you into error.

Loose yourself from: Price of life, lust of flesh & lust of eyes that would connect you & keep you in error.

I loose the Holy Spirit to cleanse, release, up-root and heal in this area. I release the blessings and peace of God to replace any curse symptoms of error, in Jesus name.

Is it better to choose iniquity rather than suffer affliction? Job 36.21. 2Tim 2.12.

......He will bring me forth to the light and I shall

Behold His Righteousness

Micah 7.8-9
James 5.19-20.
2Sam 6.7

#8

I Renounce the Ancestral Principalic Stronghold Root Spirit of Perversion Mt17.16-17   9

Heal us Lord from that which: perverts, leads astray from truth, and corrupts (defiles) or misuses. IJN. Heal us from that which distorts (twist, misrepresents, misinterprets, deceives or modifies and tried to reproduce itself in our lives unfaithfully). And from that which deviates from what is right and from, that which despises the Lord. In Jesus name. Prov. 14.2. Cleanse us O Lord. Jn 10.35.

I decree I am not the victim, vessel or carrier. Rom 9.21. Col 2.10

We plead the blood and the name of Jesus. 1Jn7-9. Exo12.23. Eph1.7. Cor 11.25.

To resist it. IJN. James 4.7.

I Take Authority

I Bind, Break & Divide it's false authority, that is no longer operate in our lives. (past, present, future), in Jesus name. Lk 11.18. Mt. 16.17. Lk 9.1.

I Break the power, curse, passion, assignment agreement and will of perversion. 2Tim 2.16. Isa 4.5.

I loose Perversion out of the bloodline body, soul, spirit life, relationships and environment. I cut it off at the root and cast it out in Jesus name. Mk16.17. Jn12.31. Lk 19.31.

We welcome the Holy Spirit to make room for the Holy Spirit in the up-rooting process of purging, cleansing and healing of spirit impurities, defilement and/or spirit violations of others. Mk 4.17. Isa 11.1. Mt. 8.16. Mt. 12.28. Zec 4.6. Eph 2.18-22. Ez 3.18-22. Jn13.13-15. Acts 2.38.

I Bind, Break, Divide, Cut-Off and Cast-Out the spirit fruit and principalic root of Perversion trying to operate in our lives through:

A spirit and spiritual work against the mind, thought & thinking process until the spirit fruit is produced.

Self (Spirit fruit Character)

Personality-Relationships / Environment
Chaff personalities: Mt. 3.12. Ps 1.4. Job 21.18-19.

Self	Personality-Relationships	Environment
Deceit	Abusive and/or Abused treatment	Abominable (customs/traditions & belief systems)
Defilement	Abominations	Betrayal
Contrary heart beliefs to truth and contrary counsel to the heart,	Accuser	Bribe
Heart intent	Arrogant	Corrupt (ion) by flattery
Eye gate	Affliction	Dark watches &/or discernment (naturally &/or spiritually so).
Flattery	Condemnation	Despise
Hate	Confusion	Disharmony (that reward evil for good)
Hard to get along with: due to one's spirit nature in need of release and healing.	Digs up evil (They look for trouble for sport. Spiritual release and healing is needed). Not the same as godly biblical discovery.	Disrespect of others
Proud Heart (stirs up strife or looks for trouble)	Division (carnal/flesh disharmony)	Fear
Perverse heart	Discord	Iniquitous family patterns
	Envy	
	Jealousy	

Perverted (by one's level of wisdom & knowledge.

<u>Perverse or twisted Disputes</u> (perverse ways & belief systems).

<u>Perverse or twisted Judgment</u> (of right ways, due to spirit belief systems contrary to truth)

<u>Perverseness</u> that can cause transgression.

<u>Self-Righteous(ness)</u>: Revealed in ones behavior or belief systems

Vanity

Pride

Fools / Foolishness, of a man perverts his way

Guilt

Hypocrite

Lying in wait (for harmful intentions)

Lying

Lawlessness

Mean

Oppressing personality

Offended (spirits can and do cause over-sensitivities) Releasing oneself from spirit impurities and defilement can help assure a right nature.

Presumptuous sins (or transgressions)

Lying vanities

Malice

Maliciousness

Manipulation

Mischief (they seemingly are continually at war (or striving ways)… simply because they are in need of spiritual release, cleansing and healing from the. Savior).

Profane

Provocations

(To Provoke consistently)

Proud looks or purposes

Reasoning (reflecting a dark spirit nature)

Other Dark

Spirit Realm Influences
& experiences.

Affects the mind, conscience, thinking/thought processes, memory, will, desire, sight, vision, <u>inclination, hearing, magnification, etc., to the point of obsession.</u>

Spirit voice of the enemy.

<u>Idol spirits defile conscious</u>

Unclean spirits

Filthy mind/Reprobate mind.

<u>Corrupt mind</u> <u>Vanity of mind</u>.

Seared conscience.

<u>Chronic worrier</u>. Unbelief (created in spirit realm)

<u>Dark spirit image fantasies/ imaginations</u>

Slander

Unbelief (vocalized) (nat/spiritually)

Unjust punishment

Adversaries or adversarial personalities, environments (render evil for good)

Unreasonable

Vanity

Vainness

Resisting Truth

Religious examining & sifting

Transgression

Ambiguous &/or unclear communications that may lead to confusion (a type of deceit).

Un-forgiveness

Un-faithfulness

Un-natural affects

Un-sound

Vile affection

Wicked (works of mischief)

Confused vain thoughts/ noise-some pestilence.

Negative to obsessed spirit image perverse thought recall.

Create un-steadfast spirit with God (through spiritual and/or natural distraction)

Breach in tongue (due to perverseness in the tongue)

Iniquitous tongue

Some types of unclean spirit activity

Frigid

Self-gratification: Masturbation

<u>Lewdness</u>

Bestiality

Any type of sex perversion or confusions.

Adultery nat'l or spiritual.

Fornication

<u>Incest</u>

Pedophiles

Hypocrites mouth

Naughty tongue/False lips

Perverse tongue.

Spirit of perversion

Destroying evil angel spirits.

Evil tongue (must be rooted out)

Compulsive speaking.

Vain/dark fellowships

Evil encouragement

Dark Watches

Desires to be with evil men.

Sons or daughters of baal (or spirit of baal teach others also how to be a son of baal and will turn ones spirit life in Christ to theirs – it's like a DNA spirit nature-release & healing needed). This connection (spiritually and naturally so) need to be broken once realized, constantly/consistently until Lord brings complete deliverance.

Chamber of perverse mindset, imaginations, imagery & memory
Any type of spirit invasion can occur by being in wrong spiritual environments or it can occur by people in allegiance with spirit activity or as a spirit assignment sent by someone in a dark spirit profession, who have located you. It's an occult attack if it repetitious.

Orgy's: can also be viewed as demonic seed breeding or ritual sex acts, for spiritual and/or natural reasons.

Sex molestation/Any sex abuse and/or sex traffic.

Pornography (spiritually & naturally so)

Nasty

Homosexuality (or its agenda.

Lesbian (abominations) We should desire release from being consistently in spirit environments contrary to truth.

Nightmare spirits: It is said to be a type of witchcraft spirit that only seems to attack the body when one is asleep. Calling upon the name of the Lord can help pull you out of this hellish nightmare &/or resist it by using our "Wash" flow chart. Also 20-inch fans close to bed can prove helpful.

*Night visitations would be hells desires to find a place in anyone's life they can't get to during their waking hours. It is a serious assignment if it is repetitious.

I would also consider binding unclean spirits on objects you are sleeping on. Just in case. The powers of the air seemingly can cause spirits to manifest in objects/things, as well as people.

(It would also be a good idea to prayer bless everything, binding and breaking powers and loosing the blessing on everything you purchase or that you come in contact with).

Naughty (one who devises evil continually)

Bisexual desires

Effeminates spirits (if male) or masculine (if female): Beware some in dark spirit professions have the ability to marshal these types of spirits into a life until the person becomes influence by the spirit. (Again, fans and/or intense Lysol spraying at point of defilement can prove effective.)

Sex spirit demons: Can be sent or assigned and ancestrally inspired/Asherah (See Asherah).

Incubus/Succubus: Spirits that can also attack the body when sleep to release spirits of lust and perversion or infestation. Again, continually calling upon the name of the Lord and praise can help pull you out of this attack. You can spray Lysol disinfectant at the point of engagement.

Wife/husband swap
A spirit influence. Consistent release is needed until broken.

---

*Note: Use any sprays at own risk, and use a nose magic.

Familiar wicked, unclean and evil spirits of Perversion coming from culture, community, business marketplaces, families any size people group to defile the soul and spirit lives of men (who do not yet realize how to maintain, guard and protect their spirit lives from spirit impurities.

Break any curses and/ or repent of any sins and reverse and mirror back any spirit transfers back to its kind or habitation. In the name of Jesus.

Bind and break dark spirit trinities, assignments and/or agreements between principalities, fallen angels or demons, rulers of darkness or demon spirits (working individually and/or through dark spirited territorial assignments). Cut them off from the power of the air and cast it out, In Jesus name. Go. In Jesus name.

Cut Cords: Pride, Vanity, Wickedness, Affliction & Sin (or any spirit belief system) that connects one to any type of perversion.

Loose yourself from: Pride of life, lust of flesh &lust of eyes that would keep one linked to perversion on any level. In Jesus name.

We welcome the Holy Spirit to help us up-root, cleanse, release, and heal in these areas in Jesus name. We release the blessings and peace of God to replace the curse symptoms of perversion or misfortune of being connected in any way to the spirit fruit and principalic root of perversion. In Jesus name.

Love works no ill. Rom 13.10. Prov.28.18.

The work of righteousness shall be………………….……….. **Peace**   **#9**

I Renounce the Ancestral Principalic Stronghold Root Spirit of Haughtiness   10

2Sam 22.28. One who show great pride in one's self and contempt for others. Arrogant. Egotistical.

I decree I am not the victim, vessel and/or carrier. Rom 9.21 Jn 8.32 & 36. Col 2.10.

We plead the blood and name of Jesus. 1Jn 1.7-9 Exo12.23. Eph 1.7. Cor 11.25.

To resist it. James 4.7.

I Take Authority

I Bind, Break & Divide its work and false authority that can no longer stand. Lk 11.18. Mt. 16.19. Lk 9.1.

I Break the power, curse, passion, assignment and will from the body, soul spirit life, relationships & environment. In Jesus name. Tim 2.26. Isa 14.5.

I loose Haughtiness from the bloodline, (body, soul, spirit relationships & environment). I cut it off at the root and cast it out. Mk16.17. Ps.16.19. In Jesus name. Ps 54.5.

To make room for the Holy Spirit in the up-rooting process of purging, cleansing and healing of spirit impurities and defilement. Mk4.17. Isa11.1. Mt8.16. Mt12.28. Thess5.23. Ez3.18-22. Zec4.6. Eph2.18.

I Bind, Break, Divide and Cut-Off this spirit fruit and principalic root of Haughtiness trying to work in our lives through:

(A spirit and spiritual work against the mind, thoughts & thinking patters until the spirit fruit is produced).

Self

Personality/Relationships/Environment

Chaff personality: Mt. 3.12. Prov 22.5. Heb 6.8. Ps 1.4.

Accusation – Accuser of the brethren

Bullying: Like vexing is a spirit symptom. Release is needed.

Contrary heart

Degrading heart

Dominating over bearing.

Ego.   Arrogant

Heart Issues.

Haughty Heart

Haughty (Character) A type of arrogance

Haughty. Could be symptoms due to victimization, abuse or hurts)

Abusive and/or Abused behavior or treatment (this can cause a victim to be haughty)

Betrayal (can produce a fruit of haughtiness)

Complain

Critical fault finding.

Deceit.

Daily Vex & Pressure.

Dissension.

Envy.

Fears (can be the fruit of haughtiness)

Flattering Lips

False witness

Foolishness

Followers of those who do evil

Gossip.

Abominations

Afflicting   (Afflicted)

Bitter words.

Bitterness.

Boast.

Dishonoring.

Drama Mimic (Unnaturally)

Dispute.   Distress (causing or being)

Evil Intent.

(also revealed by the spirits operating in people lives causing them to seek those being preyed upon, as if they were instituting a gov. duty on their own, when they are only a civilian- release is needed to stop this behavior)

Flattery.

High Look (eye gate).
Mean.
Proud.
Proud Boasting
Reputation.
Selfish/Self-Centered.
Self-Righteous.
Vain pursuit of honor

Hypocrite (activity)
Hindering or Blocking another
Lies in wait for harm.
Intruding/Intrusions /invading type(spiritually/naturally)
Intimidation.

Lusts of Flesh.
Meddlesome.
Miserable Comforters.

Hateful. (attitude & disposition)
Hate (is how some walk in darkness)
Hard to speak to
Hypocrisy.

Lying Vanities.
Ill-intent (of the heart)
Impatience
Iniquitous family patterns.
Mischief.

Oppression.
Offended or, Offensive

Partiality.
Provoke (ing).
Prejudice. Gen 37.4.   Racism
Proud tongue.
Proud Purposes.

Ridicule (or sarcastic type of mocking)
Rebellion
Rude.

Dark

Spirit Realm Influences Affects the mind, memory, hearing, thinking/thoughts, will, desire, spirit vision, sight, imagination, inclinations until "spirit" magnification occurs.

Unclean or evil spirits.
Spirit voice of enemy.
Confused noise.
Noise-some Pestilence.
Creating a idol conscience (can come from constant spirit mind bombardments-see flow chart of authority for release in this area)
Fear seizes.

Flesh mind. Col 2.18. Vanity of mind.

Unbelief. (operating in or coming from the spirit realm through mind suggestions); Can be resisted with our flow chart of authority.
Creating chambers of haughty mindsets, imaginations, imagery and memory.
Haughty fellowships.
Desire to be around evil (haughty) men.
Evil/haughty encouragement or counsel.
Spirit of error.
Destroying (evil angel spirits)
Power of Pride. (is fuel by the spirits of darkness & is the reason one must gain their ability to release their spirit life from spirit impurities and defilement of pride before it becomes a stronghold.

Religious spirit activity
Sin spirit nature
Resisting Truth
Respect of Persons
Scorner
Sedition
Slander
Spite
Smug
Strife
Strange vanities
Stubborn (Stubbornness)
Strife
Treacherous
Transgression
Tempting

Unreasonable
Usury
Vain Glory
Vanity (linked to haughtiness)
Variance
Vain Comfort
Vain pursuit of honor
Vile

Familiar wicked, unclean and evil Haughty spirits coming from culture, community, family (sometimes ancestrally) or any people group to spiritually defile. Break any curses and reverse any transfers back to its kind (or sender). In Jesus name.

Break any curses (dark angel spirits come with curses, because they are fallen or cursed spirits, 2Pet 2.4.) or repent of any sins and reverse or mirror back any haughty spirit attack transfers back to its kind. In the name of Jesus.

Bind and break dark spirit trinities, assignments and/or agreements between principalities, rulers of darkness or demons (working individually and/or through dark spirited territorial assignments). Cut them off (from N. S. E & W) from the power of the air and cast it out, In Jesus name.

Cut Cords: Pride, Vanity, Wickedness, Affliction & Sin that would keep one connected to haughtiness and/or a haughty belief system.

Loose yourself from: Pride of life, lust of flesh & lust of eyes and affliction that would keep you linked or cause you to produce the spirit fruit of haughtiness.

I loose the Holy Spirit to uproot, cleanse, release and heal in this area. I release the blessings and peace of God to replace the curse of haughtiness in Jesus name.

He will confirm you until the end that ye may be blameless in the day of the

Corin 1.8. Cor 6.9. Phil 2.15. Thess 2.10. Isa 2.11 & 17. Micah 6.8. 2Sam 22.24.

Lord, help our hearts to be sound in thy statues that I be not ashamed. **#10**

The spirit of the world is pride and haughtiness…and ultimately leads to destruction.
The Spirit of Christ is humility…and ultimately leads to honor…

Jimmy Swaggart, Expository Bible.pp.1050.

I Renounce the Ancestral Principalic Stronghold Root Spirit of Jealousy 11

Prov. 6.34. Jealousy –To be resentful and suspicious of rivalry. Mistrust and doubt.

I decree I am not the victim, vessel and/or carrier. Rom9.2. Jn8.32 & 36. Col 2.10.
We plead the blood and name of Jesus. 1Jn1.7-9 Exo12.23. Eph1.7. Cor 11.25.
To resist it. IJN. James 4.7.

I Take Authority

I Bind, Break & Divide its work and false authority that can no longer stand. Lk11.18 Mt16.19. Lk 9.1.

I Break the power, curse, passion, assignment and will…….. Tim2.26. Isa 14.5.

I loose Jealousy from the bloodline, (body, soul, spirit life & relationships). I cut it off at the root and cast it out. In Jesus name. Mk16.17. Mt.16.19. Jn 12.31. Ps 54.5.

To make room for the Holy Spirit in the up-rooting process of purging, cleansing and healing of spirit impurities and defilement. In Jesus name.
Mk4.17. Isa11.1. Mt8.16. Mt. 12.28. Thess5.23. Ez3.18-22.Zec4.6. Eph2.18. Acts 8.22.

I Bind, Break and Divide this spirit fruit & principalic root of Jealousy trying to work in our lives through:

(A spirit and spiritual work against the mind, thoughts & thinking patters until the spirit fruit is produced).

Self (spirit fruit activity)

Personality/Relationships/Environment

Chaff personality: Flesh & thorn activity. Heb 6.8. Ps 1.4. Mt. 3.12. Ge 30.8.

Self	Personality/Relationships/Environment	
Contrary heart (hard heart)	Accuse	Angry
Cruelty	Accuse falsely	Abusive spirit nature towards others
Deceit	Argue	Assault(ing)
Discontent	Bitter	Affliction
Heart – questionable Intent & heart issues.	Boasting	Betrayal (can cause jealousy)
Interference (Intrusions/Invading – violating disposition – a type of pride)	Confusion	Bigotry (Intolerance/bias)
	Condemnation	Control concerns/issues
Insecurity	Conspire harm	Complain
Pride (can cause jealousy)	Coveting	Criticism (unbiblical)
Possessiveness	Dispute	Disharmony
Resentful	Discontent	Depression
Reputation	Distrustful	Discord
Selfish	Division	
Self-Importance	Evil Eye	Envy
Self-Will	Emulation	Fear
Suspicious reasoning/doubt	Frustration	Flattery
Un-content	Fool/Foolishness	Gossip
	Hate (covered by deceit)	

- Un-forgiveness
- Unreasonable
- Vainglory
- Vanity
- Vigilante/Vengeance/Revenge

Other Dark
Spirit Realm Influences/ experiences

Affects the mind, memory, thinking/thoughts, will, desire, spirit vision, sight, imagination, inclinations, memory, hearing, magnification unto obsession.

<u>Spirit image of jealousy</u>

Idol spirits defile the conscience & mind with jealousy

Flesh mind (created by consistent dark spirit thought activity- resistance must be learned)

<u>Create negative image and vision re-call</u> Confused noise

<u>Unclean spirits</u>

- Jealousy
- Hypocritical mouth/lips
- Manipulation
- Malice
- Mistrust
- Provoke/Tempt
- Proud look
- Resist Truth
- Rage can be the fruit of jealousy
- Spite

- Spirit of Unrest
- Schizophrenia-rejection-rebellion
- Self-preeminence
- Un-godly competition
- Un-natural affection

Other Root Stronghold causes or links:
Error Sorcery. Infirmity.

<u>Iniquitous family patterns</u> (of jealousy)
<u>Lies</u>
<u>Lies in wait</u> (for harm)
Mischief
Prejudice
Partiality
Slander
Strife
Suppression (To restrain-form of oppression)
<u>Transgression</u>
<u>Troubles</u>
Threats Acts
Un-cleanness
Un-kind
Un-forgiveness

Desire (spirits can create or cause a desire to be around evil men)

Destroyer/Destroying spirits of destruction (evil angel spirits)

Oppressive spirits

Spirits can create chambers of jealously mindset, imaginations, inclinations, emotions, image & imagery etc.

*Any dark spirit violations could influence men to: attack, assault, interfere, harass, etc. through people (that may or may not be aware they are being used for the harm of another) to a certain point, then directly through dark spirit realms or environments by any of but not limit to the above dark spirit activities.

<u>Familiar spirits of wicked, unclean and evil spirits of Jealousy</u> coming from culture, community, business marketplace, families any size people group trying to attach to others.

Bind and break any curses (dark angel spirits come with curses, because they are fallen or cursed spirits) and reverse and/or mirror any spirit transfers back to its kind sender or habitation   . In the name of Jesus. We resist it and cast it out. In Jesus name.

Bind and break jealous dark spirit trinities, assignments and agreements of principalities, rulers of darkness (working individually and/or through dark spirited territorial assignments). In Jesus name Cut them off from the power of the air and cast it out, In Jesus name.

Cut Cords: Pride, Vanity, Wickedness, Affliction & Sin that would keep and/or connect one to jealousy. We resist it in Jesus name.

Loose yourself from: Pride of life, lust of flesh & lust of eyes that would keep one or cause one to connect to jealousy.

I loose the Holy Spirit to cleanse, up-root, release and heal from any spirit fruit and principalic root of jealousy. I release the blessings and peace of God to replace the curse. In Jesus name.

And I appoint unto you a Kingdom as My Father hath appointed Me.

Lk 22.29. 2 Cor 11.2.

#11

I Renounce the Ancestral Principalic Stronghold Root Spirit of Lying   12

A wholesome tongue is a tree of life. Prov 15.4. Prov 15.2. Ps 141.3. Ps 50.23.

I decree I am not the victim, vessel or carrier. Rom 9.21. Col 2.10.

We plead the blood and name of Jesus. 1Jn7-9. Exo12.23. Eph1.7. Cor 11.25.

To resist it. James 4.7.

I Take Authority

I Bind, Break & Divide it's false authority...... Lk 11.18 Mk16.17. Mt. 16.19. Lk 9.1.

I Break the power, curse, passion, assignment agreement and will. 2Tim2.16. Lk. 9.10. Isa 14.5.

I loose Lying from the bloodline(body, soul, spirit life, relationships and vironment). I cut it off at the root and cast it out in Jesus name. Mk16.17. Jn 12.31. Ps 54.5. Ps 76.12. Exo 12.23. Eph 1.7.

To make room for the Holy Spirit in the up-rooting process of purging, cleansing and healing of spirit impurities and defilement. Mk4.17. Isa11.1. Mt8.16. Mt. 12.28. Zec 4.6. Eph 2.18. Acts 2.38 Thess 5.23.

I Bind, Break and Divide the spirit fruit and principalic root of Lying trying to operate in our lives through:

A spirit and spiritual work against the mind, thought & thinking process until the spirit fruit is produced.

Self (Spirit fruit behavior)   **Personality-Relationships / Environment**

Chaff personalities: Mt. 3.12. Heb 6.8. Mt. 21.18-19. Flesh and Thorn types. 2Cor 10.3.

Self	Personality-Relationships	Environment
Arrogant mouth Cursing	Accusation	Accuse falsely
Corrupt communication	Breaks covenant	Complain
Deceitful tongue		Compromise (in a ungodly way)
Defiled mouth	Condemning	Deceived
Evil tongue (must be rooted out)	Condemnation	Deception
Evil speaking	Confusion (envy, strife)	Discord (expressed)
False tongues False lips	Contentious	Division (expressed)
Filthy communications	Contrary	
Flattering words	Crooked ways	Fear
Flattering lips	Debt	
Foolish talking/jesting.	Deceiving	Error (traditional error)
Fools mouth	Disharmony	
Feign lips		
	Exaggeration	

Fools voice	Envy	Guilt
Hardened heart	False/Unfaithful witness	
Heart intent	Faultfinding	
Iniquitous tongue	Foolish	
Lying Lips (hides hatred)	Gossip (surely release is needed – some cannot release themselves)	
Lying tongue		
Lying vanities	Hate	Lack (any area vocalized; joy, peace, etc.)
Lying words (some trust in lying)	Iniquitous family pattern (of lying)	Lies against the truth
Mouth of wicked		
Naughty tongue (also intruding interrupting tongues need healing…..)	Ignorance-lawlessness	
Piercing tongue		Mischief
Perverse tongue (breach)	Lead Astray	
Reputation	Murmur	Provocation
Selfish		Proud/Pride can be fruit of lying
Scourge (to afflict punishment w/tongue)	Prejudice	Resist truth by lying
Sin of mouth		Sin (spirit nature)
Strife of tongues	Proud speaking	
Talebearer	Shame	
Unbridled tongue	Spite	
Unruly evil (tongue)	Superstitious reasoning	Transgression
Vain speaking		
Vain words	Temptation/Tempting	Unreasonableness
	Unnatural affection	

Other Dark-

Spirit Realm Influences Can create the following:

Idol spirits defile the conscience (with lies)

Lying negative spirit image & vision recall/confused noise.

Flesh mind (bombarded with lying thoughts)

Corrupt mind (mind conditioned with lying thoughts & thinking patterns).

Unbelief (to truth) Mk5.6.   Un-steadfastness

Delusion

Desires

Vain/Dark fellowships (enforced by or that focuses on creating more lies)

Evil counsel

Lying spirits   Eye gate (that envisions lies/lying)

Breach in the spirit (can also be recognized by a perverse tongue)

Destroyer (evil angel spirits and/or warring principalities). These also can gain the ability to speak through and/or attack territorially.

Create chambers of lying mindsets, imaginations, inclinations and magnification until lying becomes an obsession. Break any bands around the mind.

**Talkativeness (and non-talkative states alike) can be induced by sudden spirit raid influences in the environment (or within). This could also be considered a breach in one's spirit realm and/or cut off this affect from the power of the air, in Jesus name. Either way spiritual release is needed. Prov 15.4. Eph 2.2. See .

Familiar wicked, unclean, evil Lying spirits coming from culture, community, business marketplace, families and any size people group to defile the soul spirit lives of men (who may not know how to maintain, guard and protect their spirit lives from spirit impurities or intrusions of the power of the air to control the lives of men.

Bind and break any curses (dark angel spirits come with curses, because they are fallen or cursed spirits, and reverse any transfers back to its kind and mirror back to any sender. In the name of Jesus.

Bind and break dark spirit trinities, assignments, agreements of principalities, rulers of darkness, spiritual wickedness in high places (working individually and/or through dark spirited territorial assignments that would operate through lying). In Jesus name. Cut them off from the power of the air and cast them out, In Jesus name. Isa14.5.Dt6.19.Mk3.12. In dark spirit assignments there may be a need to consistently drive out spirit activity until the Lord brings deliverance into your experience. (Our flow chart of authority can help).

Cut Cords: Pride, Vanity, Wickedness, Affliction & Sin that would keep you connected to the root of lying.

Loose yourself from: Pride of life, lust of flesh & lust of eyes that would cause you to lie or continue lying.

I loose the Holy Spirit to uproot, cleanse, release and heal in this area. Lord, we pray for a wholesome tongue, in Jesus name.

The heart of the wise teaches his mouth

Prov. 16.23. Prov 14.3 & 5. Ps 120.2
Job 15.6. Jn 6.63. Job 16.5. Isa 3.8.

A poor man is better than a liar.

(The wise in heart teaches, instructs, guides, develops or trains, his mouth).

#12

I Renounce the Ancestral Principalic Stronghold Root Spirit of Heaviness   13

Cast thy burden upon the Lord Ps 55.22. (burden-weight) Exo6.6. Isa61.3. Mt. 11.28.

I decree I am not the victim, vessel or carrier. Rom 9.21. Col 2.10.

We plead the blood and name of Jesus. 1Jn7-9. Exo12.23. Eph1.7. Cor11.25.

To resist it. James 4.7

I Take Authority

I Bind, Break & Divide it's work and false authority......In Jesus name. Lk11.18 Mt. 16.19.Lk9.1.

I Break the power, curse, passion, assignment, will and purpose of Heaviness. In Jesus name. 2Tim 2.16. Isa15.4 Lk 9.1.

I loose Heaviness from the bloodline (body, soul, spirit, relationships environments). I cut it off at the root and cast it out in Jesus name. Mk16.17. Jn12.31. Lk 19.31. Ps 54.5. Eph 1.7.

To make room for the Holy Spirit into the up-rooting process of purging, cleansing and healing from spirit impurities and defilement. In Jesus name. Mk 4.17. Isa 11.1. Zec 4.6. Mt. 8.16. Mt. 12.28. Eph 2.18-22. Ez 3.

I Bind, Break and Divide the spirit fruit and principalic root of Heaviness trying to operate in our lives through symptoms and/or conditions of:

A spirit and spiritual work against the mind, thought & thinking process until the spirit fruit is produced.

Self (Spirit fruit Character)   **Personality-Relationships / Environment**

Chaff personalities: Ps 1.4. 2. Corin 10.3.

Self	Personality	Relationships	Environment
Burden of people Also Moses dealt with it.	Affliction & Persecution induced from Kingdom servitude (can produce spiritual kingdom conflicts in both the spirit and natural realms of life and living)	Abandonment (concerns/issues)	
Broken heart		Demonic watches (through men, realized or not doesn't seem to be the issue, only understanding that there are only 2 spiritual kingdom activities operating among us). Therefore, spiritual release, healing & understanding of biblical spiritual kingdom activities is needed. Seeing that God does nothing without purpose.	
Confusion			
Despair Desperation			
Depression (can be included by heaviness)			
Excessive mourning	Abuse (can be included by heaviness-abuse can be by natural or spiritual means)		
Grief. (grief of mind)			
Heavy heart			
Inner Hurts/ Torn	Adversary, Adversarial		
Iniquity (can be or become a heavy burden)			
Many temptations	Chemical Imbalance		
Rejection – a certain level of consistent rejection (being sent from the operation of darkness can take its toll)	Dishonor		
	Discouragement		
Self-pity			
Sorrow			

Other Dark
Spirit Realm Influence & experiences or looking for expression to affect the: mind/conscience (thought/thinking process), memory, desire, will, spirit vision, sight, imagination, inclination, interference, magnification of a life of continual heaviness can turn into an obsession if there is no (spiritual release through prayer or resistance).

Dark realms and/or activity can try to create:
Flesh mind   Corrupt minds.

Creates idols spirits that defile conscience

Spirit voice of the enemy

Corrupt desire. (can be spirit forced upon a person with out continual spirit impurity and defiled releases, IJN).

Suicidal thoughts

Evil patterns of thinking

Noise-some pestilence   Confused noise

Vanity of mind

Self-delusion   Troubles

Fear seizes (working behind the scene but revealed by it's visible fruit of working)

Unbelief (can also be created in the spirit realm through repetitious thoughts and thinking patterns)

Destroyer spirits (spirits of destruction)

Compulsive habits from driving spirits (operating in the thought/thinking patterns and manifested spirit leadings)

Error

Foolish children
(can produce heaviness)

False responsibility

Hopelessness

Helplessness

Insecurity/Anxious

Infirmity

Intimidation (can induce eaviness)

Lack of praise

Disharmony/Division – spirit personalities

Distractions

Distressed

Fear

Insomnia (can be a fruit of heaviness)

Oppression (can be a fruit of heaviness in the natural and or spirit realm)

Plague...can produce heaviness

Familiar wicked, unclean & evil spirits of Heaviness coming from culture, community, business marketplaces, families and any size people group to defile the body, soul, spirit lives, relationships and environments.

Bind and break any curses and reverse or mirror back any spirits back to its kind or habitation (if assigned), in the name of Jesus.

Bind and break any dark spirit trinities, agreements and assignments of principalities, rulers of darkness and/or spiritual wickedness in high places (whether working individually and/or through dark spirited territorial assignments). In Jesus name.

Cut Cords: Pride, Vanity, Wickedness, Affliction & Sin that could cause heaviness in one's life.

Loose yourself from: Pride of life, lust of flesh & lust of eyes that would produce heaviness in one's life or circumstance.

(You can go to our individual flow chart to help enforce and/or release your authority and/or then end with the following prayer, in Jesus name)

I loose the Holy Spirit to cleanse, release, up-root and heal in this area. I release the blessings and peace of God to replace the curse or ill-circumstances or situations trying to influence or create heaviness, in Jesus name.
Prov. 26.2. Lk 9.1.

The **Remedy** _____

For the spirit of heaviness

Isa 61.3. Ps16.11. Exo 6.6. Ps 27.6. Ps13.2. Zeph 3.17.

#13

I Renounce the Ancestral Principalic Stronghold
Root Spirit Deaf & Dumb

14

Exodus 4.11. Mt 9.33. Mt 12.22 (Let us understand that spirit activities and influences can and will transcend into natural experiences and/or expressions, affecting even children). Mk 9.21.

I decree I am not the victim, vessel or carrier. Rom 9.21. Jn 8.36.
We plead the blood and name of Jesus. 1Jn7-9. Exo12.23. Eph1.7. Cor11.25.
To resist it. James 4.7.

I Take Authority

I Bind, Break & Divide this root that it can no longer operate …..In Jesus name. Lk 11.18 Mt. 16.19. Jn 8.32. Lk 9.1.

I Break the power, curse, passion, assignment, agreement and will. 2Tim 2.16.

I loose Deaf & Dumb from the bloodline (body, soul, spirit & relationships). I cut it off at the root and cast it out in Jesus name.
Mk 16.17. Jn 12.31. Lev 17.11. Lk 9. Ps 54.5.

To make room for the Holy Spirit in the up-rooting process of purging, cleansing and healing from spirit impurities and defilement.
Mk 4.17. Isa 11.1. Zec 4.6. Mt. 8.16. Mt. 12.28. Eph 2.18-22. Ez 3. Eph 1.7. Exo 12.23.

I Bind, Break and Divide the spirit fruit and principalic root Deaf & Dumb trying to work in our lives through symptoms and/or conditions:

A spirit and spiritual work against the mind, thought & thinking process until the spirit fruit is produced. Col 1.21. Heb 6.8. Ps 1.4. Mt. 3.12.

Self (Spirit fruit Character)

Coward   Fright (Any level of fear)
Hopeless   Hopelessness
Inferiority/low self esteem
Infirmity (body, soul or spirit)
Insecurity
Miscommunication
Pining away
Slander
Slow to understand/comprehend
Slow speech or tongue.

Personality-RelationshipsEnvironment 2 Corin 10.3. Heb 6.8. Ps 1.4. Mt. 3.12

Blindness (spiritually so)
(devil spirits can induce blindness)
Destruction   Catastrophe(s)
Dumb (this spirit can cause pining away)

Mute (can be caused by natural and/or spirit influences)
Passivity – Inactivity or procrastination
Ignorance/Innocence (inability and/or not accustomed to comprehend)

| Scorner | Scorning | Stupid/simple |
| Slothful | Unreasonable | (can cause error) |

Other Dark

Spirit Realm Influence & experiences trying to find expression to affect the: mind/conscience (thought/thinking), memory, will, desire, vision, inclination, imagination unto magnification, etc.

Self-will

Idol spirits defile the conscience

Create a flesh mind

Confused noise Isa9.5 Noise-some pestilence

Create delusions/hallucinations   Foul spirit

Dumb/mute spirits

Dumb Idol (spirit) can lead &/or defile a conscience.

Seduce hypnotism/ can also occur from not resisting dark spirit life activity influences whether you realize they are operating or not is why they call it a work of darkness, so then you learn of its influence(s) by the fruit...and this is a reason to stick to a schedule of consistent spirit releases so as to not collect spirits.

*Some go into self-induced trances, so that spirit life can use them to traffic dark spirit life into the lives of others. It's error.

Soul instability (or unstable soul can be created by consistent dark spirit life intrusions & invasions).

---

*Can arise from being targeted by dark spirit life activity and/or those in dark professions can release an assignment or as an operation of darkness to hinder one's progress in Christ. Herein lies the need to stay close to the Lord and away from the snares (naturally and/or spiritually so because dark spirit life will try to make you and/or others think you are unsound. It's what they do. It's how they operate. Jesus said, a mind stayed on Him is kept in perfect peace.

Familiar wicked, unclean & evil Deaf & Dumb spirits coming from culture, community, business/marketplaces, families and any size people group to defile or violate the body, soul, spirit life, relationships of those who have not realized how to maintain their spirit life in Christ and thereby the people begin to collect spirit impurities or spirit manifestations until the spirit personalities and characters begin to develop in the lives of people.

Bind and break any curses or reverse and/or mirror any spirits transfers back to it's kind (or habitation), in the name of Jesus.

Bind and break any dark spirit trinities, agreements and assignments of principalities, rulers of darkness and spiritual wickedness in high places of demons (working individually and/or through dark spirited territorial assignments). In Jesus name.

Cut Cords: Pride, Vanity, Wickedness, Affliction & Sin that would try to keep you connected to deaf & dumb spirit life (activity).

Loose yourself from: Pride of life, lust of flesh &lust of eyes that would keep one connected to deaf & dumb spirit activity.

I loose the Holy Spirit to uproot, release, cleanse and heal in this area. I release the blessings and peace of God to replace the curse and/or ill symptoms.

And now Lord, What wait I for my hope is in

Thee

Ps 40.11 & 13 & 17
Ps 74.21.

#14I

I Renounce the Ancestral Principalic Stronghold Root Spirit Slumber   15
Cor 15.26. Rom 11.8.

I decree I am not the victim, vessel or carrier. Rom 9.21. Jn 8.36.
We plead the blood and name of Jesus,. 1Jn 7-9. Exo12.23. Eph 1.7. Cor 11.25. Col 2.10.
To resist it. James 4.7

I Take Authority

I Bind, Break & Divide the root and it's system of operation...
Lk 11.18 Mt. 16.19. Lk 1.9.

I Break the power, curse, passion, assignment, agreement and will.
2Tim2.16. Isa14.5.

I loose Slumber from the bloodline (body, soul, spirit & relationships).
I cut it off at the root and cast it out in Jesus name. Mk16.17. Jn12.31. Lev17.11.
Lk19.31. Ps 54.5.

To make room for the Holy Spirit in the up-rooting process of purging,
cleansing and healing from spirit impurities and defilement. 2 Corin 10.3. Ps 1.4.

I Bind, Break and Divide the spirit fruit and principalic root of Slumber trying to work in our lives through:
A spirit and spiritual work against the mind, thought & thinking process until the spirit fruit is produced.

Self (Spirit fruit Character)

Personality-Relationships/Environment
Drawback (perhaps due to being continually attacked)

Discouragement (can cause slumber)
Disappointments (can cause slumber)
Love of slumber
Simplicity of foolishness
Slothful

Other Dark
Spirit Realm Influence & experiences
They try to affect the mind/conscience (thought/thinking process), memory, desire, will, spirit, vision, sight, imagination, inclination and magnification, until it becomes an obsession. They try to create the following:
Flesh mind:
Confused noise/Noise-some pestilence
Desire (to slumber, be passive and/or be inactive)
Idol spirits (defile the conscience)
Negative image or vision recall.

Fear
Ignorance
Passive-Inactive state (of body, soul, spirit & relationship)
Procrastination/Delay
Rejection (can induce slumber)
Sluggard or tired states
Slumber (or slumbering can affect productivity)
Transgression Joshua

Unbelief (can be created in the spirit realm)
Creating chambers of slumber mindsets, imaginations and imagery.
Encourages vain fellowship.
Voice of the enemy.
Destroying (evil angel spirits)

<u>Familiar wicked, unclean & evil Slumber spirit</u> issues, concerns and/or attacks (spiritual &/or natural) coming from culture, community, business/ marketplaces, families and any size people group to defile the body, soul, spirit lives and relationships and/or environments.

Bind and break any curses (dark angel spirits come with curses, because they are fallen or cursed spirits,) and reverse and/or mirror back any spirits transfers back to its kind or habitation. In the name of Jesus.

Bind and break any dark trinities, agreements and assignments of principalities, rulers of darkness and spiritual wickedness (working individually and/or through dark spirited territorial assignments) by the blood and name of Jesus. Cut them off and cast them out in the name of Jesus.

Cut Cords: Pride, Vanity, Wickedness, Affliction & Sin   **Loose yourself from:** Pride of life, lust of flesh & lust of eyes
that would cause one to slumber.   that would cause the desire to slumber.

I loose the Holy Spirit to cleanse, release, up-root and heal in this area. I loose the blessings and peace of God to replace the curse.

That ye be not slothful but followers of them who through faith and patience

Inherit the promise

Heb 6.12. Ps 121.3-4. Ps 73.24.   **#15**

I Renounce the Ancestral Principalic Stronghold Root
Spirit of Death/destruction **16**

The last enemy is death. Cor 15.26.

I decree I am not the victim, vessel and/or carrier. Rom 9.21. Jn 8 & 36, Col 2.10.

We plead the blood and name of Jesus. 1Jn 1.7-9. Exo 12.23. Eph 1.7. Cor 11.25. Rev 1.5.
We resist it. James 4.7

I Take Authority

I Bind, Break and Divide this root of death and destruction and it's system of operation. Lk 11.18. Mt. 16.19. Lk 9.1.

I Break the power, curse, passion, assignment and will. Tim2.26. Isa15.4. Isa 14.5.

I loose Death from the bloodline, (body, soul, spirit life & relationships and our work). Cut it off and cast it out in the name of Jesus. Mt. 16.19. Jn 12.31.

To make room for the Holy Spirit in the up-rooting process of purging, cleansing and healing of spirit impurities & defilement. Acts 2.38. Mk 4.17. Isa11.1. Mt. 12.28. Eph 5.26. Cor6.11. Heb 4.16. Zec 4.6. Eph 2.18. Thess 5.12.

I Bind, Break, Divide and Cut-Off this spirit fruit & principalic root of death trying to operate in our lives through:

(A spirit and spiritual work against the mind, thought & thinking process until the spirit fruit and principalic root is produced). Col 1.21

Self (spirit fruit character)

Assault/Seizure

Betrayal

Cruel Grievous

Disease

Evil (It is written: one that pursues evil can pursue it to one's own death &/or resisting any evil that is trying to pull you in to dark spirited activity and/or operations – naturally or spiritually so)

Fear

Hate (all ugly attitudes can kill or hateful spirit belief systems)

Injury Tim1.13.

Premature aging (body, soul or spirit)

Riotous behavior/Random acts of violence

Sorrow

*Please note we have also seen spirits try to cause someone to have a fake heart attack. (meaning the symptoms were suddenly with no prior heart condition and therefore can transfer from someone that had a heart attack).

Personality/Relationships/Environment
Chaff personality: Defined as anything worthless.
To annoy or be annoyed. 2 Corin 10.3. Heb 6.8.

Also includes work of the flesh & thorn personalities and war like spirit natures that can lead to death.

3Spiritual cleansing should be a part of maintaining one's spirit life in Christ)

Abortion/Aborting (Abort people, places or things)

Cancer

Chambers of death

Covenants of death

Deadly enemies (that wickedly or heavily oppressed to death or oppressive death like states of being caused by natural &/or spiritual means).

Miscarriage (inability to produce in womb or barrenness of God's blessing)

Child Abuse

Destruction (on any level)

A spirit and/or natural activity.

Other Dark

Spirit Realm Influences &/or experiences

These try to affect the mind/conscience, thought/thinking processes, memory, will, desire, spirit vision, inclination, imagination until its magnified. They can also create the following:

Idol spirits the defile the conscience.

Negative spirit image or spirit vision recall

Confused noise/Noise-some pestilence

Voice of the enemy

Deaf and Dumb spirits (can cause physical harm)

Fear seizes

Drawings (or evil pulling or releases through sorcery spirit realm environments, baal spirit manifestations or eye gates) for harmful intents. The warning is that some in dark spirit professions have gained the ability to literally spiritually draw others into dark spirit (psychic) realms and dark spirit professions.

Suicidal thoughts & thinking that can help or be the cause of death.

Suicide spirits

Drawings (in the spirit realm can affect or transcend into the natural can cause death or destruction; or death like situations or relationships)

Idolatry

Iniquity (can cause pining away)

Murder (a heart issue)

Strangling (the life or strength out of a person, place or any thing in our lives)

Death Conspiracies

Disharmony

Division Regarding people, places and/or spirit and/or natural things.

*Be mindful when you see these on any level: Whether family, culture within community. Do the first thing, bind spirits in Jesus name. Mk3.27. Lk9.1. Lk10.19.

Grief

Loveless (death-like spirit) personalities and/or issues or situations.

Persecution (that can cause prison, sorrow, isolation and/ or death states of being that can lead to death)

Un-forgiveness (can help promote or encourage death or death like situations or relationships.

Death desires or wishes   Job3.3.Jonah 4.3&8

Wrong spirit covering can cause baal manifestations &/or dark spirit infestation.

Driving compulsions/urges (that can lead to death) Job 18.18.Prov14.32.

Vain dark fellowships (can lead to death; with hidden intent(s), especially without the knowledge of knowing how to release oneself from spirit impurities and/or defilement)

Destroyer(ing) (evil angel spirit) – can include warring spirit activity and/or demonic visiation. This can also be viewed as a spirit of violence and/or the spirit of baal. It will always work in and through men if it can to always, always strive, war, oppress, defile and/or violate men naturally and spiritually so (what's the difference). Due to the spirit domination operating in their life, the person with this spirit personality is in need of spiritual release, healing, cleansing and a greater understanding of spirit life activity, in Jesus name.

Creating chambers of death-like state mindsets, imaginations and imagery.

Familiar wicked, unclean & evil spirits of Death issues and/or concerns (sometimes ancestrally) coming from culture, community, business/ marketplace, any people group size to defile/destroy body, soul, spirit, relationships and environments. Bind and break any curses and reverse &/or mirror any transfers.

Bind and break any curses (dark angel spirits come with curses, because they are fallen or cursed spirits), and reverse or mirror back any spirit transfers back to its kind or habitation (as such in the case of spiritual warfare). In the name of Jesus.

Bind, break and divide any dark trinities, agreements and assignments of principalities, spiritual wickedness, rulers of the darkness and demon desiresor demons working through human spirits (working individually and/or through dark spirited territorial assignments). In the name of Jesus.

Cut Cords: Pride, Vanity, Wickedness, Affliction & Sin that would connect one to the death process and/or experience.

Loose yourself from: Pride of life, lust of flesh &lust of eyes that would produce the spirit of death in one's life.

I loose the Holy Spirit to uproot, release, cleanse and heal in this area. I release the blessings and peace of God to replace the curse, symptoms or ailments of death, in Jesus name.

*This could be a good or appropriate time to call back to life things like promises and purposes (etc.) of the Lord that may need to be resurrected. You can list them for prayer purposes.

He is not here: Lk 24.6

He is Risen
Because I live ye shall live also

Jn 14.19. Ps 56.13.2. Prov. 11.4.

#16

Concerning the works of men, by the word of your lips, I have kept away from the paths of the destroyer.

I Renounce the Ancestral Principalic Stronghold Root Spirit of Oppression 17

(To weigh heavily. To keep down by cruel or unjust use of authority and therefore the authority is always oppressive in nature). It could also be a person or situation that presents itself difficult to understand or deal with. This person or situation could be unyielding and/or unfriendly due to the increasing questionable angel spirit activity (operating behind the scene & or in allegiance). Any of the spirit symptoms below would be a reason to reveal the need to find the time to release one's self from spirit impurities, defilement and/or spirit violations of others.

I decree I am not the victim, vessel or carrier. Rom 9.21

We plead the blood and name of Jesus. 1Jn7 -9. Exo 12.23. Eph 1.7. Cor 11.25.

To resist it. James 4.7.

I Take Authority

I Bind, Break & Divide this principalic root and it spirit fruit system of operation. Lk 11.18 Mk 16.19. Lev 26.13.

I Break the power, passion, assignment agreement and will…..2Tim 2.26. Isa 15.4. Exo 12.23. Eph 1.7. Cor 11.25.

I loose Oppression from the bloodline (body, soul, spirit, relationships & situation (s)). I cut it off and cast it out. In Jesus name. Mk 16.17. Jn 12.31. Lev 17.11. Ps 54.5. Ps 76.12. Ps 101.8.

To make room for the Holy Spirit in the up-rooting process of purging, cleansing and healing of spirit impurities, defilement and violations.
In Jesus name. Mk 4.17. Isa 11.1. Mt. 8.16. Mt. 12 28. Zec 4.6. Eph 2.18-22. Ez 3.18-22. Jn 13.13-15. Acts 2.38.

I Bind, Break, Divide and Cut-Off the spirit fruit and principalic root of Oppression trying to operate or attach itself through:

A spirit and spiritual work against the mind, thought & thinking patterns until the spirit fruit and principalic root is produced.

Self (Spirit fruit Character)

Personality-Relationships / Environment
Chaff (thorn type) personalities:

Self	Personality-Relationships
Abuse to self or others.	Angry
Accuse/Accuser of the brethren.	Abomination
Arrogant	Betrayal
Cruel hatred	Consistently unrighteous (cruel)
Control – Controlling patterns	Cruel hatred Brutish Cruety
Defiled – defilement	Contrary
	Cursing

Affliction/To Afflict (as a fruit of oppression). This is when the enemy is trying or has risen up in one's life.

Please note: that affliction(s) of dark spirit operations (and those in allegiance to it) are designed, among other things, to keep you connected to dark spirit initiatives, agendas and a "spirit" type of witchcraft government. (Some afflict until oppression occurs). Judges 16.19. Isa58.6. Mk9.29.

Deceived

Deception

Deceitful works

Despise Gov. Nat'l &/or Spiritual protocol

Hate expressions

Rough

Force (forcing wrath, obtrusive ways)

Grievous (behaviors)

Hard Speeches

Iniquity

Insurrection (in the reality that there are only 2 spiritual kingdoms operating among us – this is the only reason – inside church or not – that people will rise against another. Therefore some do not realize that they are spiritually operating against God's kingdom authority). Spiritual healing & understanding is needed.

Ill-behavior

Lying: See principalic stronghold #12

Oppressive (violating) spirit behavior/nature or presence

Reproach (dishonoring)

Selfish Self-will

Sin

Transgression

(naughty can also be considered a transgression)

Ungodly persuasions and/or activities

Wicked plots

Wicked works like: deceit, strife, violence are also works or ways of the oppressor.

Depise holy things

Defraud

Destroy/Destruction

Dishonoring

Drunk (or any addictions)

Dishonest gain

Evil Eye (hard looks)

Envy

Error (from traditional thinking)

Extortion

Fears (and/or loneliness can be fruit of oppression)

Fools/Foolishness

Greedy

Fierce Suppression

Force (ful) personality –

Harsh

Heaviness

Hardhearted (oneself or others)

Ill-Treatment (individually or territorially)

Intent (ill)

Intimidation (threatening spirit attitude and issues expressed in the flesh system-verbal or non-verbal activity)

Arrogant (obtrusive)

Adversary (returns evil for good)

Blaspheme

Covetousness

Dark spirit reasoning/thinking

Discontent

Disharmony/Divison (when these 2 surface in any people groups it would be
biblically & spiritually appropriate to bind spirits and dark spirit trinities because there are only 2 spiritual kingdoms operating among us).

Distress (causing it)

Evil Mischief

Evil ways:

Evil intent

False Lips

False accuser

Flesh (some walk after uncleanness)

Fierce Oppression

Hunting (personality to pursue others for harm due to the spirits operating in the pursuers life)....release, healing and understanding of spirit activity is needed. Sometimes certain leaders will pick up this spirit nature personality and will need release before they can rec'v God's operation in their midst.

Hostile . Hypocrite

Traitor

Haughty

Other Dark

Spirit Realm Influences & Obsessions

Tries to affect the mind/conscience thinking/thought patterns, desire, will, imagination, eye gate, voice, inclinations, sight, spirit vision, Imagnification until obsession and/or spirit domination occurs.

Iniquitous family patterns

Inheritance by oppression

Justifying the wicked
(to have evil intent without cause)

Mad Oppressive people can drive a wise man mad.

Lawlessness

Lack of understanding

Meddlesome

Mean

Mockers

Oppressors: Seek after souls.

(Often identified by those in dark spirit professions and/or those being drawn into dark spirit

These influences and obsessive dark spirit life try to create:

<u>Flesh mind</u>   <u>Corrupt mind</u>   Desire

<u>Spirit voice of the enemy</u> (repeating the nag or the thing being provoked)

Idol spirits that defile conscious

Confused noise

Constant to extreme thought image & vision recall

<u>Evil eye spirits</u>

Eye gate (enemy will try to flow dark spirit powers or his presence through or upon those not willing to serve him.

<u>Spirit oppression</u> activity is used to suppressed and oppress one into a dark spirit service. In an effort to draw you to others or others to you. A spirit type of bewitchment used to oppress a person into a dark spirit service. So beware it's not all you.

<u>Idolatry:</u>   <u>Sin spirit nature.</u>

<u>Evil patterns of thinking</u> (instigated by dark spirit life). **Use our flow chart to resist.**

<u>Unclean spirits</u> (if not released can cause: vexation, annoyances, afflictions, provoking (to bother).

<u>Corrupt spirit life</u>

<u>Unbelief</u> (This can also be a spirit fruit transfer from associations and could also be a reason for consistent spirit releases from spirit impurities and/or defilement.)

Fear seizes

<u>Hasty spirit</u>   <u>Spiritual entanglement</u>
<u>Spirit of Baal</u>

<u>Spirit of persecution</u>   Can persecute into a darkplace

<u>Oppressively fierce spirit natures or manifestations</u> (for dark spirit power releases to penetrate). Mt8.28.Jn6.15.others). **Wolf type spirit nature**

<u>Oppressed Heritage</u>   (Some dark spirit life operate generationally and/or ancestrally).

<u>Breach</u> (in the spirit can be caused by trafficking, channeling or dark spirits finding ways to manifest it's dark powers through you. Breaching another's spirit realm is another method dark spirit life activity (using men) to keep one in dark spirit realms)

<u>Betrayal</u> (first starts in the spirit realm in the thinking/thought patterns). All betrayal is not intentional it can be spiritually provoked (as an assignment).

<u>Oppress:</u> spirit type personalities that harass abuse/ abusive, maltreat & dishonor Sometimes you will see stalking spirit types operating through the souls of men. Let us perceive and understand stalking or crowding out any certain person is not a
spiritual fruit of God's Spirit character therefore revealing that spiritual healing and release is needed.

<u>Oppressive ways</u> (to include widows, fatherless, strangers & the poor.

<u>Illegal inheritance/possession:</u>

Possessions (that may not really belong to you).

Rob (Robbery)

Reputation

<u>Resist truth</u>

Persecutions (an method and vehicle used in the operation of darkness within and without the church. It is a dark spirited kingdom operation & the dark drama of the operation of the kingdom of darkness. It's their mindset. Cleansing, release and healing is needed. In Jesus name. Because God ordains His arrows against persecutors.

<u>Perverse Disputes</u>

Proud Cords (to entangle another)

Proud purposes

Practice Gossip

<u>Those who lie in wait to harm</u> (are also in need of spiritual release, cleansing and healing.

<u>Strife</u> (that is practiced)

Sin

activity. Also among those needing to learn how release their spirit lives from dark spirit activity, impurities and/or spiritual defilement.)

<u>Oppressive gain</u>

<u>Extortion</u>

Bribe

Judges

<u>Dishonest gain</u>

Thief

Ways of unrighteousness

Perversion   Rage/Fury

<u>Prejudice/Racism</u>

Pride

<u>Presumptuous</u>

<u>Punish</u> (or condemn the righteous – using unsound judgment)

<u>Practice (of vexing or irritating others).</u>

Provoke

Scorn

Scoffers

<u>Strive</u>

Stubborn

Treacherous

Treason

Transgression

Ungodly flattery Unnatural ffection (towards fatherless, widows, poor and needy & people in general).

<u>Vex</u>

(A practice of vexing or irritating another could reveal an un-addressed sin spirit nature in need of release, healing and biblical understanding)

<u>Violent</u> (fury, wild rage)

<u>Whisper</u>

Weak

Spiritual Rebellion (rebellion also first starts in the spirit realm and then produces the evil spirit fruit in the natural-or flesh). This can also cause a church leader to
not accept godly kingdom sent spiritual protocol.

Evil spirit (with no consistent release can produce evil men with no judgment-or soundness &/or cause men to pursue evil in the lives of others.

Forced allegiance to fallen angel spirits (can be caused by witch hunts, instigated by those in dark spirit professions (or false or foolish prophets who never found release from witchcraft assignments and/or other principalic assignments).

Vain/dark oppressive fellowships These can also be forced by those in dark professions.

Destroyer (evil or warring angel spirits) (wicked wait to destroy).

Wicked counsel (**naturally and/or spiritually so**)

Creates chambers of Oppressive mindsets, imagery, imaginations & memories

Self-will Titus

Suffering (caused by oppressor)

Threats

Trafficking (spiritual or nat'l)

Usury Ez 22.12

Unreasonable (including those with irrational belief system or fears)

Un-forgiveness

Unmerciful

Vengeance

Vain (vanity)

Vile

Wicked (fall from being steadfast with God)

Wickedness can pollute the land

Sorcery Professions: See Root, #2

*Pray for the city (leaders and all those in authority) to be released or stay free from dark spirit activity, powers & those in allegiance to it. In Jesus name. Pray the iniquity of the city be healed. IJN.

Familiar wicked, unclean & evil spirits of Oppression found in our culture, community, church family any size people groups to working through the natural position of men's lives and or their spirit realms to corrupt and/or defile the body, soul, spirit lives and relationships of others that do not know how to maintain, guard or protect their spirit lives in Christ.

Bind and break any curses and reverse and/or mirror back any spirit transfers back to its kind or sender if it's an assignment. In the name of Jesus.

Bind and break any dark spirit trinities, assignments and agreements of principalities, rulers of darkness, spiritual wickedness in high places and any demon wills (working individually and/or through dark spirited territorial assignments). Cut them off in the name of Jesus. Cast them out in the name of Jesus.

Cut Cords: Pride, Vanity, Wickedness, Affliction & Sin that would keep one connected to works of ppression.

Loose yourself from: Pride of life, lust of flesh & lust of eyes that would keep you connected to oppressive sin spirit natured activity.

I loose the Holy Spirit to up-root, cleanse, release and heal in this area. I release the blessings and peace of God to replace the curse symptoms of oppression, in Jesus name.

Choose not the way the Oppressor: Prov 3.31.   Trust not in Oppression Ps 62.10.

I make noise because of the Oppression of the wicked: Ps55.2-3.

Let not the proud Oppress me: Ps 119.121-122   Deliver me from the Oppression ...so will I keep your word: Ps 119.134   The Lord will reward the Oppressor:

They cry unto the Lord because of the Oppressor.

Is this not the fast I have chosen: To loose the bands of wickedness, to undo heavy burdens and to let the oppressed go free and that ye break every yoke?

The Lord also will be a refuge for the oppressed, a refuge in times of trouble

Ps 9.9

#17

Ye shall not therefore oppress one another but thou shall fear God. Lev 25.17.

I Renounce the Ancestral Principalic Stronghold Root Spirit of Darkness 18

Darkness is also a presence that depending on the level and intensity and/or spirit penetrations and/or focused powers of darkness that can be released and/or felt. It can also be a place, position, point of view, way of thinking or way of life (due to the spirits operating in the a person's life) who perhaps is also in need of learning how to be released from spirit impurities, defilement and violations of others in allegiance with negative or dark spirit activity. Thoughts can also be used by spirits of darkness as a method to lure you into dark spirit temptations, realms and/or inclinations, imaginations, etc.,...... Prov 14.19. James4.5. Pet2.11. Jn12.35. Job 29.3. Lk23.44.

A wicked man will not depart out of darkness. Job 15.2. Prov 21.12. Mt 27.45. The way of the wicked is as darkness. Prov 14.29. Ps 140.8. Lk 22.53. Isa 48.22. 1Jn 1.6.1 Jn 2.11.Rev 16.10. Dt 4.19. There is no reward to the evil man. Prov. 24.20

A Sinful Kingdom or Nation full of Darkness. No matter the religion sayeth the Lord. Amos 9.8. Habb 1.13. 2Cor 6.14-17. Rev 16.10. Wickedness proceeds from the wicked.

I decree I am not victim, vessel or carrier. In Jesus name! Rom 9. Col 2.10.

We plead the blood and name of Jesus. 1Jn 7-9. Exo12.23. Eph 1.7. Cor 11.25. Rev 1.5
To Resist it. James 4.7

I Take Authority I Bind, Break & Divide the presence and presumed authority of dark spirit activities or systems of operation IJN. Lk 11.18 Mk 16.1. Jn 12.35 Lev 26.13. Lk 9.1.

I Break the power, curse, passion, assignment, agreement, will, purpose and manifestation of darkness. In Jesus name. 2Tim2.26. Isa14.5.

I loose darkness from the bloodline (body, soul, spirit life & relationships and situations). In Jesus name. I cut it off and cast it out in Jesus name. Mk 16.17. Mk 3.27. Jn 12.31. Ps 37.22. Ps 76.12.

To make room for the Holy Spirit in the up-rooting process of purging, cleansing and healing of spirit impurities, defilement and spiritual violations. Mk 4.17. Isa 11.1. Mt 8.16. Mt 12.28. Zec 4.6. Eph 2.18. Thess 5.23. Eph 5.11. Eph 4.27.

I Bind, Break, Divide and Cast-Out the spirit fruit and principalic root of Darkness trying to work in our lives through:

A spirit and spiritual work against the mind, thought & thinking patterns until the spirit fruit and principalic root is produced.

Self (Spirit fruit Character)

Personality-Relationships / Environment
Chaff personalities: Flesh/Thorn types Mt 3.12. Heb 6.8. Prov 22.5.
Dark ways: Prov. 4.19. Job 21.18. 2Sam 23.6.

Wicked boasting Wicked character

Wicked confidence

Wicked counselor

Wicked encouragement or encourager

Wicked favor

Wicked hand

Wicked intent

Wicked messenger

Wicked mercies

Wicked plans

Wicked plots

Wicked desires/inclinations.

Wicked deceitful works (a consistent way/method in which the wicked mindset operates-healing, release & understanding is needed).

Wicked dwellings

Wicked pride

Wicked sacrifice   Wicked strength

Wicked transgressors   (no fear of God)

Wicked triumph

Wicked vanity

Works of darkness

Wicked "watch" (or watch of the wicked) **(or dark spirit watches is really what causes or stirs up a wicked watch among men-healing, release, biblical & spiritual understanding is needed. Lk 20.20 – scripture reveals that God is angry with the wicked every day)**

Ways of the wicked (is as darkness)

Dark spirit reasoning

Spirit of corruption (produces servants of corruption or of domination). Spirit of the world.

Violent (&/or violating spirit nature as a garment – sometimes expressed by using penetrating spirit attacks or trafficking spirits into the life of another to gain dominion

Sons of baal: realized or not

Anger   Accuser

Contrary   Authority of wicked

Corrupt   Crafty Tongue

Defraud   (deceitful ways)

Dark Crafty Counsel:

Deceit

Evil doings

Evil ways   (some pursue evil)

Evil men (walk in ways of darkness) Fools/Foolishness Evil speaking

Flattery/Flatterer Froward mouth

Facial Expressions:

Grievous ways (those with anti-Christ spirits think the judgments of God can't reach them. See Expository Study Bible by Swaggart.

Hardness (can reflect condition of heart & or spirit life activity)

Iniquity or iniquitous family patterns.

Justify the wicked

Mischief (a cause of harm or annoyance) Tongue of mischief & Vanity:

Oppression or Oppressed states (by the sons of wickedness in heaven or earth)

Counsel of the wicked including secret counsel)

State of blindness (spiritual/natural types of ignorance, innocence and foolishness)

Confusion (in one's life or another)

Conspiracy

Cruel

Betrayal

Discord

Death (the last enemy) Dishonor (bad attitude of others & or drawing others into dark spirit drama; or into their allegiance with dark angel spirit activity)

False matters

Hate (ful) issues or concerns.

Ignorance/innocence (avenues for darkness to work).

Law of sin (works through flesh & is expressed a spiritual operation of the kingdom of darkness)

Mixing holy with profane (where the Lord is not being acknowledged in your midst.

Mouth of cursing

Mouth of the wicked

Persecution/Persecutor: A dark spirit kingdom activity that operates by using persecuting tactics on many levels to cause or force (spiritually and/or naturally so to conform…..to what is being required and is the (spirit) reason for the persecution and affliction. Their emotions or emotionalism seems to be enough (thought not always biblically right to justify this ill-work of darkness.

Perverted judgment:

Provocation Physical Body Parts: can also be affected on many levels by intruding, dark spirit manifestations &/or infestations and must be resisted where felt &/or discerned. See Advanced Prayer Root System.

Treasure of the wicked:

Transgression
Proud cords   Chain of Pride
Cords of Sin (spirit nature)
Crown of Pride
Cords of: Pride, Vanity, Wickedness, Affliction

Paths of darkness: as well as, dark courses can be initiated &/or re-orchestrated (by dark spirited plots or operation of dark assignment against its target) to keep one bound to it by dark spirit life governing intrusions, interruptions, activity and networking, in the natural &/or spirit realm, by principalities (and/or those in dark spirited professions in allegiance to them). If you find yourself the target of dark desires, it must become your priority to and endeavor to learn how to maintain and preserve your spirit life in Christ by releasing yourself from dark spirit impurities, defilement &/or violent spirit intrusions, prayer/fasting & praise Some never rebound from dark spirit pursuits and assignments of the operation and systems of darkness. They spiritually corrupt a soul &/or spirit life in order (& is how) they gain the ability to govern a soul & spirit life & from there draw &/or spiral a soul into dark spirit professions.

Un-restful spirit: nature &/or state of being (healing/release needed)

Offensive spirits nature

Betrayal: shows up first in spirit life.

Destruction/Destroying evil angels

Unbelief: can affect the spirit of your mind.

Unfaithful

Bands of Darkness

Prince of air

Ruler of darkness (can be you or anyone in the position of your life seemingly connected to the 2nd realm operating with principalities to bring or help keep you in bondage or in or in agreement with hell's activity in your life. Whether you realize how this or any person is being spiritually used in this area seems to be irrelevant. Emissary, henchman or vessel for darkness would also fit this profile. The emissary and/or vessel could be used in ignorance, innocence or in spiritual blindness to the 2 spiritual kingdoms operating among us.

Dark Covenants Does not necessarily have to be established by words. It can also be established by allowing dark spirits to operate in your spirit and/or soul life without/or by not resisting it's dark spirit activity (in the natural or spirit realm). Can be an implied agreement, not necessarily written but can be a behavioral agreement (monkey-see-monkey-do)only spirits are operating behind the scene instigating and/or by spirit intrusion.

Dark Discernment: Healing is needed to released from dark spirit realms & activity that is causing &/or producing dark spirit discernment. One must also discover if one is being drawn &/or being held in dark spirit realms which can also be a cause.

Other Dark

Spirit Realm Influences

Voice of the enemy (must be biblically & spiritually discerned)

Desires for evil

Eye gate (influences) Some strongholds are in the eyes.

Extreme negative spirit image & vision recall and memory
(Could be initiated by those in dark spirit professions).

Evil spirit   Evil disease

Flesh mind

Fear seizes

Foolish thoughts

Evil patterns of thinking
(The thoughts of the wicked are abomination to the Lord.)

Evil speaking/speakers

Wicked reasoning

Vain mind/vain thinking & patterns

Torment (can come from transfer or traffic of spirits into your spirit realm. If you do not know how to resist them they will try to stay and could cause you to collect dark spirits.

Unclean spirits (can cause torment) And can be transferred to objects.

Spirit of baal: Violent spirited men

Wandering spirits

Chambers of Dark mindsets, creates destructive imaginations or imagery of darkness, death & destruction

Idols/Idolatry (another form of baal manifestations)

Dark spirits (or dark powers) should also be resisted (as if it is a person, because it is an expression of baal manifestation or presence if you sense them rise or come upon any parts of your body) In order to gain access a person's soul and spirit. A baal spirit is a warring spirit. He will even war through elements to try to release traffic, or transfer his spirit life in order to bring a soul into spiritual bondage. Satan must be resisted on any level of intrusion.

Familiar wicked, unclean & evil dark spirit life activity coming through culture, community, business/ marketplaces, families and any size people group to defile the soul and spirit lives of men.

Break any curses and reverse and mirror back any spirits transfers back to its kind and/or sender if assigned. In the name of Jesus.

Bind and break dark trinities, assignments and agreements of principalities, rulers of darkness, spiritual wickedness in high places (working individually and/or through dark spirited territorial assignments) In the name of Jesus.

Cut Cords: Pride, Vanity, Wickedness, Affliction & Sin that would connect and/or keep one connected to dark spirit activity.

Loose yourself from: Pride of life, lust of flesh & lust of eyes that would keep one connected to dark spirit activity.

I loose the Holy Spirit to up-root, cleanse, release and heal in this area. I release the blessings and peace of God to replace the curse, in Jesus name. Prov 26.2. Mt 16.19. Isa 26.12. Ps 29.11. Lk 1.79.

The people which sat in darkness saw great light.

Job 29.3.
Job 28.3
Lk 10.18.
Mt 28.18.
Mt 4.16.
Jn 8.12.

Commentary

Even though actions that can be seen come mostly from the body and soul realm, it is first birth or can be stirred in the spirit realm. There is no life or life form that is not connected to some level of spirit life activity. Certain levels of dark spirit activity or professions are able to "force" thoughts, influences and in the process of time can produce a "mind-set" similar to theirs through a process of spirit repetition or repetitious spirit activity. The loudness comes from or through repetitious thought patterns and is the reason dark spirit thoughts should be cast out, praised out and/or driven out in Jesus name, because of the consequences (over time/or accumulative) affect on one's body, soul and/or spirit life). Then the enemy (and/or those in allegiance with dark spirit activity) and will use other un-surrendered, un-kept or captive souls to help teach men their mute-like dark spirit language. Across the board while writing this book, I have seen more consistently, more teaching of dark spirited systems and how to walk in allegiance with dark spirit activity and fallen angels, etc, within and/or without the church than I have seen those teaching as effectively biblical Christian teaching that lines up with biblical spiritual allegiance to God's kingdom operation (within and/or without) the church. Surely, this needs to change.

Over time, wrong spirit thoughts, as well as, activity (not resisted) can produce wrong spirit imagination with corresponding behavior to follow and in this way this repetitious spirit (forced) thought life patterns will try to become a part of you and will continue to spiral you to manifest more of its spirit thought life/activity and dark ways of thinking (with behavior following). Until the principalic spirit cause you to manifest its dark spirit will in the earth through your life. Like Nebuchadnezzar.

Corrupting and defiling man's mind (and spirit life) is the target and whole goal of the operation (and systems) of darkness. *Sayeth the Lord!*

It's an operation of darkness with its own system. It's what they (and those affected by them) do! Dark spirit assignments against a soul (**targeted or singled out** by them) have the spirit ability to seemingly work over time even during one's sleep in a demented effort to pull and keep a person in dark spirit realms by and up to a continual mind/thought processes to affect the mind/conscious, memory, will ,desire, emotions ,spirit vision, natural sight, inclination, imagination (imagery) and magnify the smallest of matters to frustrate issues revealing again the importance and relevance in gaining the ability to release ones spirit life from dark spirit impurities, defilement and spirit violations of others or just to maintain one's spirit life in Christ Jesus. So far, I am still looking for churches gaining the ability to minister to those who have been singled out by dark spirit activity. It would seen like a church would need a good understanding of "spirit life activity" and its politics because often, darkness uses those in the church, if it can, to ostracize those they are singling out. How long will it take churches and nations to realize that gaining the ability to maintain one's soul and spirit life in Christ will help strengthen any church nation's reformation and also affect the overall soundness and unity of a church or nation.

The operation (and systems of darkness) seem to focus on three areas to bring a person under its (spirit to also affect natural) control of the mind and the spirit life of a person and/or the body of a person.

The methods seemingly used to bring these areas under dark spirit life control or demonic control are: dark spirit penetrations and/or spirit trafficking (the most severe can be done in a trance state – while in the spirit realm – men are learning to operate in their human spirits in this way) in the following areas, but not limited to the: eye

area, chest area, hands or into a person's spirit or spirit realm itself and then they try to control the movement and intentions of the person (if not the mind) using spirit penetrations, as a type of quickening) the areas that were being penetrated for
certain desired manifestations, in an attempt to stir the person into a certain behavior or response to what is being desired.

Darkness has an end!

The Lord makes a spiritual distinction between the 2 different spiritual kingdom personalities operating in our midst. Every nation's governmental established laws of the land are influenced by one or the other spiritual kingdom systems of operation and personality. There is no aspect of life and living that is not affected by spirit life. All spirit life represent a spiritual government. A government is not a government unless it has land to govern. Therefore ownership is a real issue even in spiritual governing.

Spiritual governing influences are so important that they literally influence a culture, church, family, community and society at large in a way that could work in harmony or inharmoniously with the already established governing laws of the land (to include local laws in every city and state (interstate) or our nation. To ignore how and why spirit life is influencing these areas and ultimately our nation, would be a real tragedy.

PART 2
ROOT SYSTEM

Strategy and Community

THE SPIRITUAL ROOT OF THE MATTER IS FOUND IN ME, is found to be an effective individual, group and corporate tool, method, system and excellent biblical strategy revealed by the Lord to help defensively and offensively guard one's body, soul spirit life and relationships from unforeseen and or un-desirable spirit transfers or ill- spiritual traditions of others as a routine biblical spirit cleansing and release method to help spiritually maintain one's life from spirit impurities, defilement and sometimes spiritual violations found in society, community and family ancestry (which can affect the land) Ez.9.11&14. Some like to begin by entering the presence of the Lord with thanksgiving, praise, prayer language and then go right into the spiritual root cleansing system. Others may like to begin with thanksgiving, praise and then go right into the root system and then end in their prayer language. Whatever would fit comfortably into your prayer style.

The root system is also a great tool, method and strategy for those who decide to partner with someone for a greater effectiveness or simply for learning purposes of how to work the root system. It just makes sense, if at least one if not both have a good biblical and sound knowledge of scripture and biblical principle understanding, as well as have access to their heavenly prayer language (while giving the other person time to grow stronger) in their bible, study time and fellowship with the Lord. Simply because one cannot stay free nor grow strong with Christ, with a demonic or undeveloped mind set. Christ said <u>let this mind be in you</u> which was also in Christ Jesus. Ignorance and or innocence could prove to be a spiritual hindrance or hazard. Acts19.15.Phil2.5.

Part of the reason being is that the root system can be more of a defensive spiritual system to help guard and spiritually preserve one's body, soul, spirit life and relationships from secret or silent invasions, undiscovered dark assignments and manifestations of the enemy to take over one's soul, body and spirit life, as well as being an effective spiritual offensive system designed to help release a body, soul and spirit life from perhaps dormant spirits or secret spirits that have been hiding in a body, soul and or spirit life as it has chosen to surface during the spiritual root system process, revealing that <u>there was a need</u> for spiritual cleansing and healing release. Sometimes the root system seemingly starts out great…then suddenly or it may seem out of the blue, one of the partners will begin to sense a silent type of spirit power attack or spirit retaliation….and now one of the partners is being troubled, instead of sensing the release once felt. **Does this mean that the root system is no longer effective?**

Absolutely not! Sometimes the enemy will attack or trouble the person that is aggressively effective in reading and/or leading (or visa/versa) through the root system process whereby, both parties were receiving spirit releases, with evidences of cleansing and the healing presence of the Lord. It is because of this effectiveness that the enemy will try to hinder or retaliate the process and progress in Christ.

Depending on how effective the root system has been is the reason that dark angel spirits will begin to interrupt and perhaps use the silent or quieter partner as a vessel to silently attack the person who was leading the root system ancestral categories of prayer; and now the dark spirits may look for ways to hinder progress. This is one reason we stated earlier that the more silent person (perhaps the one being more ministered to) may find it useful to use their inner witness to agree with the authority being taken in Jesus name, to bind, break by the blood and name of Jesus. Mt.18.19. There will always be a need to deal with different levels of faith and different levels of how the enemy is operating.

Some spirits think a body is their house or territory and will not leave without wrestling and we therefore must fight the good fight of faith. Tim 6.12. Eph 6.12.

These may be the spirits rising that were already quietly operating in their soul, spirit life and/or body or could have been transferred to them from community, culture, family or any size people group, object or ancestral spirits lying dormant and now are trying to hold on and/or revisit . Some spirits have to be pulled off or even discovered (often through a process of fishing and or revelation from the Lord) and is the reason for routine use of the root system. Dark angel spirits are definitely becoming, by seemingly finding more ways into the lives of men, more assertive and even aggressive in releasing dark spirit powers to hinder another soul's release from spirit impurities and defilement.

Change the Strategy

Like anything else worth waiting for, if the root system were not effective, enemy spirits would not attack it. Therefore the need may present itself to move from defensive to offensive.

Let's try switching roles. Allow the person that the enemy could have been trying to use to interrupt the process and progress to now read one of the principalic strongholds with its listings. After which, the other person can touch and agree for the areas of release….in Jesus name. Mt. 18.19. Spiritual things (spiritually confrontational things) must be discerned. If not they will continually gain strength, grow and manifest in areas not yet revealed or realized and is the reason they must be biblically and spiritually discerned, bound and cast out, in Jesus name. Sometimes it takes praise, dance and treading to cast out and keep out dark spirit life activity (depending on the level of spirit activity one is dealing with). Cor 2.14. Especially if, for whatever reason one cannot stay out of demonic environments…. which can (in itself) help keep you in dark spirit realms (causing you through a process of time to think you are in a normal spirit environment). If one does not gain the ability to resist and release themselves from dark spirit realms.

And now begin to jointly agree and intercede in your prayer language with authority and power in the Holy Ghost, build up your most holy faith (let'er rip) as they say, touch and agree in your prayer language for the releases to come forth in the category list renounced, in the name of Jesus! If any other spirits come up during this time (or comes to one's mind) whoever the spirit is coming to, it could be a good idea to take authority over it in Jesus name, bind it and cast it out and continue aggressively in your prayer language (or write down and add it to your list and deal with it at the next session)…..This can go on for approximately 1 or 2 hours or longer (the whole process) and/or until you both sense a peace and then try to end the prayer session according to the page titled "Root System". Mt 18.19. Jude 20. This page will give you an idea of how to address any stubborn or resistant spirits that may keep popping up by using scripture authority and repetition (you can be as determined as you want and/or need to be) in Jesus name. As you grow in your daily bible reading know that you are free to add any other authority scriptures (that you feel would be helpful) during your prayer time. Pet 5.8. James 4.7. Jude 20. Mt 8.17. Cor 12.7. Rom 15.13.

If for any reason anyone's progress is being too hindered by spiritual distractions and you seem to be spending more time with the distractions, this may be a good time to work individually on your increased faith base level of knowledge (faith) and understanding of God's word and your authority in the name of Jesus. Our flow chart could help you realize how to better enforce your authority in Christ Jesus! You may need to receive certain revelation (for greater understanding) from the Lord before proceeding. He is our sanctuary. Ez11.16. After all the healing and releases are all based on your faith in Him, His word and will for your cleansing, release and healing needs. Prov. 2.11&12. Ps. 119.129. Ps 119.144.

Then perhaps reunite (in group sessions) at a later date. It is good for both partners to both desire to be free. Because spirits are intelligent beings and will test your will, biblical and spiritual intelligence as you discover that some spirits must be pulled off (and this can be done through consistent faith confessions-even a plowing of one's way through as indicated on our additional flow chart offer. Sometimes a person could awake with a bombardment of spirit noise, to off-set this, one could upon awaking, go straight to their flow chart and just as a faith exercise begin to drive away any spirits in the environment and/or soul area by taking authority using all the names of Jesus on the flow for a least 15 min and/or until the environment and/or your soul is released from the spirit noises. In Jesus name. Yes. It really works! Others may desire to use different and/or various fishing methods to discover which spirits need to be removed. Please be led of the Lord.

Sometimes both parties will experience releases and healings but by the next session one of the parties comes back with the seemingly same spirit concerns. Also, there may be somewhere an open door evidently where the spirits are seemingly free to come back or hide and the person is either not resisting it or just from association with others who have spirits trafficking in their life can also cause association hindrances (spirits can work territorially). This could likely mean that everyone in the territory would need to know how to spiritually release themselves, just so that one could stay free. Yes, and there are those who will try to spiritually force association (unaware) with you just to traffic spirits into your life and must also find release and/or be cut off in Jesus name because spirits operating in their life will use relationship(s) to bring and/or keep you in bondage.

Scripture reveals: Do not be unequally yoked with unbelievers (and/or spirit activity that would biblically resemble unbelief), for what fellowship hath righteousness with unrighteousness or what communion baal with Christ. 2 Cor 6.14-17.

We would do good to remember and/or realize that not everyone that needs spiritual cleansing, release and healing want to be. Some people were birth into strange spirit life activity belief systems and may not necessarily think or believe that their spirit activity is wrong and/or unbiblical. Then others are spiritually trained to draw others into their dark spirit beliefs and activity contrary to scriptures, in that their spirit life activity (and dark spirit belief system) never required them to read....scripture or receive Christ as Lord and Savior; than how could one be a follower of Jesus. Even though they may go to church every Sunday, there is a need to be re-spiritually trained, that their spirit life activity may be more harmonious with the word of God.

Other Deliverance Methods

Uninvited spirits can be dealt with on 2 primary levels, yet in a variety of ways, none of which can be effective or dealt with without the word of God and the help of the Holy-Spirit. On a more-subtle, individual level or, on the confrontational (invasively offensive level, initiated by not-opposing spirit life activity coming from the warfare in the air or demon spirits operating through men in the earth in allegiance to dark spirit life activity (who perhaps never realized how to resist dark spirit life activity). Win Worley, in his book, "The Deadly Dangers of Witchcraft", tells us on page 8, that all demons are programmed to attack and destroy.

Deliverance can also be done on the conference (more personal) or corporate level. I believe there is a reason and need for both. And it is important to realize which care is needed for each situation at hand. The greater one's knowledge in the word and devotional relationship with Christ will directly affect one's confidence in serving the Lord on the deliverance and level of faith needed. Gal 2.2.

Various or alternative healing / deliverance methods

It is a good idea to begin all sessions by entering the presence of the Lord with thanksgiving and praise then begin by commanding specific demons to go in the name of Jesus, while the other assisting ministers in the room engage in prayer, praise, singing and/or reading scriptures. This should be done in low or subdued voices. The writer states that it is not the loudness with which we speak that makes demons tremble and obey but the authority with which we speak in the name of Jesus! PS 100.4.

One writer suggests that a demon can be engaged in the following manner:

> Demons I know that you are there I know of your presence
> And of your evil works. You have no right to stay in this person.
> This person belongs to Christ Jesus. Jesus purchased this person with his own blood.
> This body is the temple of the Holy Spirit. Everything that defiles is cast out.
> You are a trespasser and you must go.
> I command you to go now in the name of Jesus.

During this time the person, the author suggests that is being delivered can be helpful in the following ways:

He should refrain from praise, prayer and speaking in tongues.

These are ways, the writer states, of taking in the Holy Spirit; and the mouth and breath must be left free for the departure of evil spirits. The counselee should be encouraged to enter battle with his will. The counselee can address the spirits himself letting the demons know of his desire that they leave and want no further part of them.

This writer also suggests that the counselee being delivered can begin to expel or release his breath, this can help expel them. Or, one can force a few healthy coughs. This may be enough to get things started. The counselee may force a cough and the demons may then begin to yawn themselves out.

<u>Keep commanding them in the name of Jesus (or the many names of Jesus) until you get results.</u>
Confidence should come with experience. If no spirits have been released within four or five minutes, there may be some hindrances.

Another method, conference style, includes questionnaires to find out when and how long, etc., demon spirits entered a life or soul. Someone on the deliverance team can record the information being received and or can take notes on listing what spirits manifest for reference. The person being ministered unto may like a record to know what demons were released from one's life.

Yet there are countless others who may be believers but the deliverance arena is still too new coupled, with many unanswered questions and therefore, are still not comfortable about asking people questions or what to do with the replies they get. Even in 2007, we are still faced with more in need than help available. While the operation of the kingdom of darkness, continues to take advantage of this shortage. Hell continues to pursue subtle and aggressive ways of actively finding ways working through all levels of cultures, families, friends, associates and brief meeting situations to enlist through snares and stare pulls those near and far into sorcery group activity; spiraling many into deeper and deeper levels of spiritual bondage and captivity. As if, there were a deadline to meet, before help could be found.

It's been said that questionnaires are useful tools to help get to the root concerns of people's problems or situation. The thought here is that the questionnaire can only be as effective as the counselee is able to give the best answers possible. Meaning that some answers may be hidden in a soul's life experiences or mindsets. <u>The Spiritual Root of the Matter is Found in Me</u>, system helps to release a soul's spirit life that could possibly hinder one from a more accurate response by ministering in biblical spiritual fruit and principalic root areas that already exist where scripturally indicated.

Spirit fruit of a person could express, whether good or bad can be found in scripture. Jesus said, the words I speak are spirit and life. Herein, a person may be able to find a quicker spiritual release that if first sought by a questionnaire. Again, one may not be free enough to respond appropriate enough for immediate help, either way, healing is a process as with anything else in life worth waiting for. Eccl.9.

Many are not aware of gloom consequences of being around, those who (deliberately) secretly engage others with dark spirit manifestations and its accruing, constantly increasing accumulate growing affect. This is what is happening in the (sorcery, psychic) spirit realm each time hell uses someone to actively engage anyone with "sorcery psychic ensnaring stares". It is a type of drawing (or bewitchment) into the spirit realm. Where most people can be overcome and therefore, must be biblically resisted, in Jesus name. Acts 8.

Dark spirited practice is actually an operation of the kingdom of darkness and method to spiritually ensnare or keep spiritually bound, the souls of men. Dark spirits can't spiral a soul deeper into darkness until a soul is first ensnared and is the reason you can actually observe someone in the community in allegiance to or being hindered or troubled by dark spirit operations will go out of their way to spiritually connect or engage someone (being initiated by rulers of the darkness or dark angel spirit powers in the air) because this is how many that have been spoiled by dark spirit activity are being led in many public and private groups.

And in this respect, another reason for the, <u>"The Spiritual Root of Matter is Found in Me"</u> to help the people of God protect and spiritually maintain their soul's spirit life unto the Lord, to help keep them undefiled from hell's consistent and ongoing attempts to defile a soul's spirit life for dark operations. Just as hell is bent (it's their spirit nature) on interrupting a soul's spirit life for dark operations, the people of God must begin to make more room for the Holy Spirit to help with the cleansing and healing process of our spirits from the constant secret trafficking, channeling and contagious methods and manifestations just for being around dark operations (whether one is aware of it or not).

No longer can the body of Christ assume that our churches or any places where people are gathered are spiritually safe places due to the aggressive and advanced spirit operations of darkness against the souls and spirit lives of men. Just as dark spirit operations are trying to take over homes, communities, business marketplaces, cultures, communities, etc. and individual lives one at a time. We cannot assume churches are exempt. However, this does point to greater infiltrations of darkness in our midst trying to harmonize (even forced harmonizing) among us, while secretly ensnaring the souls and spirit lives of men with dark power manifestations, releases and transfers as part of their success is making the people of God think that they are on God's good side.

The spiritual battle is real. We must not only gain the spiritual ability and strength to deal effectively with dark spirit confrontations. We must also be able to deal with the ability to preserve our spirit life in Christ and keep it free from the accruing, accumulating spiraling effects of being consistently around those vessels who freely manifest around others, because they do not yet know how to guard and preserve and maintain their soul's spirit life. Doing nothing does not seem to work, hell Is actively taking over passive souls even those considered strong in the Lord may be challenged when it comes to resisting dark spirit life activity.

We must actively make room for the Holy Spirit in prayer, study, praise and biblical spiritual methods of cleansing the soul's spirit. Self deliverance is good with biblical and spiritual understanding, coupled with biblical and spiritual maturity. Prov. 2.11&12. Ps 119.129. Ps.119.144.

Some may find it most helpful or wise to initially team up with someone who has greater applicable knowledge of biblical principles who can effectively speak the word in faith. Even dark spirits know when one is going beyond their level of faith. Acts19.14.

Most deliverance ministers advise on not allowing demonic conversations, seeing that scripture reveals that it is the nature of devil spirits to lie. That some devil spirit personalities will even side step, question or challenge your authority, by threatening you or by remaining silent. Even dark spirits know who has the word of God abiding in their lives and who do not.

When the Holy Spirit desires, He will bring you into new levels of revelation and authority. He will give you faith and confidence to proceed.

There are many levels of demonic oppression. Strong spirits present can control the activities of other demonic powers in the mind, emotions body and spirit life; and therefore must be discerned and removed before the greater powers can be dealt with. This can also be viewed as spiritual un-layering (from spirit impurities and/or defilement).

Some desiring ministry are depressed, confused, dull of mind and sometimes feel hopeless about ministry. Some are bound by strong hereditary spirits that cause many levels of mental concerns, which in some cases have been re-enforced by other spirits received during anytime spent in hospitals or during shock treatments. Prayer priorities should be determined by the Holy Spirit during each root section.

Some people deal with deeply rooted fears that may cause panic attacks. These areas need to be dealt with and cast out before a spiritually oppressed person can have relief. Those with lesser fears can be healed with love and affirmation. Amen. Love still works! Jn 15.9. Jn 15.12. Col 2.2. Gal 5.13.

Demonic Intruders, by Noel & Phyl Gibson, Chpt. 19&20. For those needing more information or help in the areas of MPDD or SRA. See the book section at the end of this writing.

EVIDENCE OF HEALING

Expressions

Breaking a curse, casting out demons or pulling down a stronghold is not something mysterious but miraculous by and through the complete work of Calvary. Acts 2.22. Jn 12.37. It is a supernatural act of God and annot be accomplished by a man alone. A person in spiritual bondage cannot always free themselves. It may depend on the level of spiritual bondage. I suppose that if they could have delivered themselves, they would have. It's been said that, there is no set formula to cast out demons (which in this writing can also be viewed as dark spirit fruit that need to be released from a soul's spirit fruit or root tree spirit life), in this respect, we cannot put God in a box. This is why, "The Spiritual Root of the Matter is Found in Me" is a biblical and spiritual guidance manual with a step by step approach to help any one new to God's healing process get started in this much needed area that helps to sustain the soul and spirit lives unto the Lord. Spiritual maintenance of a soul's spirit life is needed because spirits are always trying to attach itself to people (using either a multitude of people or using those in dark spirited professions who have their individual dark spirit ways to release spirits into a life that has been targeted by darkness) to express themselves and their allegiance to a dark spirit kingdom initiatives and agenda. Therefore, "The Spiritual Root of the Matter is Found in Me" can be used as a biblical and spiritual system working with the Spirit of God and faith to help implement a steady diet or method to help release one's soul from undesirable spirit fruit, when some instances could have attached itself unaware, but realized once released in a spiritual release, cleansing and healing session. Some people go through their lives collecting spirits, such as the case of schizophrenia once established in a life, by rejection and rebellion, will then open the door for other spirits. How a people and generation can seemingly overlook, the open work of aggressive demonic degeneration activity of and among the body, soul and spirit life of men working not alone but through other people knowingly or unknowingly in allegiance to dark spirit activity, is a concern and can no longer be overlooked.

After a healing session, it is good to claim the freedom Christ has granted you through His death and resurrection by faith in Christ Jesus and Him crucified. You can speak directly to the demons that you believe are plaguing your life, oppressing your mind or disrupting you home. This can be done in one's personal prayer time (and then continue to drive them out using our flow chart system until there is peace in your soul and/or environment-this would indicate your release in Jesus name or during the root system process and our independent flow chart, as a supplement filled with the many names of Jesus Christ and His completed work at the cross. Don't give up….insist adamantly on their leaving. Don't be surprised if you feel certain physical or emotional reaction. Such as a blinding headache, nausea, weakness, trembling, depression, crying and so on. If this happens, it only comes to prove as evidence that what you are doing is having a direct and devastating effect on the spirits that are trying to keep you in bondage and these emotions can be symptoms of your release, as they arise, simply say, I release you in Jesus name.

Another common manifestation is that which occurs in the hands. The hands may sometimes become numb or tingle. Sometimes the body or the fingers become extended and rigid. Sometimes it may be helpful for the person to shake the hands vigorously in order to dislodge the spirits while saying I release you in Jesus name, then using the flow chart names of authority in Christ Jesus, continue driving the spirits out of the hands until there is release, in Jesus name. Tim 6.12.

Arthritic spirits often manifest themselves in the hands. The hands may become very stiff and the fingers gnarled. When the demon of arthritis is challenged the hands can take on the appearance of a person who has had arthritis for years. Some demons manifest by a twisting of the body. Death spirits may manifest itself with open eyes and/or the eye balls roll up into the head.

Odors are another facet of demon manifestations. Demon spirits of cancer may come out with an odor. Witchcraft spirits may manifest with piercing demonic screams and/or hands begin to shape like claws. Spirits of pride may manifest by folding the arms across the chest, by someone who is standing or sitting. Also, spirits of pride may manifest by tilting their head back with their nose very high in the air. Evil spirits sometime reveal their presence and nature by pantomiming (A TYPE OF SILENT MIMICKING). Someone with a demon of worldly dancing, may manifest rhythmically by moving one's body back and forth or side to side. One may begin to clap their hands with the body movements and move their lips as if they are singing a song but with no verbal sounds. Some can get very dramatic.

Some have yet to realize that often sensitivities such as, a tendency to jump at shadows or when one is touched unexpectantly jumps or one who has a constant fear of punishment are all indications that spiritual releases are needed and necessary for spiritual and physical wholeness in Christ Jesus. It's good to remember that perfect love casts out fear, because fear has to do with punishment or torment. Many like to throw out this scripture like a generic answer to everyone who is dealing with fear in their life, without expressing the other half of the issue that help to release fear in anyone's life. Usually fears in a life are created and supported by any majority in a counselee's environment who are seemingly attempting to control another's behavior and the punishment sensed by the counselee is rejection by the majority (right or wrong). However, the majority behavior <u>should be</u> questioned for not being loving, accepting or affirming because of the majority's desire to enforce a behavior silently using rejection and the unspoken punishment. This is more typical of a reflection of your average demonic spirit life activity invasion in any single environment. Since behaviors are spiritual issues and concerns (and cannot otherwise be hidden), this example would be a good example of how dark spirits could effectively be influencing or working through culture, community or any size people group.

Why? Because we are in the midst of 2 spiritual kingdoms rising in our midst. With schizophrenia or Bi-polar on the rise in our society, with rejection as one of its major tools, should not we begin to look and begin to minister to the majority more effectively because ultimately when on suffers, it will eventually affect all.

What seems to off-set fear and in some cases heal fear is love and all that expresses love and is loving; when those with "fear" symptoms are surrounded and embraced with love, tenderness and acceptance there is a release. <u>Love still works!</u> Jn 15.9.

Other spirit manifestations may include cramps in the legs and arms. Nausea. Crying. Laughing. The laughing spirit is often a mockery spirit. And the list of manifestations goes on and on and…Whatever the manifestation, it's a good thing to see them on their way out, in Jesus name.

Often times demon spirits may leave through the urinary or respiratory tract, or through the mouth or blowing the noise. As they leave, you might yawn, cough, belch, vomit, etc. Don't let this frighten you. In the course of deliverance, you will begin to feel that a heavy burden is lifting off your heart and mind. You will feel light and clean inside. Don't stop short. Persist until you feel total release from whatever is oppressing you. In Jesus name.

One of the final evidences that you have freed from Satan's grip is the noticeable change that will take place in your character, health, nerve and mental attitude, etc. Whether or not a dark spirit is seen, when the demon has left, there is always a sense of release in the spirit of both the person who is praying and the one receiving the deliverance. The dark place is gone and the Holy Spirit can now begin to fill it. Hallelujah and Amen.

Remember that demon spirits always seek to regain the ground they have lost in your life, <u>so stay alert.</u> Mt 12.43-45. There is no greater protection from Satan's onslaughts than the fullness of the Spirit. Acts 1.4.5, 8. After receiving the baptism of the Holy Spirit, it may be a good idea to ask the Lord to refill you daily. Eph 5.18. Gal 5.16.25.

---

*Please note: Demon spirits usually speak in a defiant tone because they do not intend to leave. Some like to confuse the deliverance minister. Demon spirits are tormented by the hearing of the blood of Jesus and their everlasting fate ahead of them. So tell them about the blood of Jesus and His complete work at Calvary! Corir 1.18.

IS PRAISE UNDERRATED,

We are living in a time where there is a need for everyone to gain the knowledge on how to keep undesired, invading spirits and intentional dark spirited transfers not only out of one's body, soul and spirit lives (using the root system as one method) but we are also finding that there is also a need to gain the knowledge once realized, how to also keep dark power spirits operating in the air from descending upon you or from the surrounding spirit environment with the desire to literally move your body or soul from it natural and spiritual sound abilities or course into the will of dark spirit activities or dark spirit realms designed or desired to move you literally within your environment to their dark will and purposes. Literally, pulling you into their spirit realm world (or wilderness) by hindering and/or interrupting your natural will and inclinations by spiritually invading and eroding your spirit life literally with daily distractions and delay through sorcery pulls like trance states that can work through transi-dental meditation; illusions, delusions, etc. designed by them (with our without your permission), in this way dark spirit realms and activities, and those in dark spirit professions are revealing themselves. 2Tim 2.26. Cor 10.5. And yet, one must first gain the ability to discern the demonic spirit activity before one can protect their self from it.

It seems whether we resist dark angel spirit transfers, don't know how or do know how; it seems everyone is being spiritually challenged and warred against by principalic spirit life activity. However, on many spirit levels, one thing is sure powers of the air and principalities seen to be using whoever is available to bring anyone and everyone into a captive or bound state. By even interrupting our world and our lives, they are trying <u>to cause us</u> to fit into their dark spirit kingdom activity and agendas.

Let us be mindful of the powerful effects and awesome gift of praise power, that an atmosphere of worship, praise and thanksgiving can accomplish and that the Spirit of the Lord can also release people and set the captives free because Jesus has powers over all flesh. Jn17.2. Rom 8.26. The Spirit of the Lord helps our infirmities but we must learn how to biblically apply ourselves by faith to manifest the power of God in our lives for spiritual protection. <u>I mean we need to biblically learn how to give the Lord something to work with!</u>

High praise during power engaged, even in anticipation of confronting powers of darkness has the ability to restrain (on the scene) what hell is trying to do in or with your life (at the point when spirit kingdom conflicts begin to arise even the minute before, often these spiritual conflicts are subtle in nature and must be biblically and spiritually discerned before one can begin to spiritually protect and spiritually guard from dark spirit defilement intrusions and invasions). Ps8.2. The key though, seems to be that one must be in the high praise before dark spirits come on the scene. If not, dark spirits may quickly use people like pawns one against another! It appears now that only those trying to avoid dark spirit advances and those that are about God's business in helping to set the captives free at any level are seemingly the ones that dark spirits are making the extra effort to openly descend upon, right before our very eyes to interrupt or hinder. Some are dealing with sudden open extreme spirit confrontations of darkness, from the land, earth, sea and even stationary objects as a basis (or pivot point) to release their hindering channeling/trafficking powers. These types of spirit episodes can be initiated (behind the scene) by those in dark spirit professions on assignments.

Some of God's saints on the front line are dealing with extreme manifestations and/or out-right confrontations of dark spirits rising up in their face through the lives of men out of nowhere men are expressing bazaar and abnormal behavior in that spirits have so idolized the souls, bodies and spirit lives of men (that have not learned or discerned how to resist them or who are already bound) that when certain saints of God come on the scene principalities working with rulers of the darkness and powers of the air are causing men to gather around the saints of God to spiritually pull (through sorcery powers and bewitchment) the saints into the will of Satan. Ps118.12. In this respect we are dealing with power plays and in this way satan is demanding the saints of God to give him allegiance (using men among us, police included, some willingly, some are being used in captive states as victims, vessels or carriers of darkness). Dt5.7. Isa49.25.

> But thus saith the Lord, even the captives of the mighty shall be taken away and the prey of the terrible delivered….. Isa49.25. Hallelujah!

Lord help us to just break fourth into praise to keep hell from using us! Praise power, a high praise, has the ordained God ability to pull us out of (I believe) any sorcery pulls working through those among us or forces in the environment. <u>But timing is everything!</u> So take courage saints of God, a daily working out of your salvation time has come. Sometimes having daily praise drills will help you prepare to make room for the Lord as well as daily studying of the word to strengthen our shield confessions of faith. The Lord will inhabit our praise, but we must begin to apply ourselves to make room and provision through praise for Him to come on the scene because the battle is the Lords! His glory is our defense! Ps89.18. Ps32.7. Sam17.47. Exo15.2-3. Ps106.47. Nahum..7. Ps103.6. Eph6. Ps22.3. Dt33.29.

> Save us O Lord and gather us from among the heathen to give thanks unto thy holy name and to triumph in they praise. Ps106.47. Col2.15.

Many scriptures reveal that we triumph in praise and praise can also be a perfect remedy for the nervous system:

> You that fear the Lord, praise him! PS 22.23.

Praise helps us to not give place to demon spirits and helps us to avoid taking part in their operation of dark spirit activity. Eph 2.2.

> I call it a having done all (a biblical and spiritual method in Christ) to stand. Ps46.1. Ps32.7.

Praise helps us keep our eyes on the Lord and helps us to make room for the Lord who inhabits our praise. 2Chr 20.12. 2 Chr 20. & 22.

Praise helps us to release the power of God. Scripture reveals that:

> ……………………..through the greatness of His power shall the enemy submit themselves unto thee…. Ps66.3. Ps22.3.

The garment of praise is used to resist the spirit of heaviness.

Many of us need a praise corner in our homes to release our homes, as well as, ourselves from the spirit of heaviness, impurities and/or defilement, in Jesus name. Acts16.25-26. Prov27.21. 2Chr20.15-17. 2Chr20.21-23. Ps47.6-7. Malichi 3.2. Isa48-9-11.

Some have said that praise is equivalent to the battles you/or I win!

(This would be the level of praise needed)

The author of, Evicting Demonic Intruders, reminds us that the Holy Spirit is the Divine professor of truth. He is able to cope with any situations encountered. Pet2.17. This writer tells us to **never let Satan rob you of your total victory won by Jesus Christ' blood, shed on the cross!**

GLOSSARY Terminology, common terms and commentary related to this writing

Gods. Defined in Webster dictionary as: Deity….divinity…divine being… spirit angel…idol…power…influence…universal presence…everywhere (cosmic process, potential energy) life force…energy…infinite spirit..(stars* Amos 5.29)…dreamers (Jude 1.*8). Their process and ability to quickly reproduce or transform themselves among us and in the lives of some often before others (somehow amazingly undetected) in daylight, intermingled somewhere within our daily activity among our family, culture, business, marketplace, community, legal and government systems /security and police services, youth and health care systems and within the fibers of our city, society and nation is what concerns us in this writing along with achieving spiritual recovery from active spirit violations, defilement and uninvited dark spirit reproduction and operations within our lives and among us. Some spirit angel gods are fallen angels and therefore cursed in spirit nature. Therefore, to allow them into your life (or ignore that they do not belong in your life) is to perhaps to allow the curse at some level to affect you. Mt 25.41. Isa 14.12. Dt 5.7. Know ye not that we shall judge angel (spirits). Corin 6.13. Heb 1.7.

Idols. Can be an image, idea, thought or impression of a spirit or symbolic of angel spirit power. An image or an idol can manifest into a power (or presence); depending on the attention **you** give it or should I say, the attention it (spirits/or the perpetrator causing the spirit activity to come your way) to try to force upon you to invade or gain the ability to operate in your life (the latter usually means there is a person behind the scene marshalling evil spirits to force itself into the targets or subjects life). There is a need to remember that in regards to spirit activity, nothing happens by chance, but by design. Discovery must be made and strategy sought of the Lord's protection. Many in dark spirit professions, have learned how to gained the ability to spirit force undesired spirit life activity into another's thought life, body or spirit realm and even transcending into one's natural experience(s) with enough spirit trafficking and channeling, as an entry point into your (spirit) life and then into your world. So that the person can operate in your life through and by the spirit activity they force into a life, whereby otherwise, they would not be there. This type of higher and/or deeper spirit activity you will find happening among the sons of baal looking and finding ways into the lives that belongs to Christ. They will try to enforce spirit or spiritual duality (or idolatry) into your life, like they do in many secret societies, which in itself turns out to be a type of spirit domination; because there are only 2 spirit kingdoms operating among us. Only 2. There is no spiritual kingdom King and/or Lord dualities operating in the Kingdom of God, only Jesus Christ and Him crucified has that right, claim and title King of Kings and Lord of Lords and He will not share His glory with His created and/or fallen beings. This would tell me that there is a need for us to learn how to resist the dark spirit activity that is trying to spiritually war and spiritually defile and violate against those who belong to Christ. 2Pet 2.4. This would be a reason to consistently cast down imaginations and every high thing that exalts itself against the knowledge of God and release your spirit life through the root system process (as a possible solution), with praise and/or use our independent flow chart to confess the names of the authority of Jesus Christ to help <u>resist</u> (at home or community) any confrontational spirit uprisings against the soul, body and/or spirit life, in Jesus name. Because dark spirit kingdom territories are trying to establish itself among us within our communities and many of our churches within our communities that have not as yet learned how to resist dark spirit activity. This you realize when some within the church systems resist the child of God in their midst (instead of the dark spirit activity). The spiritual resistance is there until people learn how to release themselves from the spirits causing them to behave contrary to Christ's Spirit of love and acceptance expressed in the lives of those has Christ Spirit life. 2Cor 10.4-5. Isa 42.8.

Whatever attention you give an idol (spirit, god, angel, image, etc) can become your service to the idol. Service is also a form of worship. It is through consistent worship (attention) or conjuring up attention (or spirit force invasion could apply here)….that the idol can come into being and ultimately begin to express or manifest a power or presence through or upon the body itself causing a person to collect enough spirits; thoughts, will desire and or imaginations, inclinations and memory (without resistance).

Any object, thing or person that is being given more than normal, unusual or unnecessary attention (or that is trying to spirit force itself into your life) should be questioned and then biblically and spiritually resisted in Christ Jesus and the cross as our basis for doing so because He paid the price for us at Calvary. This behavior can be seen as a way towards creating an idol or image out of the object, thing or person being consistently un-biblically exalted or enforced upon. Therefore, an idol or image can be created by giving a person's soul, body or spirit excessive attention and/or by someone marshalling spirits into a person's life. As with synchronized staring among groups of people, to single out any one person, is also a spirit type activity expression trying to come to the forefront in the area and/or place it's trying to manifest and/or reveal itself often initially, through men, and this is another way people are being demonically programmed by dark spirits and those people with dark spirit natures (realized or not) that work in allegiance with dark angel spirits to help create or help keep you in a dark spirit realm through constant channeling and trafficking and/or marshaling spirits into a life, each time they see you or by those in community who suddenly come just to hang around in a spooky type and/or unsound manner to allow dark angel spirit powers of the air to use them to attach spirits that have been trying to find entrance in your life. Bizarre but true. This is part of the spiritual operation and system of darkness working through men and women who do not really know nor understand how the true God works grace in the lives of His people. God does not work "issues" into our lives. We are actually seeing these startling "spirit activities" unfold before us, This is only some of the activity that is occurring and arising out of the spirit kingdom age. Putting a demand among us to teach spirit life activity period; to help prevent "dark spirit domination"; no matter the religion, and this will help to protect and preserve humanity, community and our society at large.

Idol spirits of devotion

Hopefully, we can perceive and understand now, how a idol can be "spirit" forced into one's life by someone in a dark spirit profession and/or led by and/or involved with continual dark spirit trafficking, transferring and/or channeling and marshalling spirits by (or sons/daughters of baal) in one way or another with or without your consent. Often it seems to be about the chase once dark spirit activity has selected its target or subject. Acts 15.20. Acts 19.28-29.Thess 1.9.Rev.22.15.

Further reading on how dark angel spirits have been (spirit) forcing their way in our midst, at the church, community and various levels of society, can be found in the writing: "Apostolic Recovery". Authorhouse, publisher. Also at the Barnes and Nobel website or stores and all books by Rebecca Brown. A sign of the times!

Idolatry. The practice of worshipping idols (images or deities used as objects of worship. False gods). Idolatry can defile a soul, family, church, city, society and/or land. Dark spirit activity can and does spread (even historically and biblically this can be seen as a type of spiritual social disease, often due to an ongoing (seemingly generational) ignorance of spirit to life activity.

Some of the ways principalic idol spirits can manifest upon men and women in community is to cause a person or people group to collectively (or individually-depending on the person strength and confidence the person has with its spiritual allegiance-not necessarily of the Lord) draw attention to a person, whose attention the dark spirits are desiring, ultimately to gain demonic attention, spiritual influence, allegiance or control in their life.

<u>Not everyone</u> is desiring to bow down to demonic systems in every city and state of our nation. However, people are being consistently spiritually attacked with dark spirit power initiatives and/or continually secretly drawn into the will of satan through various levels of sorcery (or bewitching) transformations. systems and strategies operating (if possible) even through those close to us and/or victims and vessels (those in dark spirited professions, various dark spirited covenants and/or secret societies or lodges which often seem to take on their own spirit belief system of activity). Going as far as using methods of intentional strategy and/or creating associates for hidden assignments. What is hidden in scripture that Satan can also give his ministers the ability to transform the spirit lives of saints into a dark spirit nature. Even without their concern is the concern.

Many secular jobs have been used and/or have been turned into demonic altars (places of demonic activity and/or idols of affections) where demonic allegiance is being demanded, at entry points and exit points within and about our job/business market and security systems. Recreational places, rest areas and any policing arenas would be included, often because people are in need of learning how and why it is even necessary to resist dark spirit initiatives and agendas for the souls of men (some that are unlearned among us think spirit life activity operating among us is a "joke"; these usually become sons of baal). Satan will just keep spiritually spiraling and molding them into dark spirit professions-to be bound, no longer laughing! 2Pet2.19.

These help to make up our religious, non-religious and spirit belief systems of activity operating in our cultures and communities.

It should not be a surprise, that God has a problem with idols and idolatry in the lives of His people whom Christ died for. The Lord, God not only wants our attention; He is also desiring our undivided affection and adoration. Biblically, idolatry carries a serious penalty. Scripture Ref: Ecc 12.14. Malachi3.16. Isa26.9. Isa29.24. Jere16.17, 20-21. Act17.16.2 Cor6.16.2 Ki21.11.Rev11.4. Ez20.18. Isa42.8. Isa45.16. Cor12.2. Ps106.30.2 Cor6.10.2 Cor7.1. Dt32.17.Dt32.12 & 29. Joshua24.23. Ps10.2. Ps81.9. Ps16.4. Prov16.8. Dt5.7. Ez36.17-20. Rev 22.15. Le26.21. Exo.23.24. Corin87. Exo20.16. **Idolatry** is the work (of the dark sprit life activity of the devil's ability to spiritually deceive men (by spirit force and/or constant spirit, manipulating manifestations into a person's spirit life and soul by a process of – a continual spiritual influence or invasion) working through the innocent, ignorant, foolish, spiritually blind and/or bound prisoners of war. 2Pet.2.19.

Image. Of which the Lord has said in His word…I have reserved… who have not bowed to the (spirit) image of baal. Rom 4.11. Rom6.16. Ps97.7. Ex23.24-25.

Image can come from one's thoughts or thinking patterns (natural thoughts or forced). It can be the representation of a person or thing and/or an intrusion of dark spirit life activity. A copy. A mental picture. A simile, to reflect a mental impression, perception or

God said that there is a difference between waiting on the Lord and waiting on a spirit (image) angels in the air who seek to inhabit the souls of men to keep you focused on the flesh to make idols of the souls of men and defile the flesh. 2Pet2.9 & 18. Jude 1.1-9. And they conception (magnified by dark angel spirit activity). Thought, Likeness. Mental grasp through senses, insight. Institution or observation. Ps 4.8. Spirits can come as thoughts. Col 2.18. Isa14.24. Pro12.5. Ps139.17 .Mt15.19. Mt9.4. Acts 19.35. Images can be created from thoughts.

changed the glory of the uncorruptible God into a (spirit) image made like to corruptible man... Rom 1.23-25.

Image. Another word for spirit (angel or gods): fallen angels and images can give rise to how idols are created. The bible also reveals that the word star and dreamers can also be viewed as "spirits". In this sense dark/fallen angel spirits have learned to create images in the minds and lives of men by way of consistent unrestrained and/or orchestrated thoughts from dark spirit realm activities causing men to wait on, hearken to and serve fallen angel spirit powers in the air (realized or not) in ways not intended by God. Ps 81.9. Amos 5.29. Jude 1.8. Job 4.15-16. Dr. Kurt E. Koch, Kregel publications, revealed in his book "Demonology. Past & Present, pg 11-14 that a study of one's eyes can be a method of the occult used to bring a person into spiritual bondage. Also, many emotional disturbances can also be attributed to this outright bizarre occult practice of psychic flesh/soul staring. Dt. 6.22.

We are to put on the new man which is renewed in knowledge after the (spirit - but not every spirit) image of Him that created him. Col 2.10. Prov. 25.5. Rom 8.2. Eph 4.23-24. Jn 4.24. Mk 10.15.

Confounded be all they that serve graven images that boast themselves of idols, worship Him all ye gods. Ps 97.7

....and they have no rest day nor night who worship the beas....and his (spirit) image... Rev 14.11.

And the third angel followed them saying with a loud voice if any man worship or serve the beast and his (spirit) image and receive his mark in his for head or in his hand, the same shall drink of the wine of the wrath of God... Rev 14.9-10.

...and I saw them that had gotten the victory over the beast and over His (spirit) image.
Rev. 15.2 Ex23.24-25. Ps 106.25.42. Exo 34.13-14. Hos10.2. 2 Ki 17.24-41. Isa 14.12. Exo23.24. Dt 20.3-4.

Biblical analogy of gods, idols, idolatry and images :

Dark spirits can work through thoughts to create images, imaginations, dreams, visions, etc., in your mind to the point it transcends into your natural experience and then they keep you focused in the natural on the object that was created in your mind, to keep you *focused* off and always away from God Almighty. Dan 3.12-15. Keeping in mind that there are only 2 spiritual kingdoms operating among us, this can be a serious offense against the Lord. Mt. 16.23.

So in respect, the story of Nebuchadnezzar, could be seen as a type of dark spiritual warfare-that developed (in his mind and spirit realm imagination first) and once magnified there, eventually played out in his life; or perhaps he like many of us just think we are to just let "any" spirit activity that presents itself to take place in our lives or minds, without resisting it, because *who* is really teaching how to deal with day to day spirit intrusions (or could I say that it was a spiritual battle that he lost – the bible teaches that we are to have no other God before Him) that started in his mind (and then grew into a mindset – with no resistance), and that once he heard his dream's interpretation it gripped his mind. To the point, he made the golden image, in this way he brought it into his experience and then caused other men to be subject to this image he created (or allowed to be created), by bowing down to it (but first he bowed to this spirit image in his mind until the spirit became real enough to cause him to create the image in his world-that the spirit god kept revealing to him to create).

The analogy is sort-of like today's dark spirit fetish that had caused men to gather (in certain spiritual environments among us) in demonic synchronized stares to reveal their dark allegiance to satan (realized or not) and expect everyone that would come into their dark business or marketplace environment to be subject to the dark angel spirit god(s) that any business environment would subject themselves to; that way, they literally lure "YOU" to join in, that's if you want to feel comfortable doing business in their demonic culture and business and or city community environment. Although, even before this year ends (2007), there seems to be another demonic fad that is going around flashing satanic or demonic allegiance, with a satanic hand sign. This could not happen without the influence of dark spirit activity. See the website for satan hand signs. On this website you would be concerned by seeing even past and present presidents and even well known faces in large ministries, flashing satanic hand signs. Wondering how could that possibly happened, I began to inquire of the Lord, why are your well known ministries, in the earth flashing satanic had signs? I then began to see a different type of spiritualbondage and captivity occurring even among the people of God, whereby if dark spirit powers (that are trying to rise among us all) are not being resisted every time they are sensed (either upon any part of the body, soul, spirit life or realm), then the actual rising of dark spirit powers literally rising upon flesh of men (un-resisted) will indeed begin to collect in spirit power each time it rises upon the flesh of men (un-resisted); until the spirit powers continually gain strength (from not being resisted) will gain the ability to draw men into many strange functions, physical or verbal expressions and/or places that one had not intended to go! Thess 5.23.

Dark spirit life is looking to create a spirit stronghold and/or spirit domination in our lives to gain the "spirit" ability to control and even govern your life (without your permission) a place that only Jesus paid the price for at Calvary! This is the spirit era (or Kingdom age) we are living in. Rise up America let us learn to resist the darkness on the (individual) level it is using to draw men into spiritually captive states to capture our nation. One person at a time. One family at a time. One community at a time. One city at a time….one society…one nation at a time! God is watching. I believe it is because He is releasing among us the information needed to overcome the enemy but we must apply ourselves! In Jesus name. Ecc 12.14. Evidently, when Nebuchadnezzar was judged he was found with fault because he was sentenced for a season to live with the wild beast. He had become what he was giving attention to. Rom 1.25.

Typically, it's the same scenario with Haman who was promoted by King Ahasuerus and set Haman's seat above all the princes that were with him. After this, all of the King's servants bowed and reverenced Haman at the King's gate except Mordecai (because of his faith in one God). Eph 4.6. Even the King's servants asked Mordecai why was he transgressing the King's commandment, in not bowing down to Haman. Which angered Haman continually in his MIND, thoughts thinking patterns, desires imagination unto magnification (all of the places dark angel spirits will work & operate until they make their thoughts yours, to cause you to exalt yourself (and the spirit trying to operate in your life), and believe your own press release, against the knowledge of God). Hello! We must all get and keep a grip on our minds, body and spirit life activity (by the word of God and the holy Spirit of God) due to the increased war the enemy is waging in the soul (mind (even the subconscious and unconscious)/will/emotions or desires; body and spirit life). Thess 5.23.

This is serious. I believe the flow chart called "The Wash" that the Lord helped us to create can help us all; but we must apply ourselves America! Not to boast, but I am currently in my 43rd reading of the bible, cover-to-cover; yet when the enemy rages against my mind to gain a "foothold"; I use the flow chart to plow through it and stay focused on a right mind set, in Jesus name! Depending on your level of spiritual level of warfare, some must plow with the word, just to resist spiritual advances. Some spirit activity can be aggressive due to those men spear heading any spirit occult activity against the saints (or people) of God. Often, whom of which are not discovered, until they are commanded by satan as an assignment against those selected and/or targeted. What a battle we are dealing with America but through it all, "give me Jesus". Why, because He has already overcome the enemy. What better person to cleave to in battle! Let us teach our children. We can overcome this spiritual onslaught America, (first we must recognize this rising need) and apply ourselves in Jesus name. We need to be spending our times learning from the Lord and then teaching our children how to stand in this spiritual battle and resist the growing dark spirit rage (of evil) that is coming against our body, soul and spirit life of our families, churches, communities, cities, society and nation.

The bible reveals that evil men do not understand judgment, yet you have men in positions of judgment that need healing or release from evil spirits that affect and influence their judgment. When learning how to spiritually release from dark spirit thoughts and thinking process, one is more able to maintain and retain their soundness. Can we bless the Lord, we no longer have to be subject to evil or evil influences of others because of the complete work of Jesus at Calvary I call this "grace"! Prov 28.5. Prov 17.13. Prov14.16. Prov 15.3.

Why let evil transfer into the lives of our family and children when the Lord is teaching us how to remove it and give us a hope. PS 42.11.

This is the operation of darkness, working endlessly, to get you into agreement with the dark (spirit) works they are trying to create among us and in our lives. Literally using people groups and peer pressures (of those that are already in need of spiritual cleansing, release and healing) in our environment to try to spiritually sway us with their influence, to rebel and disrespect God's will and purposes in their midst. Some of which, push social oneness (but not the oneness in Christ Eph 4.5. Col 1.5), (not spiritually realizing) in the oneness, it is easier for spirits to systematically operate and transfer into the lives of others and move about in this spirit and spiritual kingdom age. 2 Cor 10.5.

Case in point

Jesus was and is the image of the invisible God. Col 1.5. God desires us to be (continually) created and perfected in His Spirit image, <u>not compete with it</u>, with the help of dark angel spirit gods that seemingly help men to exalt themselves (emotionally) against the knowledge of God. 2 Cor 10.5... and I saw them that had gotten the victory over the beast and over his image ... Rev. 15.2-4. I so desire to be one of those who had gotten the victory over the beast and over his (spirit) image. Don't you! Lord help us to stand in every situation as we look towards you., the author and finisher of our faith, in Jesus name! Heb 12.2.

<u>Other dark spirit kingdom terminology, dark spirit fruit, professions and expressions of dark spirit life activity in our world. Other means of seeking knowledge and/or non-biblical methods of meditation for inner peace</u>

(The following dark spirit professions are biblically considered areas where spiritual release, cleansing and healing are needed. The following listings are more categorically than alphabetical. All of these are biblically considered a work on various levels of sorcery. Simply because the bible reveals that by sorcery, all nations were deceived! Rev 18.23. Rev 9.21. Rev 12.9. Rev 16.10. Dt/ 5/7. Exo 34.14. Exo. 20.3)

Cockatrice seed implants (or seizes, a seed and work of sorcery, witchcraft, and baal manifestations): infestations and/or gestations are also methods dark spirit life uses to reproduce their dark spirit activity and/or to pull a soul into a dark spirit realm of captivity and ultimate spirit bondage through a system of invading spiritual corruption. All of spirit life attempts to reproduce itself, after its kind. And this is also the dark spirit activity that we need to learn how to resist. In Jesus name. James 4.7.

Sorcery: The use of magic, art wizardry and enchantment. These also work through manifesting dark spirit powers (and descending powers from the 2nd heaven and from the earth) even maneuvering in these areas to traffic (or trance release by professional sorcerers) and channeling dark spirit powers in an effort to secretly bring their victim or prey into spiritual bewitchment, bondage or domination. Therefore consistent spiritual releases are needed until the Lord would deliver you from the situation. Acts 8.

<u>Spiraled Sorcery Professions help to create a dark governing kingdom of idols and work of idolatry</u>
Once enough spirits have been transferred (via.channeled/trafficked, marshaled, invaded and/or infested) through or by baal manifestations and dark spirit visitations (not adequately) resisted; they will then try to advance its influence in the life they are determined to influence affect and or work through. Isa 10.10. Rev 16.10.

Sorcerers seem to like to gather information relating to the birth of a person, life history and other background information (like inquiries on your family members-so they can later work against your family if you decide you want to separate from them) Using the info as a basis with which one could use, along with dark spirited luring methods to gain advantage over another. It is said, that sorcerers are also involved in meta-physics and use psychic activity to pry into people's lives by first observing their subject up close, which can be accomplished in a trance state. The caution is that these dark spirit professions can work territorially and have the ability to seek you out (even through family and/or friends unaware) especially if you are defending the cause of Christ Jesus in their territory (which may happen to be where you live). Often they are hidden as ministers of light (who never learned how to release their spirit lives from spirit impurities, defilement and spirit violations of others who pursued or encouraged them). And because of this have become false Christ, false apostles and/or false prophets. They are in a serious predicament because God shall bring every work into judgment, with every secret thing, whether it be good or evil. Ecc. 12.14. These also are engaged in demonic watches (naturally and spiritually so) just to find ways to hinder the saints and/or Kingdom of God operations.

Some have deceitfully found a place to minister as television evangelists. Mt 13.33. Some are pastor/prophets or just prophets also in need of spiritual release and healing, without which, they can be found to be spiritual predators due to spiritual confusion, perversion and/or spirit domination that has developed in their lives. Still. Please pray for their desire to be made whole by first accepting Jesus Christ and Him crucified. These can also be considered children of the devil and/or sons and daughters of baal (that cannot be taken by hands). Jere 23.32. 2Sam23.7.

<u>Magic</u>. The supposed <u>art of influencing</u> courses of events and or lives by occult control and spirit activity. Egypt was full of magicians in the days of Moses. It is said, that white or black magic can cause psychic disorder. I believe this could be a true statement with the absence of the understanding of Jesus Christ and Him crucified and the 2 spiritual kingdom activities operating among us. Exo 8.18.

Some have even found it hard to read their bible or pray. Exo 7.11. Again, revealing the need to gain the ability to resist dark spirit life activity. Joel 3.14. However it would be unsound to continue in dark spirit activity and then try to release yourself from that which you are willingly a part of.

Voodoo: A religion of the West Indies based on the belief in magic and charm. It is said that it only works if they have something of yours.

Warlock: One who practices black magic. Also can be viewed as Lucifer.

Wizards: 2Ki 23.24. Isa 19.3. Lev 20.6-7. A cleaver or skillful person who involves themselves in black magic; who is also found to associate with spiritists and sorcery.

Vampire spirits: One that preys (or seizes and or hunts) others. Like an obsession, they seemingly feed on and/or victimize. It's their mindset.

Webster's New World Dictionary, 4th ed. Published in 1999: Defines vampires as one who preys ruthlessly on others! We can find this spirit nature activity among those in dark spirited professions, depending on the level of spiritual healing, release and understanding needed, in Jesus name.

Occult: Kept secret, esoteric, mysterious beyond the range of ordinary knowledge, involving the supernatural, mystical, magical. Also seen as black arts. Mysterious arts and practices. Biblically, this "spirit" activity can be viewed as an unlawful access to and/or use of the powers and/or forces of the supernatural for ungodly reasons and purposes (which are usually emotionally based) because scripture teaches us not to allow emotions over truth to legally and biblically support an unrighteous reason and/or purpose. And is the reason spiritual release, cleansing and healing is needed if one desires to remain biblically and spiritually sound. In Jesus name. Dt 5-7.

Psychic(s): Those who tell the future by occultist means. A reading of the soul realm ... by spiritual and/or spirit means. Usually their themes are home, marriage, money, sexuality(immoral), darkness and flesh. They speak of what has already made its way from the spirit world, this could include the Spirit of God (but more perverted by the time psychic/occultist speaks it). It is said, and therefore possible, that their words can be the product of familiar spirits. The concern is that some saints (including prophets) who may believe they are operating in God's Spirit, seem to want to read others ... but I have yet to find where reading others is a past time activity of the Holy Spirit. What grace would be in it? This can and do happen among the saints that have become too spiritually affected (by spirit activity and/or by intentional spiritual influence of the operation of darkness) and have not yet realized it. How could this intentional activity bring peace, to someone in need of spiritual healing and release if you are reading what they need healing and release from and then, what do you do with that information; God will judge. This could mean that there is a need to learn how to resist psychic spirit activity. Lord, please help those of us, who want to get it right, "get it right" in Jesus name.
Corin 14.33. 2Cor 12.9. Heb 12.14. Ecc 12.14.

Spiritism (spiritualism): A spiritual belief that departed spirits communicate with and show themselves to men, especially through mediums or at séances by means of spirit rapping or automatic handwriting, etc.

Familiar spirits: See "The Prophet's Dictionary", by Paula A. Price, PH.D. Whitaker House, Publisher.

Divination: Divining insight into a discovery of the unknown future by supernatural means. Ez 21.21. Ez 12.13. Usually relies on objects, inanimate for information. Some resort to natural elements to retrieve its spiritual data. Often divination is joined with magic and sorcery to further explore nature

… using herbology and portions as offerings to petition or interrogate demon spirits or familiar spirits for audience and favor to release facts about a person. Prophetic encounters that need to know birth dates, handle objects of clothing or other possessions are said to be divinatory. They redesign or repackage ancient divinatory arts to disguise them. This definition should serve as an advance warning when you may consider that you could be dealing with prophets who may be involved with dark spirit activity when they begin to ask you for any to many types of personal items or information, of which could ultimately be used to invade every area of your life. Some are even involved in engaging in the art of trance states and transmittal meditation to gain the ability to position themselves into any life they choose, for dark spirited purposes like "spirit stalking" or to spiritually hunt individuals. Another reason spirit life activity, that invades the life of another, should be out-lawed and policed, due to the ongoing tragedy and de-humanizing it brings to community and society. A method of transcending into a life and/or any territory that they have spiritually penetrated and then they are able to observe every aspect of your life (with intrusions) and follow you around like a spiritual leech or viper. These are and should be considered transcending "spiritual crimes" into our world, done by those advanced in dark spirit activity to operate at a higher level of evil in the systems and operation of the kingdom of darkness, in a society that has yet to catch up with how to process illegal spirit activity that is operating above and below our laws, that is currently bringing great harm to society and suffering to many. Religion is not the same as spirit life activity and should be viewed separately.

<u>Necromancy</u>: Art of predicting by means of communicating with the dead. Can also involve magic and enchantment.

<u>*The downside to spirit life activity, not resisted, can cause one to be spiritually spiraled into dark spirit professions; whether you want to be or not, does not seem to be the issue.*</u>

Witchcraft and the False Prophet

<u>Witchcraft *symptoms*, circumstances, conditions or influences, could also be directed by a false prophet/sorcerer who has literally worked himself/herself to the position of "false prophet in the heavenlies" revealed and ultimately known (only) by those he reveals himself to and/or by his deeper levels of dark spirit activity or spiritual intrusions into the life of another.</u> *Often for the purposes of taking the lives of others to work through and/or to help create dark spirited environments and communities, often affecting churches. Some false prophets in the heavenlies take the lives of other for pay (and/or to try to steal the spiritual heritage of another. This is not a religious activity. It is a "spirit" activity.* Not every one in religion or in their religious beliefs use and/or allow their spirits to be used to help kill, steal and/or destroy the spirit life of another).

Witchcraft **<u>*symptoms*</u>**, can come from occultism, sorcery/witchcraft attacks that actually indicate the existence (and or spirit activity) of something, that may seemingly suddenly arise from nowhere coming from those already (spiritually) affected (or by others trying to spiritually affect or influence you or others) by or with sorcery, witchcraft, occult spirit activity and/or their resource to spirit world activity. Causing many of the above listed ailments that can spiritually and intentionally affect or degenerate humanity. Those who are also in need of learning how to release their soul and spirit life from spirit impurities, defilement and spirit violations. Usually, spirits try to reproduce itself from one life to another, when the spiritual perpetrator does not get or find spirit release. This is a spirit principle (that works spiritually and transcends to affect the natural with expressions of the "spirit" life seeking to reproduce itself) that we must understand, and increases the importance of the need for consistent spirit releases (especially in environments of active spirit kingdom activity), especially when it becomes clear that that someone has sent a spirit assignment against you. Any person being intentionally affected literally takes on a spirit kingdom personality, that is pursuing them if not resisted.

A good example spirit activity can manifest and transcend into the soul, body and spirit life is the high profile case of Jared Loughner who, according to *USA Today,* November, 2011 article, fatally shot 6 people; wounding 13 people, one of which included Arizona Rep. Gabrielle Giffords.

In keeping in step with the teachings on spirit life activity and the (spirit) fruit it produces. One way or another; sooner or later, the bible teaches that there is nothing hid, which shall not be manifested.
Mk 4.22. Corin 4.5.

This particular article tells us that Loughner started having outward expressions of behaviorial trouble when he was in high school, 2006. During this time, the article says Loughner drank so much vodka, he was taken to emergency.

By 2008, the article says that Loughner was spiraling into schizophrenia, causing him to hear voices and act strangely. By the time Loughner was in prison his illness (or spirit manifestations) raged, causing him to throw chairs and wads of wet tissue paper at the door ... etc.

Eventualy the judge ruled Looughner unfit for trial, after Loughner referred to the judge as "your cheesiness". On June 21, 2011, the prison team began giving Loughner anti-psychotic drugs. On July 1, 2011, he ordered that Loughner forced medication be stopped, causing Loughner to become significantly worse.

They said, Loughner would pace in circles up to 14 hours per day, which created a blister on his foot, which became infected and then the infection moved up his leg. In July 2011, Loughner stayed awake for 50 hours. Spun in circles on his butt for 2 hours. He also flung his feces onto his bed. By July 8, he was put on a suicide watch, where he is presently.

By July 18, 2011, Loughner had deteriorated (degeneration) to the point his prison team would begin to give emergency forced medication.

These symptoms seem to be typical of dark spirit life activity. One of the concerns is you can't ignore spirit life activity because it will spiral into more violating activity (dark spirit life to find expression in our world). We biblically learned that dark spirit life activity can be dealt with in the authority of Jesus Christ because of His sacrifice at Calvary. Prophetically, we find that dark spirit life activity (in order to protect the person) can be interrupted with drugs (other findings along this line) can also be found in Rebecca Browns books. the other concern then in high school, is when they say Loughner's trouble began ... who was the spiritual tormentor – who literally opened his life to dark spirit activity, who infested his spirit, soul and then body until the spirits themselves began to act out in his life. Just like someone was operating as a spiritual perpetrator. These spiritual perpetrators cause others to commit spiritual crimes, while the spiritual perpetrator keeps his next subject victim. These incidences are continuing examples of the effects of Satanic ritual abuse. It's not a religion. It's a practice of corrupting the spirit lives of others to commit spiritual crimes. But usually like in Jim Jones' case after the spirit activity causes crimes thru them they usually end up killing the subject they used. In this respect, Loughner was not killed but still his life will be taken once he is tried and again the spiritual perpetration walks. This is spirit kingdom activity.

The false prophet operating from the heavenlies has the ability to work territorially and/or literally hi-jack the soul and spirit lives that he has or is trying spiritually defile, intrude upon or violate so that he can gain the ability to use whomever he has spiritually defiled (via trafficking/channeling and/or spirit penetration, through a trance or TM states) he or she can literally gain the spiritual ability to *"spirit" attack* people in their own environments (or the privacy of one's home) in an effort to control the area of their life that they are desiring. Unbelievably true! Prophets can gain the spiritual ability to affect a city as well a nation for harm or for good. This would depend on their training in God and learned ability to maintain their spirit lives in Jesus Christ. There are only 2 spirit kingdom activities operating among us. Only 2. No matter the religion, man unlearned prophets often become caught up in church activity (religion) which can cause a spiritual illusion and spirit kingdom confusion which often lead to spiraled levels or spirit captivity or spirit domination.

This would include the "spirit" activity of manipulating a person's spiritual environment, family, work community and church community, etc. Sometimes the person will desire to bring you into spiritual bondage just to gain the ability to use you to affect others to hinder your life and others. Let us understand that through Christ, *you can resist the spirit attacks*, if you do not bow to what darkness is desiring in your life. James 4.7. However, there is a need to learn how to resist assigned sorcery, witchcraft, magic and occultist assignments, until the Lord brings complete deliverance, in Jesus name. Joshua and Moses, at one time, had to deal with dark spirited magicians, who in some cases seemed to challenge Moses ability in God. Exo 7.11. James 4.7. Gen, Chpt. 41.

In community we have literally seen the false prophet gain access to environment working spiritually through security and/or police officers (by intruding into their spirit realm) to gain the ability to hi-jack their soul and/or spirit life by causing the officer to pull people over, interact and begin to communicate with conversation unfamiliar to the officer but realized by the one the false prophet is intruding upon. And this spiritual activity is transcending into the natural, as the false prophet (operating in and/through a trance state) wills. 2 Tim 2.26. This is another reason our officers need a greater understanding of spirit life activity and re-discover or realize any spiritual possibilities that could affect or that could intrude into their soul and spirit lives to misuse their position as a vessel for dark spirit initiatives and agenda. A new level of spiritual crimes are being committed more often than we realize. An activity happening, above and beyond their normal policing. Using a police situations (by one who is well developed in thought transmitting or as a mentalist usually for mischievous reasons), the false prophet is then able to pull over any subject that the false prophet is desiring to gain control over, in community- in ways that could not be accomplished without the police officers position. This is critical. Spiritual ethics or non-spiritual ethics have (or should) become a issue.

Spirit life activity can also be abused, by those spiritually obsessed with controlling others. Another form of spirit domination. Officers need gain the ability to re-discover and discern (naturally and spiritually so) who or what is purposely trying to spiritually intrude (by any unsound, sudden, compelling and unnatural spiritual activity).

This is happening now among us. Some witchcraft activity operating through the false prophets; false because they have mostly been spiritually affected or defiled and/or spiritually violated: spirit life that found a way to reproduce themselves in the false prophets life (using sorcery, witchcraft, divination, medium ability and occultism activity, etc., to operate at a higher (darker) spirit realm of authority and *is also able to cause* but not limited to **the following transcending spiritual attacks into physical symptoms** and/or affect the soul (thinking/thought process) realms where the false prophet is trying to often, aggressively operate and/or intrude into the lives and/or environments of the servants of God and/or those in positions among us to spiritually defile and/or violate them , to gain the foolish ability, literally to control the lives of others; for dark spirited kingdom purposes among us. Many somehow think this is the activity of the true living God. But, God does not have any issues and He does not operate against Himself, He is holy. Their environment and their subjects or forced spiritual victims are well studied, sought out, and plotted out before the spiritual intrusion, manipulation and menu of evil begins. Spiritual control seems to be their goal against the will of God. There is no grace and mercy found outside the life of the Spirit of Christ and those who reflect and reveal His nature.

Some might consider them spiritual fanatics, Once it is realized how they are operating, because they seem to like to bring you into their dark spirit realm, their sprit domination, and keep you there (by constantly spiritually attacking you), as if they were sadistically experimenting on you because they have been spiritually defiled and violated themselves. They think perverted because of their spiritual state and spiritual corruption, some are ancestrally defiled and/or violated in their body, soul and spirit life. First, they try to cross your path in the natural, then, they reveal their presence, activity and position in the spirit realm by spiritually engaging you, seemingly nonstop. *These people are not ghosts,* even though they hunt your life like ghosts. *Some have learned, ancestrally, how to professionally operate in the spirit realm for the operation of a dark spirited kingdom*. As sons and daughters of baal, pursuing innocent lives, through a sacrifice of ritual abuse, for baal. They can transcend and move about and manipulate, by causing troubles first in the spirit realm, that transcend into the natural. They live in a house and can be located. This is serious! This is their dark spirit profession *and career* transcending (among us) into our world, interrupting (because they have been subject to *spirit domination and are under dark spirit command and bewitchment*).

They intrude always for unsound and perverse reasons, usually emotional, seemingly childish reasons, because they themselves have become spiritually defiled, servants of corruption, in need of spiritual release from the spiritual corruption and bewitchment that has plagued their lives. Let this writing go on record and be a witness of this present truth going on among us. 2Pet 1.12. 2 Pet. 2.19. Gal.6.8. Rom 3.21. Gen 31.53. 1Jn 5.7. James 4.7.

These are some of the ways the false prophet/sorcerer and son or daughter of baal, will make an effort to keep you in their spirit realm, using sorcery, witchcraft, magic, occult, etc., any method of intrusion, as their means. Rev. 18.23.

Depending on your level of faith and biblical awareness these are some helpful hints to help spiritually protect and guard oneself from demonic occultic attacks , inspired by witchcraft/sorcery, occult pursuits and, or assignments, or ongoing program of spiritually sadistic harassment satanically inspired type of ritual spirit abuses

Until the Lord bring complete deliverance and healing, it is important to protect oneself from any immediate harm, from some of the affects listed above. What gave rise to this section is the reality of the many going to "new age" seeking protection for the spirit symptoms they are experiencing or encountering. But we need to continually look to Jesus, with faith, that His complete work on the cross is finished and we are complete in Him. Col 2.10. Many do not realize that they are experiencing occultic spirit activity meaning that someone is perpetrating their spiritual symptoms and/or activity. Many are going to the doctor and/or taking medication due to demonically perpetrated spirit attacks and/or assignments. Biblically, we can see that God would use certain prophets in the Old Testament, to help with remedies. In our day however, we need to make sure that the person with the remedy, is not also being used by the enemy to cause any symptoms. Kings 17.8+. 2 King, Chpt. 6. 2 King 8.5.

*Some of the products used to help find immediate release (with prayer to the Lord which should always be the object of our faith not the items I am about to suggest) from any sudden rising heated body manifestations: Absorbine Jr.(the liquid and/or pads depending on the symptom(s) and heat locations or Bengay. With white thin to medium weight socks, you can literally find a pad to fit the bottom of your socks which will help to interrupt any spirit activity from penetrating and/or using your feet as a gate into your body. www.absorbinejr. www.bengay. We have also found that SalonPas patches could also prove helpful in this area to place on the bottom of your socks and or you could wrap yourself with gauze wherever spirits are seemingly trying to attack the body. Anything along these suggestions could also prove effective. These are only proven suggestions until the Lord comes. Corin 4.5.

For women who find their personal, private areas being heated, with apparent heat transfusions, rising day or night, can use a kotex pad or plain white towel to interrupt and, or absorb the heat that may come from your bottom areas seemingly at the most in convenient times. If the night heat spirit intrusions troubles your sleep you could also arise and resist it with a series of faith scriptures of your authority in Christ Jesus and Him crucified. James 4.7. *And, or those who call upon the name of the Lord shall be saved.* Rom 10.13. *Calling in series manner, repetitiously, could prove helpful.* Acts 2.21. *The other alternative would be to rise first thing in the morning to resist, with the previous suggestions to not only resist, but resisting helps to get out of agreement with what hell is desiring for your life.*

Also for those dealing with greater heat spirit infusions, especially at night, that seem to like to transcend to manifest upon one's body, I would highly suggest using many ice paks upon the body in the locations or areas the spirits are seemingly interested in, to keep yourself cool in those areas where the spirits are literally creating a warmth to a real sense of heat upon certain areas of your body to the point spirits are trying to release nightly heat infusions from the inside out, it is an assignment, seemingly causing one's body to steam or stream the spirit heat out of or through your body, because spirits like to reproduce themselves. It would be wise to continue in regular spirit root releases, found in this writing because you don't always know what spirits someone could be releasing upon you or community. I believe the coolness helps to stop the sense of "spirit gestation" or "spirit development" upon your body. The thing to keep in mind is that these spirit activities are assigned. The bible says; they excel in strength hearkening to his voice…Ps. 103.20. There are men who perverse truth; who hold the truth in unrighteousness, operating at a higher level of <u>spirit system operations</u>. Rom 1.18. Jude 9.

The <u>goa</u>l is to prevent, by resisting the powers and/or presence of darkness (dark spirit activity conflict) and/or "spirit infestation" in your body, soul, spirit life or realm, until the Lord brings complete healing and deliverance in the name of Jesus. Why? Because consistent spirit penetration (is an assignment) and can cause any spirit ailments or symptoms listed in any of the stronghold spirit section. If you consistently use the root system for release, yet you perceive spiritual interference when you get around others, that always seems to involve you. It could be a spiritual intruder; or another level and/or element of spirit assignment to infest and/or draw spirits into your life. Simply remember to release yourself when you get home from community. The Lord should be sought for complete peace, protection and healing from anyone's spiritual perversion. Let us not forget the idea that you could come under spiritual attack or spiritually intruded upon by someone else in need of spiritual healing and release in Jesus name.

Although the above may begin to occur on a daily basis, this section is more for those who may have or are under a trying day-to-day, determined, pursuit using a series of intruding principalic or demon "spirit" attacks of darkness, in another attempt literally take over your body functions, soul & or spirit life activity. Dan 7.25 reveal that the enemy desires to wear out the saints. This would be another good reason to stay on top of keeping your spirit life released in Jesus name, during times of seemingly spirit pursuits or attacks of spiritual pursuits. These are real people, sold out and in allegiance to darkness (in spiritual bondage on some level enough to affect those whom they come into contact with), working behind the scene, using sorcery, witchcraft, occult and magic, using trance states and TM to spirit force their way into, not only your life but your soul and body as well. When there are no consistent spirit releases, those in dark spirit professions have the ability to release many spirits into one's life through seemingly constant spirit trafficking or spirit marshaling, literally producing a breach in ones spirit realm. These dark spirit professionals can then gain the ability to change your personality, interrupt your schedule and cause you to do something you would not normally do and make you think it was your idea, even seemingly spiritually perpetuate any majority in your world to over look the symptoms of spiritual attacks of isolation in your world and refuse to believe they have become part of the symptom. A type of dark spirit kingdom politicking.

Part of their entrapment is that if you try to <u>report</u> how they are trying to take over and control your soul with mind thoughts and spirit trafficking infestation, think again. Some have the ability to observe your every move, and then go behind you and begin to cause interference and confusion to the person you have spoken to, and begin to manipulate what you have told. Causing those you have told to think you are losing it. So in essence they try to keep you spiritually and naturally captive to them (in their dark spirit twist, unsound perverse world). Therefore, there is a need to chart everything and then file the report with your local police station and our local police stations must take them (to get an overview); these are practical steps "not spooky notions" in order to help solve these types of spiritual crimes, that's unless our local police stations have become too spiritually affected whereby they lose their soundness and ability to help others who are hurting. Spiritual ignorance should not be able to hinder an officer's ability to help those who are spiritually tortured, quietly in our own nation. Yet, this is what is happening and often police defense seems to be the same as the spiritual perpetrators "freedom of religion". Only, police seem to often to use it as their reason not to get legally involved. But doesn't this undermine their service to protect, preserve and guard community.

This writing has the ability to help you release yourself. All you need is faith in Jesus Christ and His complete work at the cross. Because this the level of spiritual corruption that is infiltrating and happening among us now and in our nation's world communities.

These people have "complete "spiritually perverse personalities, they are too caught up into the spirit world and they think they are serving the real God, but **<u>GOD IS NOT PERVERSE,</u>** HE IS HOLY. <u>You can't be both at the same time.</u> And in this (spirit activity) people, are being spiritually programmed to commit crimes. Therefore, some crimes will **never** be resolved unless you make room for the spiritual aspect or influence in the equation because many crimes are being spiritually committee, being first plotted out by spiritual perpetrators. Rev. 22.11. Heb. 12.14.

*****Please note:*** *We have heard it said that some go by their experiences too much. However, isn't it our experiences that turn into our testimonies in how our faith in Christ Jesus saved and continues to save us by faith. How can anyone speak ill of any ones experience of faith testimony? Should not we use our testimonies of faith that came out of our experiences of faith to help encourage someone along the way. Laban said,...I have learned by experience that God has blessed me because of you. Gen 30.27. Even some colleges give credits for some life experiences. Scripture says: <u>**patience works experience and experience hope**</u>....Rom 5.*

Spiritual Violation, these spiritual perpetrators or false prophets/ sorcerers sometimes pastor prophets in need of spiritual release and healing, due to a obsessed desire to chase, hunt and communicate with you by sadistically inflicting and causing pain, peeping into personal cleansing and bathroom matters and times. Which they may try to reveal in someway to you. They can even provoke any emotion to surface and cause endless conversation using magic and/or by releasing the spirit to come upon you that would cause the desired behavior, are some of the areas involving their spiritual mischief. Spiritual mischief is how they spend their time and it's what they do. They can cause spiritual and natural trauma and drama by keeping you in their disturbed dark spirit world by infringing into every area of your life, stalking you daily with illegal spirits annoyances causing strife and division in relationships. Whether in the natural or spiritual God teaches us to follow peace with all men and holiness without which no one will see the Lord. Heb. 12.14. This is how you realize that a person is allegiance with darkness when inflicting these spirit symptoms, causing the symptoms to transcend into your life (or physical realm).

Spiritual confusions (The Kingdom of God does not operate against itself)

False prophets create spiritual and and natural confusion and frustrations wherever their subject goes, whether home, church or community. It's how dark or false prophets serve the operation of darkness.

Despair   Disorientation or

Depression.   Resist it in Jesus name. James 4.7.

Try to stay focused on Word, not the spiritual distraction.
(which my take a lot of praise on some days)

Spirit burns, through a trance state, those with the dark spirit ability are able to penetrate the skin on a regular basis until one can literally feel a burning sensation, pain or see a bruise. The spiritual perpetrator can cause the evil spirit to follow you around to accomplish this irritating/ harassment.

Possible Solution, ice can be applied in a towel to bring relief until the Lord brings complete deliverance. Until then we carry our cross daily. Mt 16.24

Sudden and/or increasing levels of heat that may rise upon ones skin or body. A type of heat seemingly coming from within but that will not always register on a thermometer (because it is being spiritually inflicted). It seems to happen often to women. Usually this will first arise in the female area but men can also be affected. Resist it with the word, praise and/or by calling on the name of the Lord. It is important when dark spirit powers arise to get out of agreement by resisting it. The heat can expand to the whole body one part at a time. The heat at first tries to rise only when one sleeps, rest and/or sits and can eventually cause diarrhea and other heat distress symptoms. Ice packs can and should be used to lessen the discomfort.

•Please note there is also the concern that as these seemingly spiritual stalkers can create much physical discomfort due to the heat they can generate upon a body, because you are dealing with perverse spirit personalities working through human spirit activity; please understand the heat they create upon or within your body can serve many purposes. One of which is to create such physical discomfort as to cause one to pull off your clothes, but it might be better to offset the heat with cie paks. Also it might be a good idea if you sense you are being spiritually stalked to either,only to wash up (keeping ones private parts concealed as much as possible) and or wash with underwear, so as not to feed into even the human spirits stalking desires and ill spirit fantasies they continue to create in their spirit mind, as they operate in the spirit realm some will try to pepetrate the feet to gain access to spirit rest or germinate in ones hips or private parts to try to act out perverse spirit desires. These would like to make you think it's spirit or ghost activity but it is a human spirit activity. These people need to be ??????, discovered and told this is not acceptable behavior.

Sudden bouts of sleepiness at inconvenient times (seemingly) out of the blue. Also seen as spirit hypnotic type that pulls you under (or into a sleep state). It could occur at any time as a spirit intrusion They can be resisted with consistent word confessions in a series, of authority in Christ. Also, moving out of targeted area may help, along with praying in tongues. Usually the spiritual perpetrator would be in a trance state (close enough) to affect this sleepiness, so spraying with Lysol disinfectant in the immediate environment can break the grip as you continue to pray are possible solutions. Fans are also helpful, if the sudden sleepiness occurs while driving.

And other programs and/or series of spiritual harassment that transforms into our world to interfere with ones' life to the point of spiritual abuse which seem to occur in sadistic manner and also transforms in extreme inconveniences in order to force a soul into dark spirit servitude or mental concerns if not resisted with the word of God and prayer and, or calling upon Lord in a series type manner. You'll know when a lot of strange unnatural experiences keep occurring seemingly to get your attention but usually there is a perpetrator behind it, to interrupt your life it is an assignment. Faith in the complete work of Christ must be used in Jesus name.

*Our faith chart of authority can prove helpful in resisting what hell is trying to accomplish in your life in Jesus name.

An unexplainable sudden series of throbbing pain around the back and neck shoulder area, the hand, arm or feet usually. Even while one is sleep could occur to awake you. These also can be spirit attacks. <u>Possible faith solutions:</u> These too can be resisted with the word of God and prayer. Again, prayerfully spraying Lysol disinfectant into your immediate atmosphere can break spirit grips causing the pain, once there is release one would realize it was a spirit attack. (Be sure to use a face mask). When the ongoing pain is sudden, it could indicate human spirit activity working through a trance state. When using the spray stops the pain, then the spiritual perpetrator must be discovered.

Also, these areas of the body can be covered at night for protection (for any night spirits assigned) to bodily harm and/or soreness until the Lord brings complete restoration. Any persistent nightly spirit visits hints that it is a spirit assignment to be discovered.

When there is a sudden rising of numbness rising upon the hand or feet, etc. Shake it off. Physically and, or by a series of faith authority scriptures of Christ. Again, the repetition could indicate spirit activity intrusion.

Sudden bouts or even episodes of diarrhea can occur provoked by a rising heat within the lower body area. If you catch it early you can resist with scripture. In Jesus name.

Loss of voice, you can actually feel like your throat is being spiritually penetrated at night. If this is the case, try to keep your throat, or whatever area is being affected covered, while sleeping. Again, when spirit activity is up close and personal and repetitious, there is a spiritual perpetrator operating in a trance state usually a human spirit activity on a dark assignment.

---

*Children can also be targeted or affected, www.congochildrenbattlewithwitchcraftaccusations.

Also, for those experiencing sudden sleepiness during times of reading your bible, doing "things for God" and/or driving a vehicle, we have found that an upclose fan can literally help release your immediate environment from "spirit penetrating" activity operating behind any sudden sleep states. What can help tip it off is sudden yawning. Some have had to drive with a high-powered fan operating right next to the driver's seat while praying in tongues to not be over-powered by any "sleep spirit assignments" attacking. Let us all understand and be mindful that we can know spirit activity on the scene, by the "spirit fruit" that arises on the scene. We are in the spirit kingdom age! Mt. 12.33.

• Please note a face mask should be used by anyone in the environment for safety. Please check with your physician for other questions. The concern here is someone is infesting your life and environment with spirit manifestation and, without resistance, demonization could occur! James 4.7. Our world is still needing to process how to deal with spiritual perpetrators who are attacking humanity and society as a whole because they are the ones in need of spiritual release from the "spirit domination" using them to attack humanity. Let us continue to pray, because it is not about religion. It is about the only 2 spiritual kingdom activities operating among us no matter the religion, non-religion and/or spirit belief system. Also when any spirit assignment arises to consistently attach any area of the body, it will become necessary to maintain a steady diet of exercise and proper nutrition to sustain you through any spiritual battling, while praying, doing bible study until the Lord bring deliverance and healing.

Other biblical solutions

for dealing with descending demonic risings, presence and/or "spirit attacks" upon a soul would be to: <u>Shake it off</u> <u>daily</u>, whenever you sense a spirit manifestation trying to come upon you and/or when you awake, in Jesus name. Scrip. Ref: Acts 28.3-5. Job 38.13. Lk 21.26. Heb 12.27. Ja 4.7.

This would also be a great spiritual faith exercise and release for children to release themselves in Jesus name from spirit impurities, defilement and spirit violations of others. Especially, when they get home from school and/or other outings. Parents this would work for you as well. Only, let the children shake themselves. Simply show them how; then teach them to realize how to know when there is a release in Jesus name. Col. 3.23. Corin 2.13.

<u>Position:</u>

This would work out nicely if you were already on your knees, in a prayer position. Simply continue to bend over, placing the palms of your hands on the floor. To be honest this can take as little as 15 min. up to a half an hour should you sense the need to go longer. Works best in the morning and before bed if needed. Anyway, while on your knees and on the palms of your hands, as an act of faith, because we always need the Lord's help with spiritual things and without faith it is impossible to please Him. Let's pray: Lord, we pray that you would release your Spirit to help us release ourselves from spirit impurities, defilement and/or spirit violations of others as we begin to shake ourselves, for your word declares you will shake the heavens and the earth and that which can be removed will be..... Hagg 2.21. Isa 52.2. Dan 10.10.

You can begin to sway your arms and shoulders with hands and knees on the floor and then simultaneously ,we can begin to shake the hips , we can work up to faster motions. But, if you have not shaken in a while, slow is fine then work your way into faster. You can shake your head also. Sometimes, you may feel a release begin to release through your eyes (which is good), just quickly give the command , come out, in the name of Jesus, in the name of Jesus come out......continue these body expression until there is a release. Sometimes your eyes will water and sometimes you will just *yarn*. Sometimes you may release in a sweat, which is ok. When done, simply jump in the shower or wipe dry in Jesus name. Other positions for release, would be simply to get a stool, bend knees a little with hands on the stool; then begin to shake from side to side in shaking approximately 15 min. at a time, off-and-on to start simply stating by faith in Christ and the cross, that you are releasing yourself from spirit impurities, defilement and/or spirit violations in Jesus name. You'll be surprised how this little faith exercise can go a long way. The best part is it should help keep you from "spirit" collections, using it with the first part of this writing (the root section) try to release yourself at least every other day from this manual, but try to do daily shakes (especially when coming in from community and/or when faced with spiritual warring) to help keep yourself spiritually free, in Jesus name.

Biblically, scripture reveals that we are to resist the works of the enemy, this would also include resisting any rising, /or descending powers, presence of darkness or spirit attacks upon the body, soul and spirit life in the name of Jesus. James 4.7. Thess. 5.23. The body of Christ must also learn how to spiritually resist the enemy physically <u>because</u> spiritual wounds or attacks <u>can</u> and <u>do</u> transcend themselves into physical ailments and soulish flesh. See our Principalic Stronghold section on Infirmity in this writing. Example: Any dark spirit risings upon the feet, legs and arms can be released through treading, shaking and calling upon the Lord and/or scriptures of authority consecutively if possible, i.e., without interruption, until hell backs off. Again, this section would be more for those with spirits being trafficked and/or marshaled into one's life. The alternative would be to go crazy, unless you get an immediate miracle from the Lord.

Any dark spirit risings upon the hands specifically, releases are possible by, beating both the hands upon ones bed or pillow (on one side, then the other side) until any stiffness is released (because the enemy can actually cause the hands to look deformed, depending on how long a spirit penetrates a hand) or cause hand expressions that one may not normally engage Cumulative spirit penetrations could also restrain any parts of the physical body, gripping it as he wills when there are no consistent spirit releases in any area. He can traffic and spirit penetrate into one's soul, spirit life and realm from any secret place to be discovered, ultimately (without resistance) making it impossible for the subject/ victim to escape the will of darkness and captivity. Except, by Gods grace. 2 Tim 2.26. If there are consistent "spirit" releases each time the enemy tries to rise, by his presence, and/or descend upon the body, soul and/or spirit life in Christ, it makes it harder for a person to come into spiritual bondage or a greater spirit oppression through the accumulation of (unleashed) spirit trafficking, marshaled spirits and spirit penetrations. It is the manifestations (that can be initiated or perpetrated by someone in dark spirit professions), of the spirits being trafficked in a life, that are literally (spirit training and or are leading or spirit forcing) a person to do as darkness wills, until the person learns how to release themselves or it could cause the person to become intimidated by the increased and/or amount of spirits being trafficked or marshaled into a life. These are some of the reasons for consistent releases, from spirit impurities, defilement and/or spirit violations, until the Lord brings complete deliverance. 2 Tim 2.26.

We need to be aware as a society that by continuing to openly allow sorcery/ witchcraft , occultism activity, magic and/or false prophet activity working against others (working behind and through the trafficking/channeling/trance states/TM, etc., to continually go unchallenged has found to produce, lead to their increased practice and conditions of increasing ills and disharmony in humanity, among us and in our society, causing and/or supporting the following ails, physical and social symptoms in any society and world communities www.policingsorcery.

Homelessness, in this context, many do not consider that homelessness can be due to a spiritual condition and/or something that can be caused by dark spirit activity (and/or men in allegiance to it) targeted at someone or anyone in the family church or community. If it is their assignment, those in dark spirited professions can cause those who become subject or victims (like a spiritual conspiracy) to be "spirit forced" to leave their safe place, causing a person/s spiritual environment to become contrary, indifferent and spiritually hostile, as part of a dark spirit strategy to separate their subject/target and then harass and/or spirit attack their subject in any of the above spirit methods (as a present truth of their existence, that can transcend into physical and/or mental anguish, harm or illness) and cause forced service to the operation of darkness – that's if this dark spirited method does not literally kill it's subject first, and this is not an exaggeration, spearheaded by anyone in dark spirited professions and/or anyone in allegiance to dark spirit kingdom activity. There are only 2 spirit kingdoms operating among us and there will always be only 2. No matter the religion, non-religious and/or spirit life beliefs. Lk 4.29. Lk 15.16. Mt 20.18-20. Jn 8.10.

There are no demonic graces in dark spirited assignments, revealing the reality and clear distinction of the only 2 spiritual kingdoms operating among us. Our society seem to feel at rest writing off these types of "spirit activities" as satanic spiritual ritual abuses as a solution to keep covered what can no longer be hidden nor ignored. There are thousands of spiritual ritual abuses each year in America, with seemingly no natural safe places in our culture for protection caused by spiritual perpetrators, if there were, there would not be thousands of spiritual ritual abuses a year, in America alone. Ritual abuse is still the under recognized problem, according to: www.ritualabuse. This would help to explain, why new age books were sought for spiritual remedies. People have been getting spirit attacked by occultic means and methods and they have not known how to apply the cross and/ or stand in battle to deal with occult attacks without the knowledge of God. Where are the true prophets. It is still true, God does nothing except He first reveal it to His servants the prophets. ***It has to be revealed, is a present truth.*** Just like God had to show Moses and Elijah how to deal with witchcraft and magicians during their day. Exo 8.18. Ki 18.25+.

How long can we allow perpetrators of spiritual and inhuman crimes of society to hide behind freedom of religion. There is a distinction between religion versus spiritual and spirit life abuse of others. There are perhaps a million and one ways anyone can take a person's life, but the question is why are we giving them the space and room to play out their spiritual and inhumane abuse and then call it (an expression) of religious rights. What is wrong with this picture? Clearly the abusers are in need of attention, help and accountability. Even the bible states that a child is known by what they do. Prov. 20.11.

Sex exploitation: of women and/or children whoever is being targeted and/or becomes the subject of ritual abuses can be drawn in by spirit life activity.

Unemployment, can be caused by spiritually warring against every area of the subjects or target's life spiritually will transcend and affect natural circumstances. Learning how to release could help keep your life's course.

Family Disruptions: or broken homes and/or disunity. Those in dark spirited professions do not have a problem breaking up homes, dividing it (by using spirit activity) to pull away the person or subject targeted in any environment. There are no demonic graces in dark spirited professions only spirit domination.

Distortion of reality (confusion): Due to the spirits evidently dominating the perpetrators spirit life causing them to think they have a "spirit" duty to disrupts and intrude into the lives of others due to being driven by spirit domination or too spiritually affected. Spiritual release, cleansing and healing is needed.

Culture and/or Community disruptions or invasions: those with dark spirited belief systems usually have social harmony issues. People are seen as prey.

Since there are only 2 spiritual kingdoms operating among us. Those with spirit domination will flow and in some way operate in the dark spirited systems already set up in this world. Some will only be doorkeepers and draw people into any dark place whether it be drugs, sex trafficking, etc., or dark profession.

Mental Concerns: Due to evil spirits being trafficked into a life

Paranoia: Sorcerers/False Prophets/working through the Occult, magic & spirit trafficking, TM and/or trance states can be used to stalk or cause hypnotic staring symptoms. Release is needed. In Jesus name.

Psychotic behavior: Can and do occur when spirits are trafficked and/or marshaled into a life and where there is no faith release. See root sections.

They can cause unnatural affections; sadistically operating or intruding in another's life spiritually or naturally so, for harm, is unnatural. Rom 1.31. And a distorted, perverted relationship could occur if one accepts the abuse of the perpetrator.

Relationship disorders: Can be caused and created by spiritual abuse Using any of the above spirit intrusions transcending into the natural, because the spiritual perpetrator is in need of spiritual release and healing in Jesus name.*Darkness will often cause friends, family or associates to reject or disassociate from the subject and then continue the demonic process of disrupting a body, soul, spirit life and/or realm. The battle is still the Lords. Those who call upon the name of the Lord shall be saved and a revealed truth to those in battle. Rom 10.13.

Death: Spiritual ritual experimentation can and does lead to death. The degree of spiritual experiments of how much abuse is actually harming someone is what causes the harm and trouble

Fear Can be caused and/or developed by the consistent ritual abuses. 2 Tim 1.7.

Intimidation, sorcery, witchcraft, occultism and magic, etc., used to daily afflict pain to you or anyone that comes near you can cause intimidation. One should stay focused on biblical meditation, Jesus and the cross and consistent releases.

Forced isolation: Literally by speaking negatively of you to others who are not correctly discerning God's voice, the spiritual perpetrator can work witchcraft to spiritually manipulate one's environment to help create the isolation and thereby isolate naturally by spiritual means. It is possible to be spirit attacked into isolation. It's already happening until people learn to release spiritually release themselves. James 4.7. Phil 4.8.

This dark spirit practice among us is what causes a lot of spiritual confusion among people (including the church) to think that God is speaking when its really spiritual intrusion.

Bodily Ailments A by-product of various dark spirit body attacks. Some in dark spirit professions can cause some spirit life to attack people. Some sicknesses can be caused by some spirit activity. It doesn't happen for no reason, spirit life attacks must be perpetuated by someone who has been spiritually affected (or violated) by someone else who has been affected. In this way, dark spirit life can reproduce itself in a negative way. Some in dark spirit professions have the ability to spiritually attack anyone they choose while in a "trance" state, by first continually penetrating someone's spirit realm and can be spiritually and naturally by its repetitious attacking of the first, spirit, soul and then body of another, who has become spiritually targeted. Exo. 15.26.

Stumbling: Another symptom being caused by dark spirit activity is having times of seemingly unexplained walking or standing imbalance. This too can be caused by someone literally traveling or operating in a spiritual trance state of
those in a dark spirit profession who has transcended to this spiritual ability.

Hand tremors: (and/or wherever part of the body is being penetrated). Being subject to constant spirit penetrations can eventually cause the whole body (or any parts) to tremor like a nervous condition.

Hand tingling, or other body areas (or numbness).

Muscle Spasms: Seemingly, out of the blue but always planned by someone. Usually occurs during certain times, like in the morning, done seemingly in a manner to "spirit" force activity to awake someone and/or disturb any needed rest, on a consistent basis reveals an occultic attack. Again, confessing our faith authority listed on our flow chart found in the King James version, in a series like manner and in the various names and acts of Jesus consistently (day-by-day) can literally break the power of this spirit (behind the perpetrator) causing the great sudden discomfort, thereby also helping one to perceive and realize it is a "spirit activity" operating against the person's body, soul and spirit realm. We must learn and understand that dark spirit life activity can be used by those spiritually affected at certain levels of dark spirit activity and/or dark spirit professions. Also, 911 Cramps (found at www.amazon.com) can also prove helpful, while standing in faith for complete deliverance from anyone being attacked, by occultic means.

Feet: Some in dark spirit professions or spiritual perpetrators will try to spirit perpetrate the feet (using nightly trance; Spirit visits – a human spirit activity). Once penetrated enough ... certain spirits can be sent to shoot up the leg causing extreme spasm attacks ... or, certain spirits can be sent to travel up to leg so that spirits can lodge themselves in any private area and/or sections of the body, and hen when the spirits are called out, they can release themselves by causing the subject to pass gas or feel the sudden urge to urinate.

Possible solution: either wrap the feet at night, or sleep with shoes and then wrap the feet with shoes on. Seemingly assigned spirits are able to eventually penetrate any seam area by the shoe. This depends on the level of spirit attacks assigned again, consistently spraying around the ???? when wrapped until spirits back off. May be needed for mroe aggressive spirit attacking feet (use mask whilel spraying) Spirits then can also lodge themselves in the feet causing soreness. Until the Lord brings healing.

Neck: spirit activity under an apparent assignment can also cause pressure in one specific area being spiritually exerted upon, eventually causing and /or producing a sharp pain, distress and/or constant ache whenever the spirit is sent, affecting the skin. It's almost like a spirit burn, that may eventually cause some skin discoloration, dryness, soreness and/or a tenderness may be detected by touch. Usually praying in tongues for a certain amount of time will eventually release one from this distressing experience. Also, covering this area can prove helpful while prayerfully awaiting the Lords intervention of complete deliverance. Again, this spirit activity can come to you up close and personal, by assignment of those in dark spirit professions working through a trance state.

** When one recognizes these types of spiritual activities are happening, it is a good idea to exercise regularly to help gain the ability to off-set the harm that is rising against the muscles, mind and physical stamina. Thess. 5.23.

With this type of spiritual "spirit activity" happening to any one person consistently on any given day, would eventually cause anyone to wonder, why would a person spend so much time causing another person so much pain, intrusion and interruption against another. First, we must remember this is being done by someone "spiritually affected" or spiritually dominated, this would include those who allow themselves to go into trance states or TM to spiritually operate and function in our society in this way. And among those, in need of spiritual healing and release in Jesus name. Hurting and/or suffering people, hurt others. Whether they mean to or not, does not seem to be the issue but doing what they do becomes the issue. Let's remember these are "spirit activities", <u>not religious nor spirit friendly activity revealed through men</u>. **God is "not" every spirit activity happening among us.** Because of this, there is a need for spirit life activity to be taught among us, not religion! This is why scripture says some will kill others and "think" they are doing God service. Jn 16.2. Eph 6.7. Ja 2.11. **<u>This is spiritual confusion!</u>** Hosea 2.19, tells us that God will betroth us to Him in righteousness, judgment, loving-kindness and mercies. Religion seems to be the camouflage for those who engage in dark spirit crimes. Now we can look more seriously, at the religions and/or those engaged and in allegiance with dark spirit life activity, that are killing others and/or causing conditions that help lead to the death of others and begin to spiritually perceive those who have been spiritually affected by dark spirit life activity, infestation, captivity and/or spirit violations of others working with intelligent dark spirit life activity.

Therefore it is necessary for people to understand, realize and recognize when they are under spiritual attack and lift them up in prayer. They need the correct prayer community. One with understanding of the purposes of darkness against a soul and humanity. Perhaps, even purchasing this book for them could help preserve their soul and spirit life in Christ. Many do not and have not recognized "spirit and/or spiritual attacks-including doctors" until it happens unto them because it is being done in secret or in the dark but can be realized by these like symptoms that manifest to and ultimately, can't be ignored because of its intended, eventual pain that will also manifest. This "spirit activity" is becoming more frequent by those living and walking in spiritual darkness and some in dark spirit profession who havecome to spend much time in the spirit realm (due to spirit domination); living their lives in the spirit realm begins to become more real to them than living in the natural. Yet, <u>they desire to find contact with humans who live in the natural</u> but only, seemingly by negative spiritual means are able to contact and/or affect human life through pains, hurts and attacking humanity in a variety of ways (even by attacking any individual to separate families to take the life they are interested in causing homelessness (and relational troubles) in many situations) they can eventually, pull people into their dark spirit realm experiences, even without their permission, is what helps us to recognize it as a crime against humanity. Some crimes will not be solved without a look at any "dark spirit" spiritual intentions. Just like a doctor who listens intently to his patience tell him about symptoms of coughing, a cold can be determined. Likewise, spiritual attacks (and the repetition of it) could help authorities look for the person causing the symptoms, by the number of people coming to them for the same symptoms. People that have been spiritually affected, will continue to attack because the attacking spirits behind the perpetrator and when the perpetrator finds help for his "spirit condition" will he be able to stop attacking others, how he himself was spiritually affected. Since there are only 2 spiritual kingdom activities operating among us, and by those spiritually affected and/or entrapped by dark spirit life activity, they are literally calling out to society that they need help, and because they need help, they cannot stop attacking humanity. It operates like a spiritual disease, whereby left alone, cannot cure itself. It is a dark spirit life activity, initiative and agenda. Jn 10.10. May this writing help authorities recognize how those spiritually hurting and negatively affecting society can find a step-by-step faith approach towards spiritual recovery, with those willing to help in Jesus name. Ignoring, those in need of spiritual healing, from the rising spirit diseases among us, does not seem to work for us. Just look and see.

Our policemen could be helpful in learning how to chart these types of growing "spiritual attacks and crimes" against humanity, community and society happening among us and begin to recognize who is causing the spiritual distress and where it is coming from, which means that they would need to know how to chart if certain people keep popping up whenever bizaar experiences occur among the people (especially when its happening in any one area), to *begin to recognize when spiritual perpetrators are operating or trying to move in among us.* Why should people keep suffering by those **who are not spiritually well** (who could have initially been spiritual prisoners of war). We do not allow this with any other crimes. These spend their time spiritually attacking souls, humanity, society and disrupting family life, because *they* are in need of healing, not necessarily(initiallly) the person being spiritually attacked by demonic spirit life means. Witchcraft, sorcery/black magic and occultism spirit activity can and does transcend into the above inconveniences with life-threatening intentions. This is serious.

There are too many spiritual ritual suicide abuses happening a year in America alone *by those spiritually experimenting on others while pursuing them* because they can. People are trying to report these crimes but they are not being heard. These spiritual perpetrators are seemingly hidden in society (behind their religion and magic, while spiritually **sadistically** operating among us) and the spiritual fruit they are producing can be seen above and is greatly affecting and making inroads into our society. We could also consider that continual spiritual releases and learning how to resist dark spirit life aggression, perversion and pursuits could also possibly help save a life, especially when and until society learns and recognizes how to process satanic spiritual ritual abuses. Please help us in a massive effort to help reach those in need to desperately learn definite ways to resist dark spirit life activity and attacks, in Jesus name! I humbly ask, can we look pass ourselves and see that the need is great. *We have yet to realize that some spiritual perpetrators (in the United States) will not even allow their subject/victims sleep (living like being in a concentration camp in their own home, trying to wear them out by continually sending marshaled spirits to fill the body, soul and spirit lives of others they are desiring to pull into the spiritual operation of darkness! Lord, please help us to cause others to be aware of how serious dark spirit life (and those they use) are making inroads into the mainstreams of society of the United States.*

Witchcraft Websites: http://wildhunt.org/blog/2009/09/witch-hunts-are-now-an-international-epidemic.html or witchcraftinafrica.com.

www.policingsorcery. www.witchcraftdestroyingthecatholicchurchinafrica.

Witchcraft: Another type of spirit form and activity of sorcery and/or use of magic. Also seen as, black art. Other witchcraft expressions would include: WICCA   Druid & Celtic   Indian Charismatic   Island   Witch Doctor

See, www.overviewthedifferencesbetweensatanismandwitchcraft. It is said Satan also uses witchcraft to fight against humanity.

Dark spirit infiltrations among us has also given rise to the false prophet and sorcery, activity among us and the seemingly growing "psychic houses" among us seem to be due in part, as a

discovery, to prophets of God that did not know or realize how to release themselves enough from dark spirit impurities, defilement and spirit violations of others who found spiritual ways (through trafficking, channeling spirits or marshaling spirits into a life) as inroads into their personal lives and dwelling places. And it is from this activity, that the enemy used to back door many of our churches, by first spiritually defiling many at their homes and then when these saints or people went to church the spirit assignment upon their lives would begin to release themselves and then start to manifest in the churches. The book of Acts reveal that spirits can transfer even independently of the person they were with. Some manifested in the church belief systems of operation. Some in keeping their traditions. Some manifest, while people would come up for prayer right in the front of the church. The church prophets who may not yet have learned how to spiritually release oneself, from spirit influences enough, once seemed to be willing to receive all people, now have learned to discern prophets and/or others by the spirits they have yet to be released from. By not receiving any "true prophets" of God into their midst was also a way of protecting themselves (and cause a type of spiritual warring in the foundation gifts), who did not know how to spiritually release themselves from spirit impurities, defilement and spirit violations of others. Whether any outside prophets coming into any church system came either looking for a church home and/or had a word from the Lord, they would not be received. This same concept could occur in any church leader that had not learned to effectively release themselves (or I could also say, maintain their spirit life in Christ). Causing a type of spiritual and/or unbiblical indifference that can be remedied or restored by consistent release. Bless the Lord.

One of the tactics the enemies of our spiritual warfare, is to continually, spiritually war with you-the-desire is your gift in Christ, using anyone close enough to you to spiritually war for your body, soul and/or spiritual life in Christ. This could mean everyone around you would need to learn and understand spiritual warfare resistance, just to spiritually protect one another, from dark spirit intrusion(s) and invasion. In this sense, "The Spiritual Root of the Matter Found in Me" could help act as a spiritual _**safe guard**_ (inside or outside the church) to help all to spiritually be on the same page, so to speak, in learning how to preserve their spirit life in Christ. In the midst of only 2 spiritual kingdoms operating among us. We pray this writing ministers to you, wherever you may find yourself.

False Prophet Activity in the Heavenlies: It is said that it (the False Prophet's work) is designed and set up to attack deliverance ministries and ministers. Well, we can confirm this and wondered why more was not written on them. A False Prophet minister is said to be the satanic counterfeit of the **true biblical office of prophet.** He or she operates under a spirit of the False Prophet. They are often hidden under the guise of religion and/or religious activity in/or outside of the church system. In other words they seem to "fit in" because they are a part and recognized as a part of the church and/or religious system (evidently the concern is, is that they are being un-discerned, naturally and spiritually so). And often seem to "fit" in more than the true prophets! They help to create this spiritual delusion and spiritual confusion in any church foundation it helps, to secure them.

The purpose and reason that the office of prophet and/or sent apostolic prophets and sometimes house prophets experience various levels of attack within/or without the church and/or religious system until they conform to the spirit of the False Prophet, who secretly sets up and orchestrates the operation of darkness within or without any church and/or religious system reflected by that, which does not receive any legitimate sent apostolic prophet (s); who may arise within and/or without the church system; directed and released as part of the operation of the Kingdom of God in the earth can be attributed to infiltration. Non-acceptance of them is an indication of "spirit infiltration" in need of restoration and healing from the religious operations and/or systems of darkness that is somewhere set in leadership (un-discerned) – headed by a spirit of the false prophet (or spirit influence) because **the Kingdom of God does not operate against itself**.

This causes a continual spiritual hidden or secret warring in the spiritual foundation of any church system to which this scenario applies. The False Prophet in one sense will war with any true prophet that comes on the scene (usually a familiar spirit will signal them); even if it's just really for the purpose of trying to hide their spiritual state. Meaning, not all False Prophets (this could also be a pastor/prophet) intended to be one. From what we've seen, still seems to hold true; and that is when a true prophet is spiritually warred against by any False Prophet (the False Prophet's spirit will automatically stir them up simply because dark spirits are very, very possessive and often too sensitive of the territory they have acquired or are in) and if the true prophet does not overcome the False Prophet's spirit in spiritual battle (because there are only 2 spiritual kingdom activities operating among us) the False Prophet will then try and/or cause them (the true prophet; whether in the office, apostolically sent and/or church prophet) to come under their dark spirit submission, dark spiritual allegiance and/or the same spirit domination of the False Prophet. This is serious because this is their system of the operation of darkness (and spiritual dynamics among us) in the church, any religious church or community that allows this dark spirited system to be erected, enforced and/or established; in like manner, Pastors with the true Spirit of God operating in His life will also be spiritually challenged sooner or later by those with a different spirit life, which could be due, by not learning how to spiritually release themselves or are prisoners of spiritual warfare. This is a reason spirit life maintenance can't be ignored, because "spirits will clash", it's what can cause seemingly personality differences and/or cultural difference. People are simply over-due for spiritual maintenance. People of God, there is NO ORDER IN DARKNESS (or in dark spirit life activity); there is only continual spiritual warring for the souls (mind, will & emotions), bodies, spirit lives and realms and territories (whether homes, churches, establishments, etc., against the saints of Christ Jesus. We are in a spiritual kingdom era. Whenever, spirits manifest they will always reveal their spirit kingdom initiative and/or agenda, always!

Many, many, too many of our church leaders were seemingly not prepared (seemingly for this last move of darkness across the land) and is the reason for this book to help bring restoration to our leaders as well as their flock and our communities where needed, but first we must recognize our spiritual need and reality of appropriately affecting the work and power of the cross and locate ourselves. **Keeping our body, soul and spirit lives free from spirit impurities, defilement and spiritual violations of others (who did not realize how to maintain the condition of their spirit lives and victory in Christ) is a great part of our spiritual warfare**. Hopefully, this writing will break things down enough for us to understand that there is power and salvation at and in the cross and how to appropriate faith and power in the cross in Jesus name and even war with His name (with the spirits operating in ignorant and foolish men, defeated by satan and because of it think satan is more powerful, and so these will wrestle, strive and war with you) and the power of His blood; until all realize the spiritual reality that we ARE complete in Him who is the head of all principalities and power. In Jesus name. Col. 2.10.

The job and authority of the False Prophet in the heavenlies within or without the church system is very broad, which can and does include and is not limited to:

> His or her ability to pass false spirit judgment and statements of evil purpose over the sent and/or assigned apostolic prophet and/or other legitimate deliverance ministries and/or ministers. This should be a flag!

From the heavenlies, this spirit of the False Prophet can reinforce and give strength to lesser spirits of False Prophecy or house prophets or those with the gift of prophecy, who have been affected (or turned into counterfeits of the true gift of prophesy); when there is no longer discernment of the true prophet among them because the False Prophet will affect anyone and everyone below or around him because it's not really any longer him, because he at some point, missed the ability to maintain his spirit life in Christ Jesus and now is subject to spirit domination and since spirit life like to reproduce itself, everyone under and around him that is in any way connected or that he tries to connect to will sooner or later become spiritually affected.

The demon (or I call it spirit domination) behind the False Prophet, ranks very high among the witchcraft spirits within or without the church system with a religious influence.

When working against the body of Christ, he/she has the ability to marshal evil spirits and assign them to any chosen target (or of those in legitimate deliverance ministries and/or with a true office of the prophet call) which causes a warring in the spiritual foundation of the church system, producing spiritual confusion because False Prophets are disguised under religion /or religious activity, by confusing the 2 spiritual kingdom systems of operation. How is the Lord dealing with the False Prophet in our day? I heard a minister on Sun Life Radio in Cleveland, say that in the OT, False Prophets were killed. However in the New Testament they are exposed!

In this "flesh" work of the False Prophet and the supernatural you may find the following dark spirits operating: error, hersy, witchcraft, deception, lying, mind control, false prophesy and/or other religious spirits. The writer (Win Worley) tells us that to counteract these types of spiritual dynamic tactics of dark spirit activity, dispatch angels of the Lord against the False Prophet's work in the heavenlies operating under witchcraft.......curse.....his works.....and decree that everything that he does will be returned, mirrored back to him and satan; 2 for 1 and then send the angels of the Lord to enforce this prayer of protection daily and continually until you begin to see a turn and a release from the assigned darkness and release of marshaled evil angel attacks, in Jesus name. There would also be a need to bind up all personal spirit spirit attacks of: slander, backbiting, accusation, error of judgment, dissension, division, Leviathan, pride, maligning and strife, hate, intimidation, jealousy, lying, error, deception,....etc. Throw the False Prophet's plans down (along with the sent and assigned marshaled evil spirits) into confusion and disorder......etc., and loose the angels of the Lord to stop their work and activity immediately, in Jesus name. Ps. 91. Ps. 35. For more information and detail see: End Time Mind Control, by Win Worley, Booklet #25 and the Demolishing the Hosts of Hell.

This book, "End Time Mind Control", by Win Worley, tells us that the False Prophet from the heavenly job duties are broad. Such a False Prophet of the Heavenlies, acting as a counterfeit of the true office of the prophet, continues to broaden his job duties for the operation of darkness by warring against the true prophets of God's kingdom. These False Prophets from the heavenlies work territorially and so adept at working and operating in the spirit realm that whoever they war with in the natural, that once their deceitful plot of meeting their target has been achieved, they begin immediately to pull them (any legitimate prophet calling & or gift that they have targeted) into their dark spirit realm. Those they target and establish a (usually deceitful relationship in the beginning to hide their dark spirit side); then they try to bring their target into spiritual bondage by using the method of constant trafficking, channeling and marshaling evil spirit assignments into their lives, until their subject is literally forced into a dark spirit position to serve the operation of darkness. You may wonder how someone could be spiritually attacked constantly. The answer would be that some False Prophets from the heavenlies have been so spiritually indoctrinated in dark spirit life activity (in laymens terms – spiritually corrupted) that once they (the False Prophet) locates and connects with their subject in Christ, the False Prophet then begins to submit to the "spirit dominating" in his life through a trance state process to spirit penetrate his subjects house, who will also try to guide it's subjects life, from there the False Prophet will begin to spiritually violate his subject within their own home by spirit penetrating it's subject; which is actually a process of demonization. Literally, spirit forcing dark spirits into its subjects life, to either spirit attack it subjects body parts, causing some pain and even loss of sleep tiring its subject out until there is little to no resistance to the False Prophet. Literally, changing a servant of Christ Jesus, spirit life and realm by spiritually defiling and violating it. And then forcing them to serve the dark spirit, that is spirit dominating the life of the False Prophet. This type of spirit violation of another's life is nothing short of a spiritual crime and can cause a person to lose their soundness (naturally and spiritually so); and it could cause them to lose their job and literally rip apart family and relationships; all because of a minister who has been clearly spiritually corrupted by dark spirit life and who serves his religion by "spirit domination".

Greater Understanding Proverb 4.7-8

The Lord has given us the understanding that when any government allows religion, in the name of religion, to do evil to another; then you literally <u>undermine</u> righteous /civil laws of the land and civil laws set in place to protect its citizens.

In plain terms, I believe I actually heard the Lord say, it could be thought of as plain "stupid" to do so, in light of scripture that tells us that there is only One body, One Spirit (but different levels of spirit life activity) and only 2 spiritual kingdom activities operating among us, One Lord, One faith, One God and Father of all who is above all, who judges every work, and makes a distinction between right and wrong. So why would we undermine Truth, in the name of "religion"; placing religion above the laws of the land and even God, Himself; making religion a idol and work of idolatry ……. Eph, Chpt. 4. Ecc.12.14. Isa 42.3. Isa 42.4. Chr 29.11. Gen18.25. Hosea 6.5. Heb.12.28. Zeph 3.8. Isa66.3. Zec2.11. Ps22.8. Dan2.44. Lk1.33.Isa55.11. Mk.11.22. Jn.19.30. How absurd and what a lack of intelligence and judgment to do so, for any nation. STL!

There only one God (and there is no spiritual confusion in heaven as to who is operating in the Kingdom of God in the heaven and earth) who reveals in His word that there are only 2 spiritual Kingdoms operating among us (regardless of the religion, non-religious and/or spirit belief system). May this writing help you clarify any doubts or spiritual mis-understandings because only one of them is coming out in victory (regardless of any ones religion, non-religious and/or spirit belief system). His victory is already determined.

Other pagan high-places: (in thinking/thought patterns and belief systems where spirit release is necessary for healing to occur)

Higher consciousnessKarmaReincarnation

Please note: Infatuations with dark spirit worlds and activity could be spirit symptoms of sorcery (witchcraft) or baal spirit drawings, pullings, bewitchment and/or pursuits after you. And such like…..

Gal 5.19-21. Wherever the enemy can get into your thought, and thinking areas.

Observer of times: Also a type of soothsaying and or form of divination. Dt. 18.10 & 14. Gal. 4.10. Which God also forbids. Dt. 18.10.

Numerology: (Considered a type of divination by numbers and use of birthdates)

Birth Charts   Horoscope   Zodiac   Astrology
(it is revealed that any of these can potentially produce psychic disorders-due to the "spirit activity" attached)

Handwriting Analysis

Iridology: Based on Iris of the eye

Palm reading (also a type divination)

Phrenology: Based on shape of head

Fortune Telling: A type of divination, wizardry, spiritism or sorcery. Fortune telling and the occult can cause one to develop a (spiritual and natural) resistance to anything or anyone holy or divine in our world and/or society.

Tea leaves or coffee grounds: Can also be used for predictive purposes.

Ouija board: Used to convey messages from spirits.
Scrip. Ref: Lev 19.26. Lev 19.31. Dt 18.10-12. Corin 10.14, 20-21.

Yoga: Mystic…..Hindu discipline for achieving union with a supreme spirit through meditation, posture and breathing. Which can also lead to spirit domination.

Seducing spirits (bewitching spirit activity): Another way and method that satan is using, that is causing dark spirit activity, to come upon people to cause, stumbling, a seeming drowsiness and/or deep sleep naps, or suspended immobile states; and this can happen when a person and/or their spirit realm has been spiritually penetrated enough. A type of "spirit oppression" is trying to take place and the enemy will make it seem like an *infirmity* to hide behind the symptoms. No, it's a spirit thing and should be resisted until it lifts by continually calling upon the name of the Lord, confessing the names of the Lord and scriptures that reveal His authority and remind Him that you are the redeemed of the Lord and His work was complete at Calvary, and so on, until its power is broken in Jesus name. Our flow chart of Christ's authority and His complete work at the cross can help until one becomes more developed in bible study. Acts 8.9 & 11. 2Tim 3.13.

If not the enemy will keep coming in that area until he builds a stronghold. Lk 13.16. It could also cause a <u>trembling</u> on the part of the body that is being daily penetrated (if he can) and/or this could occur when spirits try to rise (or descend) upon the flesh, even while you sleep. The goal seemingly is to gain control of one's body as well as the soul and spirit life. Sometimes consistent release is needed in this writing (found in this writing) until the Lord brings release. Release is needed to help prevent these "spirit symptoms and/or spirit domination". Gal 3.1. Acts 8.9 & 11. Tim 4.1. 2Tim 3.13. Thess 5.23.

Séance: A meeting at which a medium seeks to communicate with a spirit of the dead. Also defined as a meeting for exhibition or investigation of spiritualistic phenomena, where demonic delusion reigns supreme when mediums try to consult.

ESP: (Extra sensory perception) A system of mind dynamics. It is said that no mind bending techniques should be used by Christians.

Hypnotism: A type of mesmerism. Believers are advised not to allow their minds to be taken over by another person and/or power (through whatever the present day means to do so or fetish is. Psychic stares to draw others could also fit this category). Nor would it be wise for one to engage in this spirit type of activity for (what some would call) entertainment purposes. This would be a way to give place (room, space and time to demons and their spirit activities) Eph 4.27. Eph 5.11. Evicting Demonic Intruders, by Noel & Phyl Gibson. Synonymous with bewitching and/or seducing. Acts 8.11. Tim 4.1. Prov. 12.26. 2Tim3.16.

Santeria: And its spirit fruit. Its followers believe in the god of Olorun who works through orishas spirits. These spirits have the ability, it is said, to be found under the hierarchy of Santeria and has affected the Catholic church. It is also said that other spirits found under the hierarchy of Santeria have also affected the Catholic religion. More information can be found in "Shaking the Heavens", by Ana Mendez Ferrell. www.VoiceofTheLight.com.

It is also been recorded that Santeria is gaining members in the Central and South America. The Netherland. France and Southern United States.

Please note: It has come to light that some in dark spirit professions have the ability, even through and/or by ancestral training in induced trance and/or hypnotic states have the ability to pull and/or draw others into trance or sleep-like states which must be resisted, in one finds oneself in such an experience for preservation of one's soul and spirit life, in Christ Jesus. Some call it a spiritual based manipulative method of mental control over people and/or situations. Another reason one should gain the ability to release oneself from spirit impurities, defilement and/or spirit violations of dark spirit belief systems of others.

It has been said that satan loves to see Christians operating under the power of his spirit rather than the Holy Spirit.

Halloween and/or Ghost activity:

It is said that many families use the Halloween season to spend time with dead relations at the cemetery (graveyard) or gather photographs of the deceased and relate to them through the pictures. All I wonder is, "why"? It is possible to attract undesired spirit life activity into your experiences through graveyard incidences and occasions. See: "The Prophet's Dictionary", under familiar spirits found wandering in the family lines, looking for a new home, pp. 466. Due to the analysis of information in this writing and the information in the book, Haunted Houses Ghosts & Demons, by Roberts Liardon. We are seeing that ghosts can also be a cause or a result of one accumulating spirits without gaining the ability to release oneself from spirit impurities, defilement and/or spirit violations (of others trying to affect their spirit life); spirits can literally release themselves into an environment and/or attach to another person at will. 2 Tim 2.26.

Also, during this time it is said that Catholics…..celebrate the passing away of saints to purgatory, called: "All Souls Day", on November 1st. They say that "All Souls Day" on November 2nd is when Catholics perform a consecration of sin and prayer for the dead. Sounds like a way to invite necromancy, mediums and/or spiritism, etc., into one's life and/or into the family. Halloween is also considered a high season for spiritual contamination and can affect the innocent, ignorant, spiritually blind and foolish. Where naïve persons can suffer spiritual attacks as well as a season of open initiation, indulgence and spiritual interference and invasion; because Halloween is a season of casting spells, bewitching (or the bringing one under sorcery powers by way of trance states and/or Transmittal meditation, trafficking and channeling of spirits into a person's body, soul and/or spirit life) and the hunting of souls of the innocent, ignorant, foolish and spiritually blind. A season where the willing and unwilling can be/and are lured into the practice of witchcraft. Jn 10.10. And always any season seemingly, that when it looks like reincarnation, it's really a residence change for a disembodied demon spirit activity whose previous residence has passed on to the land of the dead.

The operation of darkness, among many things, is an illegal satanic interference and invasion of the enemy into any life and environment (of which our world seems to offer little or no help), until after the spiritual damage has been done or the crime has been committed. Lord, please help. Our society has yet to learn how to process (which includes judging spirit actions and spiritual activity); sound vs. unsound spirit activity that transcends into our natural experiences obviously affecting citizens of the land. This is when dark spirit activities make illegal moves within and around you without prior notice (warning) OR WITHOUT ANY EXISING RELATIONSHIPS to bring anyone into spiritual captivity. Some relationships are established (only) for this specific purpose (realized or not) by dark spirit operations. And through this illegal spiritual move, hell is trying to instigate a relationship by finding a place (spirit place) in your life. At times, men can be used as an instrument to help those in dark spirit professions and/or sons or daughters of baal, as an entrance into the life of another causing much harm among us. Rom. 6.13. There are only 2 spiritual kingdom activities operating in the earth, among us and in the heavens. Every religion and/or non-religious person will fit or be "spirit forced" into one or the other. Some work really hard to fit into a religion and or a denomination but it's not about a denomination or religion it has always been about spiritual kingdoms. Denominations and religion are the distraction, while dark spirit kingdom life and activity continue invading, defiling and spiritually violating the body, soul and spirit life/realm, relationships and one's life work (trying to spiritually conform men to dark spirit life activity) often with little or no resistance because many are not being trained how to resist dark spirit life activity and thereby are becoming victims or prey to those in dark spirit professions and/or the activity of the sons of baal among us, those actively seeking to expand satan's kingdom and seemingly operating above and below our legal system and civil laws. Isn't our laws supposed to help defend all who need it, yet we've created a big gap whereby many are not being defended, because our laws have yet to learn how to process "negative spirit activity" transcending into dehumanizing and destroying its inhabitants. Therefore, our laws in-fact are not protecting those being greatly harmed, by that which it has yet to learn how to process that part of "spirit life activity", which it has not yet properly labeled (it is not a religion issue but a "intentional harmful spirit activity", which is transcending and growing great harm among and towards the people of the land. What a tragedy continually happening. May this writing help bridge the gap, between the spiritual and natural, that place "evil spirit activity" is freely operating because our society is seemingly not yet being made aware and/or knowledgeable enough to understand the importance of processing that which justice needs to attend to.

A deep tragedy and spiritual reflection on our nations level of spirit and spiritual intelligence and/or ability or lack thereof to the growing number of many being spiritually victimized by those under " spirit domination" – either by being a willing subject of trance states allowing oneself to be used willingly by dark spirit life (in error) or by those who literally force dark spirits into the life of another for sport and thereby become or are made to become victims of spiritual abuse by those seeking to expand satan's kingdom (or even by those who fell prey to it); for us not to have laws concerning "spirit activity" that continues to bring harm to many, on a daily basis.

We must allow and encourage all of the spiritual gifts of God and in God to be released especially and specifically when spiritual hostile environments arise as we work together as one in Christ towards our nations spiritual recovery. The gift(s) should be biblically released by the Spirit of God based on the gift and release of the Lord, as the Lord allows and ordained for His gifts to make room and prosper us. The approval or non-approval of the church, denomination and/or religion does not biblically take precedent in releasing the gift(s) of the Lord, over His word and leading of His Spirit. How could It, Jesus is head of the church and man. Herein lies the significance in listening to the correct spiritual kingdom and understanding spiritual activity and then distinction.

Baal Brides

Similar to the brides of Christ, under the sorcery group professions (or principalic strongholds also realized as spirit domination), you'll find counterfeit brides of baal, of which means some have been "spirit forced" into it. Wed by spiritual deceit (or by constant/consistent dark spirit activity (of trafficking and channeling; sorcery seduction or bewitchment activity) behind the scene ordered (or targeted) by someone – <u>yet to be discovered</u> in one's life (in need of spiritual release and healing) and the father of lies. Jn 8.44. Rev 18.23. Hence the saying, its usually someone you know or knows you. Prov. 24.15, Prov. 12.6. Not all of those operating in professions of darkness began voluntarily; but often through a dark spirit relentless and demonically, dehumanizing processes of pursuing and seemingly endless "spirit" hunting and attacking of the soul and spirit life-which can occur in any profession and religion and level of life-to attack the soul, body and spirit lives and realms until one conforms to what dark operations are desiring of the pursued life. A very un-American activity, happening among us. Through a spiritually detailed and defined or fine tuned and planned process of trafficking, channeling, bewitching magic and possible strategy of trance states and transmittal meditations.... etc. Methods used to release dark spirit manifestations and transfer of dark spirit life (with its activity into the body, soul, spirit life and realm of individuals of another to spiritually defile, affect, infect and infest individuals, cultures, communities, cities ... and eventually a nation. And once the individual is spiritually (completely spiritually captured and indoctrinated into dark spirit life activity) then they are spiraled into dark spirit professions for the initiatives and agendas for the operation of darkness. There is a great need for spirit activity to be taught and better understood even on the growing level that people are being taken by spiritual abuse activity and religion has nothing to do with it. Not directly anyway. Religion is more like the camouflage, to make you think it could be about Jesus.

These are not isolated events or activities. These are now a daily on-going operation of darkness among us and who is defending them (the spiritually hunted and pursued). How is it that our nation only seems to be able to process "spirit activity and spiritual concerns" after the crime has been committed or after the harm or death has occurred? We have preventative treatment for health care and even our cars but not necessarily maintenance of our spirit lives in Christ Jesus, making it easier for many to be preyed upon, spirit attacked and seducing spirit violations that are happening, by those often in higher levels of dark spirit professions, and/or by the sons and daughters of baal. What wisdom is in that? **<u>Surely, evidently help is needed before this!</u>** Is a government of democracy set up to only help every one except the growing number of those pursued, fallen prey or victimized by those with dark spirited belief systems (who perhaps also fell prey to dark spirit activity, who upon finding no help was pulled into allegiance to it (or dark spirit domination)? Whose to break dark spirited activity that is bent on destroying every level of life and living? <u>Only, a society that has learned how to spiritually processed that which is continually harmfully transcending into our world</u> (who in fact need help being processed because many have fallen victim to it and really need the soundness of those who can help (instead of currently rising against those who can help because others been too spiritually affected); because spirits never die, people must ultimately be release from it for healing to occur, naturally and/or spiritually so-otherwise, it will continue to be self-inflicting, infectious and destructive to the point it causes people and society to begin to destructively operate against itself – as it has been). No matter the religious, or non-religious or organizational face it wears. It is not, nor has it ever been about religion. It is deeper than religion. It is the spirit life activity by the only 2 spiritual kingdom activities operating among us in the land.

Proverbs 24.11-12, from the Expository Study Bible, by Jimmy Swaggart, tells us that it is incumbent upon government to help and thereby protect the innocent….and that it is the obligation of every Christian to rescue the perishing….and that inaction could invite the Judgment of God to render to every man according to his work:

> **"If you forbear to deliver them who are drawn unto death and those who are ready to be slain; If you say, behold we knew it not; does not He who ponders the heart consider it? And He who ponders the heart consider it? And He who keeps your soul, does not He know it? And shall not He render to every man according to his works?"**

Is it possible that spiritual and/or natural help for many could not be found? Strategies for deliverance needed in its season must be sought from the Lord. Even then, the forces and the operation of darkness fights those gifted to help (within and without the church, community, marketplace and city; realized or not) from releasing this information to the body of Christ and our world. In this we reveal the need of learning how to release oneself from spirit impurities, defilement and/or violations in our world and society at large.

I believe the Lord is revealing that one can break undesirable spirit realm habits and connections trying to spirit force its way into a life that has a legal and spiritual right to live in peace but can't because of those in need of spiritual healing, etc. Isa 14.25. Rev 10.15.

Sure, scripture says that we as individuals have authority over the powers of darkness, however when darkness has infiltrated and infested a people and environment, things become a bit more serious in that we can begin, even through this writing to see that dark spirit life activity is an operation, by which the Lord told me, **you can't cast out an operation, you must be healed from it!** Sure, by faith the saints of the Lord have authority over dark spirits, but the underlying (spirit) conditions and concerns of dealing with why a person continues to seek others for harm, hurt, control and/or danger, etc in a society that literally makes room for the (spiritual activities and realities that transform into disasters and catastrophes) under the guise of freedom of religion, is a bit deeper and much more to chew on.

Hear me dear ones. Some may not be operating knowingly in any of his dark spirit professions and/or be in a dark spirited individual covenant but may be serving darkness through and/or by a involuntary bound servant-hood way. Another good reason, to learn how to spiritually release oneself from spirit impurities, defilement and violations of darkness.

There are many illegal spirit-led ways that dark spirit life will use to try to attach and/or connect with any of us, some of which could include people and/or relationships that are in need of spiritual cleansing, release and healing. It could be people collecting a certain amount of dark spirit life, to the point that spirits themselves are able to (act out or) release themselves from the person. And let us not forget that biblically dark spirit life can work through elements of the earth graves, air…etc., some dark spirit life work through elements or vehicles of a dark spirit assignment sent by anyone in dark spirited professions (and/or sons and daughters of baal) to those they are desiring to pull or draw (by bewitchment) others into their dark spirit arena or realm and then try to keep them in dark spirit realms for eternity. For demonic reasons, in our world, people are being kept in demonic-like grips whereby their subject/victim is visited daily, continually for spiritual ritual abuse purposes. There are some dark spirited assignments (placed by spiritually affected men) that cause and/or hinder people from having certain or any normal relationship with others. All of these things (are backfiring back) into our society because release and healing are needed. A grace that can only be recognized and found in Christ Jesus.

These people need to be recognized and located when they are found trying to perpetuate spiritual control of the lives of others in our society (communities and churches, etc.,) and they should be legally stopped from being a spiritual nuisance and for distracting and interrupting another's normal life functioning abilities (even hindering their bodily functions) in an effort to gain control over a person's life. Why, should those in need of healing, be allowed to operate to the point of interference with another's life. No, it's not a religious matter, it is a spiritually and biblically unsound matter and indicates a troubled soul and spirit life.

This is what scripture meant when it said, suffer not a witch (those working sorcery powers and magic) to live or (in laymen's terms) they should not be allowed to operate to the point of interfering with the life and normal function of another to the point of harming the life and/or livelihood of others, while they go searching for their next subject victim. In some extreme cases I could see the need to remove them from society – because some are so spiritually affected (by dark spirit life mind-sets) that they might not realize how much they are harming others due to being spiritually affected by dark agendas. In the last Quarter, of 2009; a Cleveland, Ohio man killed 8 to 10 women and buried them in his back yard. In the first Quarter, of 2010 a guy shot a policeman and it was stated over the radio that a spirit influenced him. In the 3rd Quarter of 2010, a woman, who is said to be a marriage counselor, had gotten an Injunction for protection against her husband, due to his behavior. Shortly after the Injunction, her husband killed her. They said he stated that something came over him. Laws are needed as well as experiences correctly labeled and processed more accurately what people are experiencing: Laws for the people by the people! It was later discovered as a response to the injustices that happened to most women needing protection, that who get Injunctions are women and they usually end up dead, by those they filled Injunctions against for protection. So then, we have laws in place "symbolically" representing what they would like to do but never accomplish. So then, how can you establish and/or enforce what is not protecting what it was designed to do? Now the men are in counseling and the women are dead. Our society needs help in spiritually processing that which is negatively transcending, that which is need of healing. Our society needs to learn how to process spiritual concerns before the crimes have been completely committed and the harm and hate has all the time it need to complete its cycle of destruction.

Our society must understand how to get a grip spiritually and help the many in our society being spiritually violated and victimized on a continual daily basis. These did and do not need a aspirin or conference they need spiritual release and healing (as outlined in this writing as a real solution) from spirit life activity. People trafficking dark spirit life into the lives of others should be (considered a spirit violations or offenses and/or crime to spiritually victimize another and) is first being done or plotted out in the spirit realm by those in need of spiritual release and healing and due to not finding it, is now submitting to dark spirit initiatives and/or agenda. We cannot ignore dark spirit life activity.

IT IS A FULL COMPLETE ORGANIZED OPERATION GOING ON AMONG US. **Why** are we only dealing with dark spirit life activity after the spiritual crime has been committed and transformed into our world into pain, hurt, harm, danger and/or death? While the multitude of spiritual crimes and the attitudes that go with it of (defiling and violating another person) is free to continue to harass and mock all of life and dignity of humanity one person at a time.

Dark spirit life activity count on people not knowing how to spiritually release themselves, from their dark spirit operation to defile and violate another(through a process of spiritual/natural degeneration and corruption that first comes from dark spirit life activity.

Once dark spirits can continually grow in a person's life, undetected and/or without release, as the bible reveals some spirits can bring in other spirits (contagiously coming from other families, cultures, churches, marketplace, business, police, security services, media/art/edu., and legal and government systems, health and youth care systems, etc.,) environments; however and wherever the spirits are desiring to attach from until principalic spirits can develop themselves into a dark spirit professions in a person's life and the area of that person's influence, in an effort to strengthen and expand the operation of the kingdom of darkness. Then the spiritual process repeats itself, using those who have been spiritually forced to conform before them. Many are being spiritually forced into a dark spiritual union, deceitfully and illegally(naturally and spiritually so), even with those who claim Jesus as their Lord and Savior and who perhaps did not know nor realize the need to know how to resist dark spirit advances for their life on a daily basis. Yes, we have authority in Jesus name. Yes, we are complete in Christ Jesus who is the head of all principality and power.

However, one of the concerns is that the people of God need to be trained (including our officers and security personnel) how to resist dark spiritual intentional infestations and/or on-going pursuits of dark spirit activity to wear out the saints on a consistent basis is how the saints are being spiritually warred against in a personal way and then how to stand, when they are tired, in Jesus name! In this spirit kingdom age, we are dealing with those in dark spirited professions and/or with the activity of the sons of baal, who are literally targeting the saints, literally pulling them out of safe arenas, even away from the safety of saints, by spiritually warring against those targeted (often using those around them-that do not realize how to maintain their spirit lives in Christ or are not yet able to biblically discern-and therefore, darkness has enough influence over them to cause their surroundings to become contrary and/or behave indifferent towards them, literally, and this is how darkness is targeting the saints in their surroundings and pulling them out of their environments and then continually finding ways to war with them even in their homes until they spiritually conform to what darkness is desiring). Then you have the saint, trying to make peace with those in their surroundings that the enemy is using to war against those targeted, neither of which may realize what is actually spiritually happening. There are no co-incidences in the spirit realm. Things are plotted and planned around us because there are 2 spiritual kingdom activities operating among us continually and everyone should gain the ability to spiritually and biblically locate their spirit life activity, in light of grace, truth, Jesus Christ and Him crucified. You know them by their (spirit) fruit is not a suggestion. It is a reality happening among us and reveals those in need. The concern is how this (spirit) fruit is manifesting among us. Many people are having spirit manifestations but do not realize that they are manifesting because someone in their life is actually causing the manifestations, by someone (that may need to be discovered) in need of spiritual release and healing. These are some of the spiritual dynamics occurring among us by those in dark spirit professions and/or considered the sons and daughters of baal (on assignment among us). There are no spiritual coincidences among us only 2 spiritual kingdom activities with their own initiatives and agendas closing in on us!

Nelson's New Illustrated Bible Dictionary on marriage

Describes how God used marriage in the OT to reveal God's spiritual relationship with His chosen people. Scripture ref: Ps 45. Isa 54.6. Jn 3.29. Eph 5.25-33. Rev 21.2. Gen 6.1-2.

Baal bride spirits could actually be a person connected by him in the spirit realm due to the spirit activity operating in a person's life (realized by the person or not and/or forced (or mated) by those in dark spirit professions).

There is a biblical need (to find out how) to stay out of agreement with any demonic systems of influence among us because the enemy will use it to keep you connected to dark spirit realm activity. For some it may be difficult because, some dark spirit professions have gained the ability to spiritually pursue and/or hunt you (in any arena) and the Lord must be sought to break the enemy's purposes for trying to stay spiritually connected to you. 2Corin. 6. Rev 19.15. Micah 2.13. Dt. 33.29. Isa 14.25. See "The Wash" flow chart, as another biblical method of resisting dark spirit advances for more information.

I am reminded of a story, whereby a certain young woman had joined a congregation. During this time, it was revealed to the pastor of this congregation during his time with the Lord, that this woman was cursing pastor. The pastor thought how can this be, a curse causeless shall not come, but he did check with the Lord, just in case. Prov 26.2.

Well, to make a long story short, when service started this young woman showed up for prayer and the pastor asked this young woman is she was cursing people? He did not want to make it seem like the question was personal.

This young lady with tears began to say pastor, I wake up in the middle of the night and just start dancing and doing things with my hands. That she did not know why and could not help herself. In the spirit realm it was revealed to pastor that this woman was a sorceress.

I thought this to be a good example, for what's happening today to help reflect the great need among us, for people to learn how to resist dark spirit realms and activities that try to descend upon them and stories like this happen when you don't. People end up being spiraled into dark spirited principalic professions, until you lose any (soul and spirit strength and ultimately biblical soundness and) ability to resist dark spirited expressions, manifestations and mindsets. At the same time, like in this story, people are trying to go on and live their natural lives as if there is no need (or are just plain clueless) as how to deal with the condition of their spirit life.

In this example, satan had found a way to create a union (type of spiritual marriage) where evidently this young lady was not aware of how to resist him and thereby was spiraled into any sorcery profession (behind the scene) to operate against the church and body of Christ. This is serious. <u>Accessing and using her gift from God</u> for his dark will and purposes and disturbing her sleep to do it all the while she is still trying to have "a normal life", but how can you with sometimes severed spiritual interference? How can this be right? 2Tim 2.26. An involuntary abiding place in the spirit realm, where satan will also try to grant you the desires of your heart, fulfilling Jn. 15.7 (in the negative), making you think it's God while networking you in the spirit realm making and demonically causing what you want to happen as another demonic anchor to build dark spirit strongholds in your life with connections in the natural and in the spirit realm. It's like a demonic spiritual politicking.

There is a need to make sure that those we associate with, as well as yourself, are fellowshipping in the spirit realm and in the right spiritual arenas with the Lord only through bible times, prayer and praise times, anything that spiritually "pops" up (trying to contact you in the spirit realm) outside of this biblical practice should raise a red flag to be resisted. Ignoring dark spirit unction and manifestations does not work for those desiring a healthy spirit life with Christ. Dt. 5.7. Isa 42.8. James 4.7.

This is similar to what Ana Mendez speaks about in her book regarding, complex structures in the spirit realm, a type of demonic macro-structure being built in the land and in the cultures and communities of our society but first structured in the spirit realm, where permission is given, founded and accumulating generationally on past sins, but now seems to be structuring or mantling itself in the spirit realm (in some culture circles) contagiously on the spirit sins (some ancestrally) of others in cultures, marketplace/business places, community and society itself; thereby connecting structurally through relationships and associations. So then, the question that presents itself, how then do you come out from what is trying to spiritually structure around you (wherever you go)?

Where there was or is no reconciliation the enemy will continue to work progressively in the spirit realm, not just structures of our society's economic system, etc., but in the spirit realm of people's lives, demonically bonding or bringing people together (for dark spirit purposes) or dismantling society through cultures and communities using division, strife, dark spirit reactions to people of faith, etc., in the natural simultaneously demonically bonding people (realized or not especially in the marketplace) or dismantling people of faith in God by principalic strongholds in the spirit realm. Surely, satan is trying to permanently capture and bind those not knowing how and or not realizing how necessary it is to resist principalic spirit activity. Using relationships and/or associations, as their demonic means to spirit war (force, or press) their way, into another's soul and spirit realm. One way it seems, to find out if you have been connected or reconnected with someone who needs spiritual release, healing in their lives is when the spirits operating in their lives begin to rise up against you; out of a relationship that you thought was safe. Ultimately, there would be a need for both people to war (spiritually war together) if peace is to be found and/or restored. Otherwise, the spirit (uninvited or not) will begin to work against the relationship.

So it is apparent, that it is not enough that just a few know how to effectively war in the spirit realm or deal with uprising spirit confrontations in the natural or spirit seizes in the environment; like vultures or fowls descending upon those they (dark spirit life) are trying to affect. We should never lose sight that some are being affected more by questionable spirit activity than others and are literally crying out for help. May this writing find those, being more affected by dark spirit activity than others, even against their will? Yes, we have authority in Christ Jesus but we are dealing with an operation. In many situations dark spirit life activity can be found trying to break the will of the saints in order to bring them into captivity, so then it isn't so much an issue that Jesus is Lord, even though HE IS! It is more a matter of resisting the hounding of the saint with continual/consistent "spirit" activity attacks to literally try to wear out what the saint believes even in moments when their strength fails, while someone in the spirit realm is orchestrating and tampering events around the saint(s) and causing them to feel isolated. Seems like a strategy, using a high level and high spirit profile and assignment to literally pull any saint out from their surrounding and then attack them until their will is broken. This is happening now!

There seems to be a need to spiritually grasp how dark spirit life is able to target and attack a saint to cause forced servitude for the operation of darkness. This is an area we need to be able to gain the ability and reality of how to reach and minister to these also. They are part of the body, but attacked into isolation, left to fight the great fight of faith alone. This I believe is one of the reasons there have been so many "psychic houses" rising up among us. They were pulled out, isolated by dark spirit attacks, then infested with dark spirit life, until they conformed to dark spirit life (or hells will) for their life. They need more than prayers they need to learn (in practical ways, by those who have been spiritually and naturally challenged) how to fight the good fight of faith on the various levels that many are being, in most cases, spiritually warred against through and /by spirit life activity and the operation of darkness using society, community, families and territory against any one individual. Who is able to minister in this area other than what we are offering as a society usually a mental institution or 12 step program, by those who perhaps was never challenged to fight the good fight of faith.

> And when the fowls came down ……………, Abram drove them away….Gen 15.11.

In some instances, there is a need to realize how to drive spirits away (especially, if and when someone in dark spirited professions and/or the son(s) of baal have released and/or marshaled evil spirits into a life to attack it). We are not discussing religion but apparently skilled and dark intelligent spirit life activity operating among us and the need to biblically know and realize how to protect oneself, not pretend – it's church as usual.

It would seem that the impact of our effectiveness would come from helping others also to learn how to better understand spirit life activity in the midst of 2 spiritual kingdoms operating among us, otherwise people will continue to be lost and submissive to the growing operation of dark spirit dynamics happening among us. My people are destroyed for lack of knowledge. Hosea 4.6.

Shaking the Heavens, Ana Mendez*It is important to be able and/or to gain the spiritual and natural ability to distinguish the works of evil spirits and wickedness that help to make up dark spirit life activity and the operation of darkness vs. the Spirit life activity of Christ and the operation of the Kingdom of God because to continually and consistently work and/or strengthen dark spirit life activity and the operation of darkness will ensure you spiritual allegiance to their dark system of operation and deeper levels of spiritual bondage whether you are in the church or not. There are only 2 spiritual kingdom systems of operation among men. Everyone will fit or be spiritually forced into one or the other. Everyone. No matter the religion or non-religious belief. Let us consider our ways and turn again unto the Lord. Mt. 22.29. Lk 20.21.Mt. 16.23. Mt. 7.20. Mt. 15.14.

Spiritual History

The reality of the affects and influences of "spirit domination" playing out in societies and nations in need of learning how to judge and release oneself from spirit life impurities, defilement and seducing/bewitching spirit violations that operate against its own humanity continues to escalate (or increase) seemingly multiplying among us by itself (exponentially), year to year, generation to generation. All of life is, continually, at some level of spirit activity. Jn 6.63. Some only can understand and perceive spirit life activity on certain levels. Yet, anyone's limited knowledge and/or awareness of spirit life activity never seems to hinder and/or thwart it's growth, because of its growing reality and affect on society and humanity at large, it therefore, becomes necessary and even crucial to understand the only 2 spiritual kingdom activities operating among us and the greater need among us to see the bigger picture of spirit life activity, how it is affecting, eroding in many instances and operating among us with its own initiatives and agenda and our need to realize which spiritual kingdom activity we have become a part of either by our will to choose or by the reality of those being taken or who could have fallen prey through one's own environment, family, ancestrally, family hereditary or that of others, to spirit life activity and operations due to not understanding the reality of the need to gain the ability to release oneself from spirit life impurities, defilement and/or seducing/bewitching spirit violations that takes a soul and spirit life that does not know how to protect itself in the truths, reality and power of Jesus Christ and His complete work on the cross.

Historical human spirit life activity, accounts and influences that have and continue to affect our cultures, national government, communities, families and society at large which ultimately can be biblically and/or spiritually traced to some level of spirit invasion and/or domination.

Governing affects and influences of spirit domination

The causes, affects of spirit life activity and influences continuing to cause national and international generational spiritual kingdom genocide and slavery among us. It's not a race thing, tribal thing or a culture thing, it's a "spirit" thing!

Genocide, seemingly intertwined with slavery, of which both are still affecting and warring against humanity, cultures and civilization as we've known it. Genocide and slavery are recognized by the United Nations as "world crimes". Genocide (intertwined with slavery in many parts of Africa, still) continues to press its way (in our world community) as if it were meant to be a continuing part and purpose of Africa's society. Many of Africa's redemptions (are being made possible by those who buy the slaves to free them), such as Christian Solidarity International (CSI) Zelglistrasse 64. P.O. Box 70, CH-8122 Binz (Zurich) Switzerland. Ph 41 (0) 1 980 47 07. E-mail:csi-int@csi-int.org. Who reveal startling stories or current accounts of where slavery began and how its cruelty still exists as it did in America over 150 years ago. And the mystery, of why the UN, US and the European community have seemingly joined the world community by negotiations not to create tension by confront ting the movement(s) seemingly creating, causing or feeding into the genocide and slavery issues. Concluding, in this writing, that help from Europe and the United Nations has pretty much stopped in southern Sudan, based on their remark that the world community should work with the government to solve the problem. One question that arises is how do you work or confide with a government that is clearly supporting if not causing and creating the genocide (and slavery) concerns? See: www.sudan.genocideandslavery.

1. Pharoah

And Egypt's government said, when ye do the office of a midwife to the Hebrew women and see them upon the stools; if it be a son, then ye shall kill him but if it be a daughter then she shall live. Exo. 1.16-20. Jn 10.10. Jesus came, that we might have life and that more abundantly therefore killing the innocent is not necessarily an acceptable expression or custom spiritually or naturally so in the operation of God's kingdom, again helping to distinguish the only 2 spiritual kingdom activities operating among us. Only 2.

Mostly all genocides seem to be initiated and/or supported by government. Governments found to be in need of spiritual healing because of their spiritual and religious beliefs that would spiritually transcend itself into genocide, slavery and/or sex. When spirit life activity manifests itself it will always reveal or spiritually transcend into our natural world. Since the 1930's the following have and some of the following continue to experience the affects and results of genocide.

The Holocausts of Russia	The Holocausts of Germany	Uganda
Angola Rwanda	Bosnia Cambodia	Guatemala
Turkey China	Ukraine Sudan	

Various reasons have been stated for genocide. Some of which are ethnic cleansing of people tribes to slave trade; some for sex trade intermingling in some way with religious purposes to the systematic killing of a whole people or nation through systematic discrimination and/or acts of violence.

When a part of Sudan called Darfur, looked for a measure of freedom from Sudan's authoritarian Islamic government, that took over a black nation of people, the Sudan , now 75% Sunni Muslim, decided to end the revolt by trying to wipe out all of the native Africans in Darfur to clear the territory for Arabs. A Islamic people, invading and conquering a government to then take over the rest of the nation, using genocide as a tool.

While indoctrinating the native Africans to become African Arabs (keeping in mind that dominate spirits can transfer. It would be good practice to spiritually release oneself after being around community and/or those with different spirit natures unless you want to pick up their spirit nature), and then renaming them "Janjaweed" to help the Islamic Arab government to wipe out the remaining tribal blacks.

The Janjaweed are described as a grotesque mixture of the mafia and the KuKlux Klan with a racist ideology that sees the Arabs as supreme over the non-Arabs. In the biblical view of their being only 2 spiritual kingdom activities operating among us. We can perceive that the native of Africa have been spiritually invaded and then divided the people through and by spirit domination (spirits duplicate themselves and try to reproduce through the people) with like kind domination. Not to offend anyone, but it's also how sexual confusion and perversion, etc., seemingly spread so fast. Spirit life is spirit life. It's how they operate. It's how they increase among those who have yet to learn how to release themselves from spirit impurities, defilement and spirit violations of others. Gem 1.25. How the Janjaweed are attacking their own people can be found at: www.witnessinggenocideinsudan-60minutes.cbs. Rom 14.12.

Like a government-made hurricane, the Janjaweed African Arab militias are chasing the native Africans out of their own nation, towards Chad. Seemingly, religion behind the scene being used militantly to divide and kill a people of a same tribe, now strategically turned against one another, affecting the unity of a culture.

All of which affect our world community. Yet, no matter the religion or non-religious views there are still only 2 spiritual kingdom activities operating among us, which makes any of the above concerns and/or issues something more profound than religious.

Only when government leaders find spiritual healing from spirit impurities, defilement and/or spirit violations of self or if affected by others can their nation begin to heal through repentance and Jesus Christ. All of life is affected by some level of spirit activity. Jn 6.63. A healthy spiritual condition and life would cause healthy relationships. A unhealthy spiritual condition (state) or life would cause or transcend into unhealthy relationships. Rom 14.12.

See: www.sudangenocideandslavery. www.genocideinthe20thcentury:rwanda1994. www.whatcountrieshavebeeninvolvedingenocide. www.crimesagainsthumanityand genocide.

2. **Nero**

It is said that Nero of Rome was a confident leader, yet he had a love/hate relationship with his mother.

Nero ordered his brother (Britannicus) execution because his (Nero's) mother showed favor to his brother over Nero in 55AD. Four years later Nero ordered his mother's death in 59AD. Around 62AD, Nero divorced his wife Octavia and married Poppaea, then a friend of Nero help him to frame his wife Octavia for an immorality charge, then Octavia was exiled to an island and then executed.

Nero was heavily into parties, orgies and gluttony as well as, arts, education, music civil engineering and architecture. He slept with beautiful young women and young boys including his brother, Britannicus. It is said, that he also slept with his mother and had relationships with older men and eunuchs.

Nero often left his empire unattended and when he heard of conspiracies against him or treason he would order their execution or force them to commit suicide. Finally, one conspiracy led Nero on a rampage to root out any opposition with daily executions. Finally, when Nero's bodyguards deserted him he fled for his life and ended up committing suicide himself with the help of his secretary. See: www.neroscharacter.

3. **Mao Zedong** – China

Helped to give rise to communism. It is said that he was poorly educated as a child but highly intelligent. When he left home he became a member of a Nationalist Army, when revolution began around 1911. He too, was influenced by Marxism system of thought. A thought system, that serves as a basis for Socialism.

Zedong would sense the need to rid China of all foreigners. He massacred all missionaries and Christian converts.

> ...of the increase of the Lord's government and peace there shall be no end. Isa 9.7. Jn. 10.10.

(again we can consider the distinctions of the 2 spiritual kingdoms when they manifest in the earth, in the lives of men or in our environments).

China's citizens experiences of extreme poverty, starvation and grief which stem from the loss of many innocent lives and times of chaos and despair seemed to set the stage for the acceptance

of Mao Zedong and godless communistic philosophies of Karl Marx. 85% of the nations farmers that supported him. Zedong started a society for the study of Marxism and in 1921 started the Chinese Communist Party. Zedong's communist defeated the nationalists.
See: www.maozedongpersonalityandidealogy.

> Because they have forsaken me and have estranged this place and have burned incense to… and have filled this place with the blood of innocence. Jere 2.34. Jere 19.4.

The basis of traditional communism is common ownership and production. Karl Marx started communism as a journey into rational eschatology. But through Lenin's soviet communism, this was discarded and only tyranny and atheism were left. It is said that Marx believed that a man's worth reflected his efforts and that the state of equality was one's final stage in life. However, this philosophy shows Communism to be not only anti-Christian but anti- any divine deity, as well.

> God so loved the world He gave His only begotten Son. Every individual's value is found hid in Christ Jesus, not measured by man's ideology. Jn 3.16-17. Ps 103.19. Corin 4.5.

Would this be the reason the China government, prevented it's Christian leaders at the airport by retrieving their luggage, to forbid their attending the Lausanne III, Cape Town 2010 International Congress on World Evangelization this year (2010). There are only 2 spiritual kingdom activities operating among us no matter the religion, non-religious and/or spirit belief systems. When a government is in need of spiritual healing and release its citizens also suffer, as well as its government. See: www.riseofcommunisminchina. And, www.lausannecapetown.

4. **Hitler** – Germany

Hitler's policies, as stated by others, who studied him, seemed to be more reflective of his personality issues than of sound judgment. Some say his policies were based on 2 main ideas or thoughts: **1.** An aggressive expansion….regarding the war in Europe, from 1939 to 1945. **2.** The extermination of the Jews. Some say the latter was due to being kept out of a school of the arts, called Vienna Academy, by the Jews. According to: www.personality,idealogyandpoliticsofhitler.

And as Nero, Hitler also, has had a seemingly unhealthy view of women as well as of the Jews. It was said that he had rigid prejudices, was quick to anger and flew into rages over small things and had an infantile perception of the world, with a personality to match. It was also revealed that Geli Raubal, Hitler's niece committed suicide just to escape his attentions. See: www.adolfhitlerkillerfile.

And even as they did not like to retain God in their knowledge, God gave them over to a reprobate mind, to do those things which are not convenient….being filled with all unrighteousness, fornication, wickedness, covetousness, malicious, full of envy, murder, debate, deceit….whispers, backbiters, haters of God and inventors of evil things. Rom 2.28-32. Prov 25.28.

And he liked to kill, to say the least. In 1939, in January, Hitler declares that a new world war would lead to the annihilation of the Jewish race in Europe. www.adolfhitlerkillerfile. Prov 29.2.

5. **Vladimir Lenin**

Established the first communist government and he lead the Russian communist into power in the early 1900s. After a party split, he (or his party) became the majority with an administration called the Bolshevik regime. The Bolshevik's intended on extending government control by trying to control most aspects of economic life, factory workers and they initialized to bring all forms of communications under state control. Some of their policies failed coupled with a failure to implement a coherent cultural policy. Lenin felt that the rich abused the poor instead of help them. He believed everyone was equal. Lenin also realized that the poor Russians were incapable of organizing themselves because they had no education. See: www.vladimirlenin.

6. Josef Stalin

After Lenin, Stalin assumed power over the Soviet Union in 1933, as Lenin's successor. His number one goal was to make the Soviet Union into a major player. But it's the way he did it. He built up the Soviets economy and modernized his military. He had guns and tanks made over food, housing and consumer goods. He did a lot of good but at great expense of the people. He went from a poor peasant to the ruler of the largest country in the world. He industrialized Russia and defeated Hitler in World War II as he teamed up with President Roosevelt and Winston Churchill of Great Britain, to stop Hitler from expanding his Nazi empire. Before Stalin's death he had brought Lenin and his revolutionary Bolsheviks back into dictatorship (absolute power). Then, after Stalin's death a de-stali-ni-zation period of the soviet began. www.josephstalin.

After Lenin, helped Stalin get appointed as General Secretary in 1922, Lenin got nervous when he saw Stalin **_begin to deviate from his ideas_** (is when Stalin's spirit activity began to manifest) and in Lenin's last testament he requested that he did not want Stalin to succeed him. Stalin stepped in and began to cover up and/or rid all disclosing information that would oppose him. And Stalin was able to exile and assassinate Trostsky in Mexico, one of his greatest enemies. Then Stalin, was able to get other enemies to kill themselves and remove each other, so that by 1928 Stalin had control. Seemingly, this was only the beginning of killing those who opposed him. And began to lose popularity because of it, even his wife committed suicide. Jn 10.10. See: www.josephstalin.

> _Could this be considered a type of genocide (or a systematic killing of a whole people – within a nation)_
> He that rule over men must be just.

Stalin became a reclusive, in fear of assignation and very suspicious and began to destroy all those in his party who might possibly be against him. He went on a killing spree, in 1936-37, he purged the Red Army of those he thought were in conspiracy with Germany and 50% of the officers died, afterwards he killed everyone who had too much information about what he did. Yet, it is said that Stalin was the mastermind of World War II but was the people's lives the cost! Stalin continued his pattern of purging and destroying his enemies until his death from a brain hemorrhage in 1953. Jere 2.21. Lk 6.43. Tim 6.5. Lk 11.34. Rev 16.10.

Those affected and/or infected with dark spirit natures take on the dark spirit initiatives and agenda, of only on the spiritual kingdom that reflects that activity that kills, steals and destroys through various levels of degeneration and corruption of mankind and/or goes through a process that defiles and violates humanity on every level of life and living. The other spiritual kingdom promotes life, healing, wholeness and blessings. When spirits manifest in a person's life it will always reveal it spiritual kingdom's initiatives and agenda, (within the life it is occupying), always. And there are corresponding angels, belonging to either kingdom, that will be released to assist, in whichever spirit life kingdom a person is operating in either on purpose or ignorance in not realizing how to maintain one's spirit life in Christ Jesus, from dark spirit captivity and corrupt activity. This is the reason some would consider those infected by, especially by certain levels of dark spirit activity "diseased". Disease defined as a: particular destruction process. Dark spirit life, has to do with the fallen angel spirits which are cursed, and they affect and infect mankind spiritually like a spiritual disease that will eat a-way automatically at your spirit life once affected by them, then they will proceed to eat a-way at the soul (corrupting and trying to infiltrate the mind with dark spirit thought and thinking patterns literally until the person being contaminated by them think the thoughts are theirs – if there is no adequate resistance), causing the person to lose their spiritual and eventually natural soundness, and then perversion and error will set in causing one to lose discernment and they will not be able to soundly judge which spirit life kingdom is operating among them or even if they are a part of a dark spirited kingdom system or God's spiritual kingdom system and things can really become a "mess" especially depending on what position one is placed in life, that darkness will either use them to affect their area of influence (whether they realize it or not is not the issue, nor does dark spirit activity stop operating because anyone chooses to stay ignorant or spiritually blind to it because spirit life has a life force all its own and is a good reason to study the bible that we may be able to spiritually and naturally locate ourselves, so as not to get caught up in the mix or hindered by those too spiritually affected (to know if they are or not) and are now working more in allegiance in a dark spirited kingdom system instead of God's spiritual kingdom system and can't discern it because they have become too affected. This is when it becomes dangerous to community, family, a nation and society itself. When the spirit life activity begins to act out in and through the life it has spiritually corrupted or affected. Jezebal could also be considered a failed personality type. she too, was spiritually affected.

This is why, Lyndon LaRoule, called Nero, Hitler and there is one more President, listed on his website as "failed personalities" because he claims they are diseased and have the same types and/or similar defective personalities. And because of their "failed personality types" are more of a threat to society and any civilization they are found in. Case in point, from the information on Nero and Hitler listed above, LaRoule's issue seemed to be what do you do when you recognize that the majority voted for a Nero and/or a Hitler. How do you stop them from doing damage to a system they as leaders are to protect, just from being in a place they are not (according to LaRoule) meant to be, due to what LaRoule calls "failed personalities". I wonder why he didn't add Idi Amin to this category?

From LaRoule's website, these seem to be "failed personalities" due to being affected (my input) in their spirit life, whether they realized it or not doesn't seem to be the issue, but because they are seemingly (biblically and spiritually) affected by this spirit disease (that seemingly causes certain behaviors), this will be the reason for why, they do what they do or why they don't do what it seems like they should do and why they behave in a certain manner. Reflected on, by when a person, even with good intentions, seem to cause more harm to a place, position or situation, just by virtue of being there. This could be a hard pill to swallow for someone seemingly groomed for any position. The point being, when spirits manifest, they will always reveal their spirit kingdom's initiatives and agenda. This also proves out biblically when you consider Daniel's lifestyle versus Ahabs. Dan 6.10. 1Ki 21.2. Tim 6.8.

Some do not openly promote darkness. Especially when they are too spiritually affected by it. Just sitting in a dark spirited environment alone could accomplish this over a period of time, literally causing people to become immune to it. Idi Amin, grew up around the Islams in southern Sudan. And even now the Sudanese trained Africans to become radical Africa, Ahabs who were trained to war and chase out their own tribes, out of African's native country, to make room for more Ahabs. Spirit life can transfer and through this transfer, can 2 natives of the same country and tribe, now begin to war against their own flesh and blood. Spirits can also be viewed as personalities, and God is a spirit (God is righteous), but not every spirit, because He is holy. Why did not Vladimir not seem to be as concerned with other religious religions who cause hate, division and terrorism among family and those who once lived in peace. God is Holy. This is what I began to understand as I was trying to comprehend LaRoule's website because I did not see the character traits that was seemingly upsetting him. But as I pondered it, in my heart, the Lord began to give me understanding by revelation. I hope not to hurt anyone's feelings, that's not my intention, but I need to reveal what was biblically revealed to me for greater understanding of spirit life activity, of why (as one of the on-going theme in this writing) you can't really ignore "spirit life" and the other theme being if, spirit life activity (as a force) will try to use the wise as well as the ignorant, no matter one's position in life one is found in, nor their religious or non-religious views. We are in a "spirit kingdom age" therefore, there is a need to understand it, spirit life activity (conceptually, biblically and spiritually, just to gain the ability to protect oneself from it.

Just like David said in the Psalms, I'd rather be a doorkeeper in the house of my God, than to dwell in the tents of wickedness. Ps 84.10. There are doorkeepers for both spiritual kingdoms operating among us. Darkness is always plotting on how to get into a individuals, family, community, city, nation and even societies of life. And because everyone does not understand spirit activity – biblically nor spiritually, the (people) become easy to use as access into these arenas and/or lives of others. The higher level or position a person holds in society the more serious it becomes. Some people (or religious movements) or even family members or some in government positions, even so like some local officers can and do become doors, gates and/or doorkeepers for darkness to gain access through, regardless of whether the person realizes it or not. Some ignorance is by choice. Some ignorance can come from spiritual blindness....being in wrong spirit belief system environment can also produce spiritual blindness. God is spirit, but not every spirit acting out is God (but it does reveal the area of healing needed). In any case, ignorance can cause sin against the true God. They could already be affected by dark spirit life operations and so all darkness has to do is see to getting a person in a certain position, that is very personable and on many levels likable, they do not have to understand the bible or spirit kingdom life activity-and so they can become a nuisance and spiritual hazard to the people of God, all they have to do is be in a position to open the door for those to infiltrate a place and occupy that place that spiritual invaders of life and humanity (like false prophets, sorcerers and sons and daughters of baal) could have not gained access to without them being in "that" position among us. Often an employer thinks he is hiring a person for their abilities and later finds that when the spirits in a personal life began to manifest, there arises spiritual conflict, even with common job interests.

So how can you not be concerned with the person, giving access to that, which could bring us harm (like Idi Amin, like Judas was the one who brought the men who took Jesus away – Jn 18.2-3) when they are ignorant of true biblical and spiritual intent of the only 2 spiritual kingdom activities operating among us-it's almost like they are out of place to the purposes and divine plan of God and this is why the prayers of the saints are so important and why we need to pray, Lord place the right people who are in line, will and purposes with you in areas of leadership among us. Especially in our national and local government, along with local police officers who can also appear to be "out of place" among us because many are clearly operating from the initiatives, inclinations and directives of the operation of darkness and they too would need spiritual release so they can work more fairly among us. He (or they) are not actually the one(s) directly killing or harming anyone. No but he or they, have the (earthly) authority to open the door or gate of our lives, communities (sometimes families), cities, nation and society to those who have already been spiritually affected by dark spirit life (diseases). Like Manasseh, he rebuild the places that Hezekiah removed and offended the Lord. 2 Ki 22. <u>Would you think the person opening the doors or gates to make us vulnerable *to those who are spiritually affected*, are in the right place for the good of everyone</u>. If it doesn't make spiritual since, how could it make natural sense. If you are fighting in a natural army and in the midst of battle, you find out that more than half of your people have different spiritual belief systems (because they have been spiritually affected in their personal lives and were not taught how to rule their spirit life (maintained in Christ) and maybe didn't think anyone would notice) and so in the midst of battle, friendly hate spirit-fire begins to erupt and they turn against each other, due to spiritual confusion that will and does transcend into the natural.

What would you think? Just look around. Lord, please help us not to be more dangerous to ourselves than our real enemies in our midst, for your name sake, that You may receive glory, not us. To You be the glory, only!

We live in a society that does not yet realize how to deal with those spiritually affected until after the harm, pain, hate, destruction and/or death cycle has completed its course. www.likeneroandhitler:o. www.larouchepublcom.

7. **Mussolini** – Italy

Founded the Fascist Party in 1919. It is said that he used force and intimidation against political opponents and took power in 1922. He also became Prime Minister of Italy in 1922 and he was a leader of the Italian Social Republic. The Fascists viewed Pluralism (regarding various ethnic, religious groups existing together in a nation or society) as a <u>dysfunctional aspect</u> of society. Fascism also rejects the idea of egalitarianism (equality, that would advocate full political, social and economic equality for all people). See: www.fascism-wikipediathefreeencyclopedia. There are only 2 Spiritual Kingdom belief systems operating among us.

For many years he was popular as he expanded government service and public works. In 1930, Italy invaded Ethopia and Albania, and in 1939 made an alliance with Adolf Hitler, of Nazi Germany. Italy's failures in the war led to Mussolini being removed from government.

In June of 1940, Mussolini led Italy (as dictator-ruling with absolute power) into World War II and when the war ended, 3 years later he was arrested, removed, tried and incarcerated (or executed).

8. **Idi Amin** – was from Africa (but studied within the British colonial regiment and subject to strict discipline and control)

What's in a name. Well, why would they call this man the following, if it did not indicate what he does and what he is about:

Idi Amin, Dada Oumee. AKA, Big Daddy.
ADA 'Butcher of Uganda, Africa. (for his despotic/tyrant rule and the most notorious)
AKA 'Conqueror of the British Empire.
AKA 'Lord of All the Beasts.......

They say and rightly so, that he left Uganda a legacy of blood thirsty killings and economic mismanagement. They say that he was neither well educated nor particularly intelligent. But he had a peasant cunning which put him ahead of his clever opponent. They say he also possessed a kind of animal magnetism. Which is seemingly used to obtain and entertain casual women (he liked bordellos or brothels), concubines and he had 6 wives at one time. And it seems he had problems with repeated infections cured of venereal disease. On the other hand, he used his animal magnetism, with his sadistic skills, when he wanted to dominate.

It seems he also felt, he was selected by God to walk with kings, prime ministers and felt he was directed by god/God in a mystic dream to humble them. And the foreign secretary of Great Britain, would be one Amin would cause to grovel to Kamala, to plead for a British residence life. Yet, scripture teaches:

> …..and what doth the Lord require of thee, but to do justly and to love mercy and walk humbly with thy God. Micah 6.8.

Another concern that arises is that Idi Amin payed attention to his dreams on 2 different occasions, each dream indicating and/or revealing how to either check someone (or put them in their place) and the other time he had a vivid dream showing him how to kill someone which he shared with his men before they carried out the assignation. Lets not forget the enemy also tried to pursuade Jesus in a vision to bow down to Him. Only Jesus was not tempted or persuaded in the least bit. He understood spiritual kingdoms.

Idi Amin grew up with Islam observing bloodshed and violence. Did he pick up their "god" spirit activity. Jesus came that we may have life and it is satan that comes to kill, steal and destroy lives. If Islam's "god" was the only spirit "god" he was around and aware of, how could he know another God. Why, would he call on any other "god" but the Islam "god". When people assume there is only one spirit "god" they often don't feel a need to even wonder if there is another. God is a spirit, but not every spirit acting out.

There are 2 spiritual kingdom activities operating among us and corresponding speech, activity, discernment and revelation to go with it. In other words God is not "every" spirit activity. Neither did Jesus receive everything that every spirit spoke to Him. The bible teaches us to submit to God and resist the devil (spirit activity) Lk 4.5-8. But it seems like people have learned to do just the opposite. This is not only error, a lot of people are suffering because a lot of people are following "spirit voices" activity contrary to scripture, spirits of a different spiritual kingdom, seemingly because they do not know enough truth and/or are not being trained how to correctly nor resist dark spirit activity, in Jesus name. James 4.7. 2Tim 2.15. Tim 1.10. Corin. 14.10. Like Idi Amin, and Charles Manson, they behaved as if you are just suppose to let any "spirit activity" work in and through their life to hurt others and don't even seem to question it. The bible also teaches us that those who err in spirit shall learn doctrine. And again, once a person becomes too spiritually affected, there conscious becomes seared.

Estimates from the Int'l Commission of Jurists in Geneva, said that he killed not less than 80,000 to 300,000 people. Another estimate by Amnesty Int'l say that the numbers are more like 500,000. He is also remember for being responsible for the "Turkana Massacre".

Idi Amin's reign to terror seem to continue with this need to order the killings of anyone who stood in his way or who witnessed any of his killings. He went on a rampage of killing leaders and prime ministers who supported Obote's government, like a killing spree. Almost similar to Josef Stalin.

Born in 1925, Idi Amin's father spent most of his life in southern Sudan, with the KaKwas, who were Islams. Where Idi observed violence and shedding of blood. Sudan's homicide rate is still one of the highest in Africa. Now, the Sudanese are clearing the area, by turning some of the Africans to radical Arabs causing them to kill other African native tribes to make room for the Arabs. www.witnessinggenocideinsuddan-60minutes.

Towards the end of his life he (Idi Amin) suffered with syphilis, causing brain damage, he would begin to draw more attention to himself when he would begin to kill people internationally. However, it seems like his "spiritual illness" or disease which seemed to begin to manifest when he was promoted to a commissioned officer, in 1962, is when he gave the order that lead to the, " Turkana Massacre." When spirits manifest they will always reveal its spirit kingdom initiatives and agenda. He seemed to have a lot of "spirit" manifestations which no one seemed to recognize. People seem to let spirit illnesses and diseases run their course, which according to satan's spirit kingdom system is to:

Kill, Steal and Destroy. Jn 10.10. Rev 16.10.

What is very interesting, is that Idi Amin seemed to upset Vladimir, who said that Africans have a _history_ of _cannibalism._ However, from my research, study and the attacks I have suffered to get this writing out for the Lord, it seems the concern is a bit deeper than cannibalism. What is being revealed is that it seems more like, the Africans have been spiritually targeted _and still are being spiritually exploited_ (like there is no one else to practice on) by those in dark spirit professions, spiritual perpetrators which is also what is behind the genocide, slave trade and sex trade, any race confusions and homosexual confusion and it is why they have suffered undevelopment and why help has been far and few between.

And now, some of these spiritual perpetrators that are and/or were operating in Africa are now operating in America also and is a big reason many are suffering spiritual confusion and physical ailments among us. People are not being trained to resist dark spirit activity, they are going to the doctor, for spiritual symptoms that are transcending into the natural. It is why they can't hear and/or retain the teaching of the cross. They are being spiritually distracted often unaware. It is an inside job. Spiritual perpetrators are working under radar, causing havoc and much spiritual confusion even within and among cultures causing many to think the "voices" they are hearing is God, if so where is the unity. Where is the message of the cross. Where is mercy and forgiveness.

Many need to be trained on how to discern and then resist dark spirit manifestations and/or presence of darkness. Therefore, it is necessary for people to know the word to a greater degree and learn how to release themselves on a regular basis from spirit impurities and defilement and spirit violations and intrusions of uninvited dark spirit life activity being brought on by those in dark spirit professions often found in community-often unaware, if not we'll get more individual hate crimes being spiritually provoked and mass suicides within cultures, because of demonic henchmen who are quietly spearheading satan's dark spirit kingdom initiatives and agenda among us. We need more united prayer among and within cultures going 24 hours in every city. Lord, help us pray in one accord wherever we are according to your word in Jesus name. www.masterpieceofconfusion.idiamin.

Idi Amin began to lean on his childhood Islam faith, as fanaticism towards the end of his life, which is recorded that this did not please the Islams. Maybe they did not want anyone to know he was a "product" of their spiritual cultural influence, like the radical African Arabs are now. And the now rising Latino Muslims. DVD: "The New Barbarians", by Caryl Matrisciana, at 1800.897.5080. www.caryl@carylmatrisciana.com or 301141 Antelope Rd. Suite, D228. Menifee, CA 92584.

They say he gave no interviews and stayed close to home. He liked to watch sporting events, attend gym sessions and do aimless shopping. They say he lived a selfish life that had no redeeming qualities. A soldier and politician. Born around 1925 and died August 16, 2003.

People group affects, influences and symptoms of spirit-domination (and its affect on society).

1. **Brief Account of Witchcraft Activity** *(before Salem)*

After witch craft hysteria began occurring in Switzerland, Scotland, Europe, France, England and Germany, persecution began to arise (not against the church) but those seemingly involved causing witchcraft activity as if it were a "spiritual fad" sweeping across the land began to take form as crimes against humanity. A period that seemed to rise to the forefront during 420, to approximately 1692. After this period, this witchcraft activity seemed to move from one side of the Atlantic to the other side, as it began to rise again in the Salem area in 1692.

So you could say that since the documentation of witch craft in 400 began with St. Augustine has never really stopped but seems to continue to look for places to operate, nor can it be hidden even though it uses spiritual means to ultimately commit crimes against humanity and society itself. There is a pattern. It is a spiritual operation. A form of dark spirit activity that continues to be measured by the harm, hurt and uninvited spiritual invasions and interruption of our natural lives they continue to seek to affect or find expression. 1 Pet 5.8. Until the area they are operating in has had enough and begins to drive them out from literally attacking and destroying humanity and society itself, like an assignment.

It's what they do. This is a part of the operation of darkness by those in allegiance to it and/or by those being spiritually forced into its dark spirited service. Some are spiritual POW's, again revealing the need to learn how to release oneself from spirit impurities, defilement and spirit violations and which can become a part of our spiritual warfare, literally learning how to spiritually and naturally protect ourselves and our children from being *taken* by those in dark spirited professions. This is seriously rising in America.

It wasn't until after King James was on his way to Scotland, to meet his wife to be, Princess Anne of Denmark, who ran into trouble trying to meet with King James due to a bad storm that changed their plans, causing them to take refuge in Norway. The wedding finally took place in Kronborg Castle in Denmark. After a long royal honeymoon, the royal newlyweds continue to encounter trouble on the seas. The ship's captain blamed it on witches. Such is the seeming paradox that many may find it hard to sympathize with those who find themselves targeted and attacked by sorcery/witchcraft activity, until it happens to them, trying to find help is another aspect of their nightmare. It literally takes learning how to fight the good fight of faith, when one is being subject to witchcraft/occult activity and it is another way they can gain the ability to spirit force others into dark spirit service. It can be devastating, to say the least. They would make you think, with their constant spirit attacking, that they are not subject to the name or blood of Jesus. That's the lie because the bible say at the name of Jesus every knee will bow. Phil 2.10. Remember when Moses had to deal with witch craft, sorcery and the occultic activity of Pharoah? When, 6 Danish women confessed to having caused the storms that bedeviled King James, he began to take witchcraft seriously. By the time King James reached Scotland, he was paranoid (which is exactly some of the things witchcraft try to cause or create in those they have targeted) which caused him to authorize torture of suspected witches. One of the largest witch hunts in British history. He would begin to address witch craft activity with prosecutorial abuses, which in affect abated witch-hunting somewhat. www.ahistoryofwitchcraftpersecutions.

What is interesting is that they say that the Salem Witch Trials were a result of fear of those who had no safeguard and/or protection from those who accused them falsely and of the young girls who appeared to be too spiritually affected by spirit life intrusion and therefore could have been spiritually compelled or driven to accuse others of witchcraft, but seemingly were the ones who needed spiritual release and healing from spirit impurities, defilement and spirit violations of others, which without, can easily lead to accusations of others, due to a type of spirit intrusions or spirit domination.

All of which are biblical symptoms of dark spirit activity. And another reason for all to gain the ability to release one's self from spirit impurities (which would include emotionalism), defilement and spirit violations of other. The only true safeguards in dealing with spirit life activity is realizing how to make the word of God a part of your life and gaining the ability to release oneself from spirit impurities, defilement and spirit violations of other (in need of learning how to release themselves from spirit defilement which means repentance from ignorance and accepting and believing in Jesus Christ and His complete work at Calvary and for such a time as this. People need to be more aware of how to apply our spiritual safeguards in Christ because of the great price paid at Calvary that backs our authority in Christ Jesus. Lk 8.29. Rev. 12.10. Gal. Chpt.5.

See: www.illusionsinthecrucible   www.seewitchtrials.
www.inthecruciblethesalemwitchtrialswerearesultoffear   www.thecrucible

Radio

There was a radio program that aired on a FM/90.3 radio station in Ohio, in October, 2010, with the American History Guys from Virginia.

Part of their program would include a call-in segment. When I caught the end of the program, they were discussing whether or not witchcraft really existed and/or does it still exist and how it seemed like those who appeared to be witches, even though they were in community or society, didn't really seem to be a part of community or society. Etc., etc.,…..

My first thought was surely if witches are included in the bible, they must exist. 2Chr 33.6. Gal 5.20. 2Ki 9.22. Nah 3.4.

My second thought was, do we think that **everyone** that is or that could be considered a witch, was or is one voluntarily? Do we realize that like eunuchs can be made or born, that witches can be also. Usually eunuchs will be one or decide to be one on their own, it may be a rare to nonexistent, that one is forced into being a eunuch. Mt. 19.12.

But this is definitely not so when it comes to all witches and turning them (people into witches) seems to be a strategy of some of those involved in dark spirited professions, especially if it involves a saint, who may not realize how to resist dark spirit pursuits. And in many cases, especially if the saint happens to be a prophet. Some in dark spirit professions target them to spiritually defile them to either discourage them and/or to mar their witness for Christ or, as I said literally pull them out of church circles and community into the operation of darkness if they can. And it would be great if churches could learn to reach out not only to the prophets but others in their church, to make sure people are learning how to release their spirit lives and/or the condition of their spirits from any spirit life impurities, defilement and possible spirit violations of others (those in dark spirited professions) and this in itself could prove to be a safeguard for churches and church leaders desiring to preserve their church environments from spiritual contamination. May this writing help to minister to possibly help churches function in this area also, because keeping our spirit lives free from dark spirit pursuits can become a part of our spiritual warfare. Eph 6.11.

And the next question that comes to mind that with all of the evil spirit activity rising among us, what is to stop evil crossing anyone's path and/or trying to camp out in anyone's life? How do we prevent another Witch Salem Hunt experience?

Do we realize, whether we can perceive it or not doesn't seem to be the issue when you have witnesses, that there are sorcerers and/or false prophets of the heavenlies (of the heavenlies) that have been spiritually elevated into a high spirit realm and position for their work and activity for the operation of darkness _among us_. Who have the ability to so spiritually dog-attack a life (once they can get close enough to befriend their subject/target) then, they will proceed to spiritually infest a soul's spirit life by trafficking and channeling spirits into a person's life and at the same time spiritually cause influence others even unaware, because many think any voice or unction concerning others they hear, especially in community is the true voice God-there is no discernment-not biblical or spiritual) even cause longtime friendships, that were in their subject's life to begin to reject their subject/victim for their selfish dark purposes. Perpetrating, provoking and causing a spiritual ostracization that will then transcend into the subjects natural environment making it seem like they are loners. No, these are signs of someone under spiritual attack and they need prayer support, not amazement and curiosity of why they appear to be distant from community. I have yet to see serious support, even prayer support for these people being targeted by hell, who are confident enough in their God that rally around these with prayer until hell backs off. Rom 15.1. Part of the concern or reason this is not happening is because people are in need of learning how to release themselves even from spirit personalities that would keep them from reaching out to others. Many need to learn how to release themselves from spirit impurities called "attitudes" and "vanities" etc., that would hinder this kind of sacrifice. In other words gaining the ability to spiritually release our selves will also help us to get pass ourselves because God needs us! He so loved us that He sent His Son to die for our sins. He can't get us ready without our help or participation.

These people, as a part of the operation of darkness, can and will literally pull a person out or away from society (and their family-there is no demonic graces in families in dark spirit operation and they will cause family to suffer if that's what it takes to hold on to you). Scary but true. This could also put a new twist on the Jim Jones and Charles Mason's situation, especially since they were both in the San Francisco area at one time or another and one event happened right after the other.

Similarly there is one, that I know of, who holds himself out to be a servant of light and he literally works out of the Upton, California area, but he is operating territorially in Ohio big time, spiritually defiling it, causing much devastation, to many unaware, because he knows how to hi-jack the souls of men by spiritually infiltrating innocent lives , using trance states to spirit stalk, harass and spiritually infest the lives of others with unwanted spirit activity. Do people realize this is happening? And so our nation allows him this freedom under the protection of "freedom of religion". Ohio is not the only State he is causing spiritual confusion that is transcending into much trouble in the natural. Because he seems to spiritually persecute, defile his subject/victims all day, making you think, he could be stuck in the spirit realm, working full-time, bringing families and communities and cities into dark spirit realms. So where are people's spiritual safeguards in a society that does not seem to know how to deal with spiritual crimes until after the hurt, pain, death and destruction against an individual has run its course?

There was a guy, in Ohio, at the end of 2009, that literally killed approximately 11 women and buried them in his yard. This was clearly a man not in his right mind. Ok, but people do not go crazy by themselves. For anyone to behave unsoundly there would have to be some level of spirit activity causing the unsound behavior. www.sowellmurders. www.elizabethsmartabduction.

See <u>End Time Mind Control</u>, by Win Worley. Ps. 103.20. Jn. 10.10. Mt 4.6. Mt 25.41. Ps 55.3. Gal 3.1. Acts 8.9,11. Tim 4.1. 2Tim 3.13. Eze 13.10. 2Ki 21.9.

The website for The American History Guys (could be in this title) or www.backstoryradio.org.

2. <u>KKK</u>

The Ku Klux Klan is said to be America's oldest, most visible and most in-famous "hate" group. Originally formed in December, 1965, …..following the American Civil War. Vigilante groups, such as the Former confederate soldiers and white sympathizers joined together in order to "undermine" political and social reforms, primarily those which involved the greater political participation of freed slaves.

> Hate is a spirit personality and without proper release can turn into a spiritual force against their subject and can also be viewed as a type of spiritual bondage by those clearly affected by this spirit disease called and expressed by hate, in which sooner or later the Lord will judge. Exo 20.5. Acts 22.8. Acts 26.14. Ecc 12.14.

> And this is the condemnation that has come into the world and men loved darkness rather than light because their deeds were evil. Jn 3.19. Gal, Chpt. 5.

They developed a bizaar mystique due to their apparel which included white robes and titles such as, Imperial Wizard and Exalted Cyclops and claimed to represent an "Invisible Empire". Likewise, a more modern right-wing group came on the scene called Moral Majority, which claimed to represent a significant, <u>but silent</u>, majority of Americans. There are only 2 spiritual kingdoms operating among us. No matter the religion, non-religious, group or spirit belief system.

> Like those in the operation of God's Kingdom will try to label or entitle their service to the Lord appropriately, likewise those whose spirit life begin to manifest will also select a label or title seemingly appropriate for their service to who they holding out to serve because when spirits manifest they will always reveal their spirit kingdom's initiatives and agenda. Always!

> Scripturally speaking, there is nothing hidden that shall not be revealed. Corin. 4.5.

> Therefore, those revealing themselves to be in dark spirited systems are only showing the areas they are in need of healing (or literally where spirits caused them to get stuck); because God created us in His image and He <u>does not</u> operate against Himself. This also reveals if one is operating in a dark or light of Christ discernment. Gen 1.27. Jn 3.21.

Jim Crows laws would follow to ensure the political and social domination of whites and literally eliminated basic civil rights for blacks.

After the original Ku Klux Klan disbanded, it was restored again during the 1920's only this time in opposition to Catholic and Jewish immigration to the United States. The commonality between these targets and the blacks who were originally targeted is that they were, in a since, competed economically with the low-income whites, who were the primary constituents of the KKK. The most recent KKK incarnation started as a reaction to the Civil Rights movement during the 1960s. However, the original Klan used lynching's and midnight raids in order to intimidate blacks, which bombed churches and murdered civil rights workers, only this time it did not have enough political support to get away with it.

> When darkness secures any grip whether upon a individual soul, church, culture group, movement or government, it hates to let go and will continue endlessly to seek reentrance. They are like leach spirits (reflective in the people they can work through for harm. Pet 5.8. Acts 28.5. When some of the people tried to escape Jim Jones camp they were ordered to be killed.

Wasn't this pretty close if not the activity that helped or tried to birth genocide within our American government?

The Ku Klux Klan had over 5 million members by 1925. In some states they had quite a lot of political power. However, political exposes and internal strife, along with sex scandals helped to end this episode. Does it seem like when the enemy could not get our President, at the time (Lincoln) to support slavery, he began to rise up through culture and extremist to push his dark spirit initiatives and agendas. Let us continue to pray for removal of slavery and healing among the African nation and the offenders need to be healed and released also in Jesus name.

What is interesting is that even though the Ku Klux Klan group is primarily an American group, they have been able to redevelop and reduplicate themselves internationally in such places as Great Britain and even larger Klan organizations have extensive contracts and continuing working relationships with <u>other racists hate groups</u> (like the religious groups infiltrating Africa an ongoing spiritual aggression always seeking to express itself in our worls and the people need to learn how to release themselves from it because the enemy works in the masses individually. Turning radical African Arabs against their own African tribes), in particular the neo-Nazi groups in Austria, as well as Germany. How great is prayer needed for those being spiritually consumed by dark spirit hate activity. Some people can release themselves. Some need help. For more information see: <u>ww.kukluxklan</u>.

Today it is said that the KKK has been greatly weakened, yet their views have become even more radical. They <u>*seem*</u> to consider themselves a Christian organization and base their doctrines upon their own reading of the bible. 2Tim4.3-4. This writing indicates that they (the KKK) have a desire to reconstruct the United States along biblical (OT-mostly) lines to help them establish a "white dominated theocracy". Isn't that what Islam did, decide to use only the OT? Whether they chose to use the OT or no testament, there is still only 2 spiritual kingdom activities operating in the earth. No matter the religion or non-religious beliefs and every religion and/or non-religion will fit into one or the other. Spiritual healing and release is needed. *Please add these to your prayer list.*

If Jesus died for the sins of the world and scriptures reveal that love fulfils the law, how do you get a <u>*"white dominated theocracy"*</u> out of that? Jesus has not changed. He is the same today, yesterday and forever. Heb13.8. Jn 13.15. Eph 6.7. 1Jn 3.15-16. 1Jn4.11. Just like there are only 2 spiritual kingdom activities operating among us, there are corresponding revelatory activities too. Mt 4.5-7.Rom1.18.

3. Charles Manson

Born in Cincinnati, Ohio, November, 1934 to a 16 year old girl, who had run away from home at 15 and who spent her time drinking too much with periods of time in jail.

This left Charles Manson, to spend his youth at various relatives' homes, at various (special) reform schools and boys homes. By 9, Charles had begun stealing and he was involved in burglary.

(Even a child is known by his doings….Prov 20.1. Prov 22.6)

By the age of 23, between being in and out of prison, Charles Manson, was married twice and by this time had fathered 2 children (both boys) by 2 different marriages (No, not at the same time).

Charles Manson learned music in prison and became obsessed with it. Once released from prison in 1967, he headed to San Francisco, CA, with drugs and a guitar. In 1968, others would begin to follow Manson and they drove to southern California. Charles Manson had one song recorded by, "The Beach Boys", otherwise his music career never took off, which would ultimately upset him.

Then Charles and his followers would move to a place north of San Fernando Valley, called Spahn Ranch, which ultimately turned into a cult. Defined here as:

> When others become a part of a system of religious worship or ritual, where people devotedly, (or could be spiritually drawn into the devotion, which is a part of spirit life activity) attach themselves to a person or principle….(which also could be considered a type of idolatry; which is an excessive reverence for a devotion to a person or thing). Scripture teaches us to flee idolatry.

Not recognizing "spirit" life activity nor "spiritual influences", Charles would begin to take, or would begin to collect certain information from various religions to form his own philosophy (another form and/or activity of an unrestrained spirit life). It is recorded that he used religious information to manipulate his followers (who also did not seemingly understand biblical spirit life activity). 2Pet 3.17.

Charles Manson, was able to release another song called "Helter Skelter" (which means in haste, confused and disorderly) and he believed this song would predict a upcoming race war (this is a type of dark spirit revelation, because it has no biblical support for soundness). Titus 1.9-11. Titus1.15-16.

> Whenever spirits manifest, even in a song, it will reveal its spiritual kingdom initiatives and agendas. Rev 16.10. Jn 10.10.

There can <u>only be</u> 2 kinds of spiritual revelation **because** *there are only 2 spiritual types of spirit activity, revealing only 2 spiritual kingdom operations in the earth that would either biblically express spiritual soundness or spiritual unsoundness, revealing what spiritual kingdom activity is in operation.* <u>There is no spiritual confusion</u> in heaven as to who is spiritually operating in God's spiritual kingdom whether in the heaven or in the earth (what's the difference) whenever, the "spirit fruit" it produced, the bible reveals you know them by their fruit (all fruit whether we see it is first being spiritually produced). The enemy works overtime in finding ways to cause people to fear, using spiritual illusions of fear is a part of dark spirit life activity. Causing one culture to become fearful of another (using spirit illusions and imaginations) is another effective tool of spirit life activity, however the bible reveals how to handle any spirit illusion and imagination, *<u>not by giving place to it</u>* but by resisting it, because God has not given us the spirit of fear…. 2Tim1.7. Phil 4.8. When the enemy rises against another culture, (like he would any family member or person at work) it is a type of spiritual warfare to bring division and disharmony and therefore indicates the reason to resist it because if you do not the enemy will use that place (in your mind) to destroy those whom dark spirit activity is targeting in your mind. People (our nation) need to be taught more effectively, the reality of how to not let dark spirit life prevail against them (their friendships, relationships, family, community, wherever darkness is trying to destroy). Most warring is being done in the flesh because people are not being taught spirit life properly causing the people (spirit life activity are using) to become more of the problem (through ignorance, innocence and spiritual blindness). The bible is a spirit book. Jn 6.63. You need spirit words when dealing with dark spirit life activity. The "Cross" and the "blood" Jesus shed is a Spirit thing that will protect and guard your life if you hold it up. If you apply it! Jn 1.1-5. Col 1.20. Jn 6.63.

> "…Knowing that the law….is for………....and if there be any other thing at is contrary to sound doctrine". Tim 1.8-8-10. Speak the things which become sound doctrine. Titus 2.1. Mt. 12.33. The enemy's is always to kill, steal and destroy. All he needs is one soul to (ignorant of spirit life activity) accomplish this. Jn 10.10. Jn 6.63.

God is not every spirit life activity happening among us!

Manson believed, that this "race war" (illusional and imaginary not biblical race war) would occur in the summer of 1968. Where he would again "imagine" that blacks would rise up and slaughter all white people. 2Cor 10.5.

> There is a need for people to recognize when spirit activity is rising against their soul, body and spirit life and then esist it like the plague. 2Cor 10.5. James 4.7.

Charles Manson, told his followers they would be saved by their going underground, literally travel to an underground city of gold that is by Death Valley.

> Dark spirit life has the ability to either spiritually draw or lead people to you and/or cause them to reject you. It is a spirit activity under the bewitchment and/or seducing spirit heading and should be resisted. One way to do this is by not lingering in crowds because this spirit activity can affect people in greater ways and/or keep a list of authority scriptures that you can quietly bind spirit activity when you need to be around the public. This is done in Jesus name. Phil 2.10. Gal 3.1. 2Tim3.13. Prov 12.26. Acts 8.11.

When this Armageddon, Manson predicted did not occur, he told his followers that there was a need to reveal to the blacks "how to do it"! Lk 6.39.

> Yet, scripture reveals that we do not war after the flesh. 2Corin 10.3. Scripture also reveals That we are to cast down (spirit) imaginations and bring every though into captivity. (Neither of which, Charles nor his followers took heed to (scripture will help protect us from dark spirit activity and tragedies) when we learn to comprehend that there are only 2 spiritual kingdom activities operating among us. Dark spirits are intelligent spirit beings and even they recognize who is spiritually and biblically blind and/or ignorant and they will proceed accordingly). Can we see what happens when the blind lead the blind and how we can learn to recognize by scripture when someone is getting "off"; or is off, it would be because of a level of spirit activity being allowed to operate without resistance which will produce spirit domination and whenever spirit life activity manifest, it manifests only to reveal its spirit kingdom initiatives and/or agenda.

> All dark spirit life initiatives and agenda will always lead ultimately to kill, steal and destroy. Those who are in need of spiritual release and healing will operate, with a passion and/or lust to harm, kill, steal and/or destroy, and will not be able to help it until they find release from the spirit causing it. Dark spirit life, is a type of spirit disease that keeps degrading a souls thinking and thought processes (then the body will follow) that we must learn and/or be taught how to conquer it through the grace and mercy of God (though Jesus Christ) or be destroyed by it.

Manson then directed 4 of his followers to go to a certain address and kill the people inside. This residence happened to be a man that was previously was not able to help Manson in his music career. A man named Terry Melcher (who happened to be Doris Day's son). However, this man (Melcher) no longer lived in this house. The house occupied by others (who happened to be an actress, her baby and her director husband) who did not even know of Manson. On August 9, 1969, 4 of Manson's followers were ordered (by Manson) to murder those in the house. Can we see how Manson seemingly lost the battle of imagination that chambered in his mind to hurt the person that could not help in his music career. We must resist continually enemy advances in the soul (mind, subconscious and unconscious) to draw us in the dark spirit realm thinking and thought processes until the enemy is able to act out or express darkness through or in our lives (or innocent others). Lord, help us.

Once the trial began, Manson was found guilty of 1st degree murder and <u>conspiracy</u> to commit murder. On March 29, 1971, Manson received the death sentence. But, before Manson was sentenced, California had outlawed the death sentence, where Manson was tried. Charles Manson now serves a lifetime sentence and it is said that he has received more mail than any other prisoner in the United States. For more information see: <u>www.charlesmanson-bibliography</u>.

4. **Jim Jones** (Jonestown Massacre).

Approximately 9 years later from the Manson story, the Jonestown Massacre would transpire.

On November 18, 1978, 912 followers of the American cult leader Jim Jones, along with Jim Jones, of Peoples Temple, died in a remote part of the South Africa jungle compound called Jonestown, in British, Guyana. Some were shot. Some were forced to drink poison. Some were able to escape. A revolutionary suicide. A mass-murder suicide.

It is said that many complaints surfaced, regarding the member's families, asking for an investigation around 1977, regarding a man, it seems, that was able to capture San Francisco's liberal elite. A man that had business in San Francisco, like Charles Manson.

Conditions were so bad in British, Guyana that half of the Jonestown members became ill with severe diarrhea and high fevers. (These are also what dark spirit activity can cause through men in allegiance with darkness, using their human spirits, working through a trance state, to gain the dark ability to attack an individual or people in a more up close and personal way.

This website article, also revealed that, Jones would have compulsions (somewhat like Manson) about conspiracies against him (these are spirit thoughts imposing itself into one mind). He told his followers the time would come when it would be necessary to die by their own hands (where is the soundness in these types of comment. There are places spirit activity is beginning to press its way and express itself through Jim Jones it spiritual kingdom initiatives and agenda concerning Jim Jones and those being pulled into dark spirit realm activity. Manson would also prewar his followers of death to occur(regarding his spirit illusional race war), which should have been biblically resisted in Jesus name, because when spirits manifest they will always reveal their spirit kingdom initiatives and agenda. Always!

Jim Jones and his followers would have "White Night" and/ or a rehearsed state of emergency which was <u>often</u> (to bring others into his "spirit" illusions) declared at the compound and within this context mass-suicide was rehearsed.

Biblical and spiritual analysis would reveal light and truth versus those who err in spirit to signify which spirit kingdom activity was actually in operation. Jn 14.17. Isa 29.24. Jesus said, judge nothing before the time, until the Lord come who will bring to light the hidden things of darkness and will make manifest the counsels of the hearts.... Corin 4.5. Some of the <u>key phrases</u> expressed concerning Jones such as, compulsions, conspiracy and paranoia are really "spirit reactions, terms and/or responses" (or spirit initiative) to the types of spirit activity operating in his life that he needed release from, even the symptoms of severe diarrhea and high fevers, suffered by his followers can be triggered by different levels of spirit activity operating behind the scene, transcending into the natural. With grace I'm trying to say and express that what he needed was some prophetic in Christ to come in and battle and wage war on the level the enemy had found a place. We are in a spirit kingdom age. All of life reveals some level of spirit life activity. Some can be seen. Some cannot, and must be biblically and spiritually (according) to truth be discerned. Scripture reveals that those who err spiritually must learn doctrine (how to apply truth to war against spirit domination on the level it is warring against you... using whoever has been spiritually affected. (Spirit activity always tries to reproduce itself). Jn 14.17. Isa 29.24. Again, depending on what spirit life level one is choosing to operate in or is being "spiritually forced" to operate in by those in need of spiritual release. Jn 6.63. We must always remember that spirit(s) will <u>always</u> manifest to reveal the initiatives and agenda of the spirit kingdom it is operating out of (always). Spirit life never dies and should not be ignored-due the apparent, lasting consequences some of which were biblically developed and revealed in this writing and must according to scripture be cast out, put in its correct biblical place and/or healed by the grace of God. Christian leaders are not exempt, no one is. Just like no one is exempt from death. Heb 9.27.

And as it is appointed unto men once to die, but after this the judgment. Heb 9.27.

Everyone needs a Savior. Everyone will need Salvation. There is only one Lord, our Savior and only one God of our Salvation given to us by the sacrifice of Jesus Christ and His complete work on the Cross.

There is no other Salvation. No other name whereby men must be saved. Acts 4.15.

There is a need to teach people and our nation how to better recognize and understand spirit life activity, for the soundness and spiritual preservation of life and our nation. To know and recognize when our spiritual leaders, as well as when we ourselves, need spiritual release and healing. Jn 8.32. Eph 3.5. There are only 2 spiritual kingdom activities operating among us. Only 2.

Often, people only know how to deal with spirit life activity after the hurt, pain, disaster, tragedy and even death has occurred, <u>*yet there is a lot going on*</u> before this and people are being victimized and spiritually abused, even spiritually *traumatized* by those who have seemed to mastered spirit activity, spirit penetration and trafficking dark spirits into people's lives (or who have fallen prey to dark spirit life activity-<u>affected to the point even they can't help themselves</u>) dark spirit life activity that is causing a major portion of our society's ills and <u>who are not being heard when they do cry out</u> for help, how can they be heard especially when *many churches have also become victims of spirit life abuse activity or are spiritually preyed upon, often unaware*) by those in dark spirit professions and/or the sons and daughters of baal who have learned to blend in with the Church of Jesus Christ (please read Rebecca Browns books), who also are in need of spiritual release and healing if and when they become concerned about their souls. They make a living doing this and these are the growing dark spirit symptom diseases they are helping to manifest in our world. This is the whole point. And we want to label it and/or excuse it by classifying it "freedom of religion". Yet, we have no places of refuge for those being spiritually victimized and who need proper biblical/spiritual training in how to release from their body, soul and spirit lives from what hell is trying to bring, often force into their lives.

Dark spirit activities that transcend into our world, causing bad health, homelessness and broken families, etc, at varying levels and degrees. We are talking spirit life activity, where people can become so affected by intelligent spirit beings with an agenda, that one could not get out of its grip by their self. Jesus said:

For though I should boast somewhat more of our authority which the Lord hath give us for edification and and not for your destruction… 2Cor 10.8. 2Corin 13.10.

> Therefore, when there is any negative religious activity happening among us, how could it be a part of Christ Spirit system kingdom of activity, when He said, I came that you might have life …. He did not come to take life…. however, dark spirit life operates to kill, steal and destroy, therefore to the degree either one of these spirit life activities are operating, is to the degree revealing the level of spirit involvement or grip, and its expression of whether healing is needed and/or how spiritually sound one is in Christ Jesus. There is no spiritual confusion in heaven as to who is spiritually operating in whose kingdom. Therefore, these spiritual and natural tragedies; like that of Charles Manson and Jim Jones, could have been prevented with a better understanding of spirit life activity. When our society's leaders decides to learn how to recognize those in need of spiritual release and healing from spirit life impurities, defilement and/or spirit violations of others. Doesn't this sound better than continuing to look the other way, when someone is being pursued by hell and then just wait for hell to run its course, and then just write off another spiritual ritual abuse victim (another gynie pig that someone affected by hell caused) because they could not find help. And the demonic cycle and spiritual crimes continue to go unaddressed, because why, O yea, "everyone has a right to freedom of religion" even though it's killing us. Can't we pass on something a little more helpful, to the next generation regarding the matter. Like hope. Like Jesus Christ and Him crucified!

It would take the knowledge of the Spirit life of Christ Jesus, whose sacrifice at Calvary would become our break through. His Cross is a "spirit" thing, a "spiritual kingdom thing" and our salvation for those in need, for those who have been spiritually captured and are now servants of bondage. <u>And</u>

all servants of bondage can do is reproduce itself. This is the work of dark spirit activity. They have a need to reproduce themselves (their dark spirited kingdom in the soul, body and/or spirit lives of men is where they actively seek to express themselves and not necessarily with our permission and this activity have become part of our spiritual warfare when we realize the need and then learn the ability to spiritually release our souls, so that dark spirit life are not free to reproduce itself (his spiritual kingdom) in our body, soul, spirit lives and environments. Even Charles Mason and Jim Jones could be our examples and our reality check concerning the only 2 spiritual kingdom activities operating among us. If it seems like they took lives, it was because they themselves, became subject victims of darkness and were preyed upon by dark spirit life activity, by someone in a dark spirit profession, and this is the person that was spiritually diseased, sick and affected who took those lives. Jim Jones and Charles Manson where their instruments who did not know how to recognize who was spiritually affecting them. And the spiritual perpetrators have moved onto their other victims and prey, operating under our society's radar and laws of the land. And, our society appears to be helping them. What a ongoing tragedy. They have an agenda and we as a society need to recognize and understand this. It's not a "do-do-do-do-do-do-do, flaky, mysterious, can't understand it thing" It is spirit life activity. 2Corin. 11.20. 2Pet 2.19.

> For ye suffer, if a man bring you into bondage.... 2Corin 11.20. 2Pet 2.19.

Scripture reveals that every man's work shall be made manifest, for the day shall declare it, because it shall be revealed by fore and the fire shall try every man's work, of what sort it is. Corin. 3.9-15.

Hopefully, this writing will teach how to recognize those in need (including ourselves) of spiritually healing and how by faith in the complete work of the cross, we can through Christ release ourselves (and those in need) of spirit life impurities, defilement and/or spirit violations of others. Lk 9.1. May the Lord grant us a greater understanding from this writing. Prov. 8.33-34. Prov. 12.1. Prov. 19.20. Prov. 23.12. www.jonestownmassacre. Written by Rick Ross.

5. **Columbine** (May, 1999)

Another example of those affected by dark spirit life activity. What we think and ponder on is important and it is important that we do not let our minds and thoughts run in the wrong direction. The word of God can be very helpful since there are only 2 spiritual kingdoms operating among us. Keeping your mind on the word will seriously keep dark spirits from manifesting in your mind and thinking processes. Only Jesus alone and His truth can keep our souls sound and in peace. There is a need for everyone to gain the ability in realizing the need of how to resist the influences of dark spirit life activity because whenever spirits manifest, they will always reveal their spirit kingdom initiatives and agenda. Always!

In spirit life activity nothing happens by chance. Everyone must locate their spirit life activity. And make sure there is no outside spiritual influences trying to keep one in dark spirit realms and/or activities. If so, they must be resisted before they become strongholds. Other's lives may depend on it, as well as, you own. Lord, may this writing minister your strength, protection and soundness to our youth, in Jesus name!

Individual affects, influences and symptoms of spiritual intrusion and/or spirit-domination (and its affect and influence(s).

Then there are the spiritual symptoms and signs revealing that even our movie stars (as everyday people) have become public spiritual targets, as well, are also in need, of learning how to release themselves from spirit impurities, defilement and spiritual violations of others

1. **Julia Roberts**

Is in the tabloids this year (2010) for her part in the movie, " Eat, Pray & Love". It seems that after doing the movie Julie has fallen in love with the Hindu religion which did not seem to sit well with her husband who was raised Catholic.

Hopefully, we are able to see and comprehend, in this writing, that the bible literally has the potential to reveal the rising and ongoing spirit activity behind the scene. The article goes on to say that Julie is desiring to bring her children also into the Hindu religion (with the spiritual belief system) that goes with it automatically. It is actually spirit life activity (or energy) that can be found to help create and institute any religion it is trying to affect, therefore religion itself is a dark spirit life activity. It is not just enough to generically like religion, one must realize the spirit belief system operating behind and through it, for spiritual and natural protection because spirit life (not of Christ) will try to transcend into our world one person at a time through religion. Jesus said:

> Thou shall have no other gods before me..... Dt 5.7.
> (Is not a suggestion, it is a commandment)

Do we recognize and spiritually that devotion to any other spirit god whether done or engage through meditation, yoga or peeping, etc., will eventually lead to idolatry and spirit domination and by giving them place the spirit itself will begin to manifest, eventually as a strong hold in the place and area you give them (or that those in dark professions force upon). Realized or not does not seem to be the issue. O Lord, help us understand the reality of spirit life activity, in Jesus name.

The article also revealed that Julie also seemed to enjoy and engage in the spiritual activity called, "peeping". Scripture reveals:

And when they shall say unto you. Seek unto them that have familiar spirits and unto wizards that peep and that mutter, *should not a people seek unto their God?*.... Isa 8.19.

Do we realize that "spirit domination" is what is causing a lot of unnecessary deaths in all societies and in our nation and many (too many) are feeding into dark spirited system activities by participation? <u>Lord, have mercy, until we can get it right!</u> *Lord, help us get it right!* www.julieroberts.com.

May this writing also speak to and help give encouragement and a greater understanding to:

Marie Osmond/Magazine, 2010. Michael Douglas/Magazine, 2010. Glen Beck/Globe, 11, 2010, Lindsay Lohan/Magazine, 2010, Whitney Houston/Magazine, 2010 and Mel Gibson/Magazine, 2010 and I want to mention Uma Thurman because some dark spirit activity will attack inwardly (physically or mentally) and some will attack outwardly, like the same guy that seemed to have a unnatural interest in Ms. Thurman, to the point a particular person was following her around.

I do believe Tyra Banks (TV Host and Model) had to deal with a similar situation and from what I have seen, this can also be interpreted as, methods that dark spirit activity uses to find a way into people's lives to begin to affect their lives, ironically like the person themselves have been spiritually affected, spirits (through its spirit activity) like to reproduce themselves, like kind, in the lives of others (it's a biblical principle). Gen. 1.24 & 27. And my last, but not least concern is for Christina Hendricks/ Movie: Mad Men, Globe, 2010, article mentioned how she not only is attractive to men but seemingly to women that the article reveals are hitting on her. Like her husband in the article thinks it odd, so do I, from a more spiritual/biblical perspective. It appears that many women as well as men among us are need of spiritual cleansing, release and healing from spirit impurities, defilement and spirit violations of others. It seem s that one of the most noted characteristics that women and/or men alike have been spiritually affected is when, spirit life start using the people among us to try to affect and infest others. Some reveal they have been spiritually affected when they engage another with unnatural "spooky" type stares and/or some who are spiritually affected will just oddly have a unnatural interest to just come around those "that the spirits in their lives are literally drawing them to" and they will just stand there like a statue, like they are lost. Because even those who are in allegiance with spirit activity realize that all they have to do is go around the person their spirit is leading them too so the spirit can release and literally attach themselves to the person or subject of interest. So I would say to all who are have these types of questionable experiences to learn how to release yourself from spirit impurities, defilement and spirit violations of others found in community. May this writing help give you understanding in this area. I pray this writing find its way to you. Acts 8.9 & 11. 2Tim 3.13.

We are talking spirit life activity, and its affect on humanity. It's not about religion (sometimes I wish it were that simple). It's about maintaining your spiritual liberties and soundness in Christ Jesus. Which will transcend into our natural world as wholeness and peace in Jesus that passes all understanding. Jesus Christ and Him crucified for our sakes. He is the best that this life and the one to come can offer! Lord, help your people find You in this life and the reality of You in their world even in the truth that teaches us that they that call upon the name of the Lord shall be saved.

Summary

Lord, I pray that if you can bring the nations together as a world community for global warming, I pray that you would give them a greater cause or reason for them to come together, that repentance and remission of sin be preached among all nations as a world community *to receive* the only one true living God, Your sacrifice and mercy that You have provided for our salvation, and the salvation of all nations, Jesus Christ and Him crucified. That we may all realize that life is by You, from You and only about You!

Lord, be glorified again and lifted up before all nations, in Jesus name. Lk 24.47. Lk Phil 3.16. www.witnessinggenocideinsudan-60minutes-cbsnew. www.religioustolerance.org. www.christiansolidarityinternational.

The purpose of spirit molding

God created us in His image, therefore everything we are made up of concerning the body, soul and spirit life is to glorify God. Today, we find many denominations, organizations and groups teaching and supporting their own type of spirit life activity that does not give glory to God, some realize it, and some are unaware. 2Corin 4.3-6. Part of the reason seems to be attributed to all of the gifts of God either not operating at all or not being permitted and/or operating properly. Corin 7.7. People are literally being subdued and/or seemingly bewitched by the "spirit of the denomination, spirit of the organization, culture or work group, society to which one belongs and/or lodge, etc., even before the people realize that they have been caught up in spirit life activity with its own "spirit belief system". Almost a monkey see, monkey do-thing (no offense intended); it's just what is actually happening. Spirit life activity is being taught and transferred, without the biblical soundness to accompany it. Job 10.22. Ps 43.7. Corin. 6.20. Rom 8.29.

The imagination which is a part of the soul life (also considered a part of the soul's chamber) is supposed to be used only to commune and fellowship with God's Spirit life in Christ to help us operate and function properly in His Spirit kingdom. Dt. 5.7. Not doing so intentionally, even unintentionally can bring or cause spiritual confusion, spiritual corruption and/or spirit domination. Corin 14.33. 2Pet 2.19.

Imagination can be defined as: The act or power of forming mental images of what is not present. The bible does not teach us to be led away with any spirit imagination but to submit to God resist the devil (spirit activity) and they will flee, in Jesus name. James 4.7. Gen 6.5-6. *********

Form can be defined as: Shape. Structure. Mold. A particular kind, type….Arrangement. Style. A way of doing something. A customary or convenient way of acting. Ritual…

Mold can defined as: A frame on which something is modeled. A pattern. To make in or on a mold. To form. To shape.

God has created us in His image, though His work in us and through our lives often goes undetected, seemingly by most, not only in our world, but in prior worlds before us, since the fall of man, it has been the job of principalic activity to run interference in God's plans, purposes and destiny of our lives. Principalities have learned to reshape, reframe and remold God's plans and purposes through prideful, rebellious, hellish, etc., patterns of thinking (through and by a series of mind and/or spirit intrusions) to the point we begin to take and accept them as our own. To the degree, it could grieve the Lord and His Spirit. If we do not catch it and then refocus on the Lord when the enemy tries to side track us and/or run interference. James 4.7. 2Corin. 10.5. Eph 4.30. Eph 5.10-11. Thus revealing an important aspect, of engaging in daily bible time with the Lord.

> And God saw that the wickedness of man was great in the earth and that every imagination of the thoughts of his heart was only evil continually (Dark spirits will work continually to try to erode your thought/thinking patterns). It is part of the of the operation of darkness. Biblically, it's what they do!

> And it repented the Lord that He had made man on the earth and it grieved Him at His heart! Gen 6.5-6.

Where principalities and demon activities are trying to create dark spirit images and mindsets through demonic spirit mind forming and molding, thought and thinking patterns; the Lord desires that we allow our fellowship with Him, through much study, devotion and praise time and service to Him as a strategy and method to draw near to the Lord to off-set what darkness is trying to do. How else would the people of God learn the ways of the Lord and gain the spiritual ability to withstand the enemy, if they have a demonic mindset? I heard one dear sister say of the Lord that some of His people are connected to the church in the earth, but are not connected to Him in the Spirit (and His Spirit life activity)! God is a Spirit, but not every spirit! Jn. 4.24. Rom 8.6. Phil 2.5. 1Jn 1,2,5,6,8. Jn 15.26. See: www.overview of the differences between satanism/witchcraft.

Since there are only 2 spiritual kingdoms operating among us. One Kingdom operates in a system of good the other kingdom operates in a system of evil. Therefore the frame (or framework) by which principalities use to reform and remold the mind, thinking and thought…..etc., process is evil in nature. Evil is used as a pattern (or blueprint) by which all dark spirit life operates in and is used to identify and locate those (people or other dark spirit life) operating within its system (which can also be viewed as dark discernment). Evil is their way of doing things, their style, ritual, structure and witchcraft system of governing, spirit belief system and evil helps to create their spiritual custom, and dark spirit traditions. Just as evil can also be and/or carry with it a presence; there is a presence and/or power that comes and/or manifest when one actually carries out the evil thoughts and/or plays out (behaviorally) the evil thinking in one's life. Therefore, to avoid a dark spirited presence from occurring and/or developing in one's life, one must first biblically correct any wrong thinking and/or thought patterns (in this writing the bible sets the standard for "right" behavior, if it is our desire to please the Lord and if one is desiring to be a candidate for His blessings, protection and goodness. Sometimes spiritual release is needed in the appropriate root area, before one could even gain the ability to better and/or biblically correct their thoughts, in Jesus name. Otherwise, the enemy will continue to build dark spirited strongholds in one's mind. 2Tim 2.26. Exo 10.21.

Overtime, many have tried to give more attention to the character names in the bible as measuring methods by which to blindly judge others by the person (per'se) instead of by the spirit nature (or sin spirit nature) of the character (that has the ability to create the influence of its character of its spirit nature in anyone's life it can find a place in). Eph 4.27. Gen 1.21 & 24. In the first circumstance (of this sentence), or going by the character name in the bible instead of their spirit nature activity dark spirits (and their activity) have been able to hide behind the personality/character flaws within the character (per'se) and/or within our society and our world, which dark spirit life and dark governing methods continues to mesh and be hidden within plots undiscovered advances among us as dark spirit life literally has come to the forefront and exploded in our culture, nation and our world seemingly unbothered or unhindered by ignorance, innocence and/or foolishness. Gal. 5.7-9.17-21. Nor realizing that it has been dark spirit life that has been serving a dark spirited kingdom system (among us) that has been eroding our spirit lives, and society on all levels of life and living (transcending into our world by dehumanizing humanity through hate crimes, mostly ignored seemingly due to our negligence, ignorance, foolishness and innocence of spiritual kingdom life, spiritual blindness and our busyness. Let us pray for greater understanding concerning spirit life activity; release from it, restoration and a reviving, in Jesus name. Ez 9.9. So that we can get pass being or getting seemingly "stuck" in spirit life activity that is seemingly molding us, for the purposes of "fitting" un into dark spirit activity and systems of operation and then causing us to think it's GOD. Isa 14.13. 2Tim2.26. Ez9.9.

We've squeezed or should I say, allowed darkness to squeeze (by its dark spirited activity of distraction and operation among us) the Lord out of our lives, families, cultures, communities, business, marketplace, police/security services, edu./arts, media, legal and government systems, etc., as well as out of our nation, yet without Him spirit life issues cannot be resolved nor properly addressed. What a paradox. Jn 4.24. Rom 1.25. We have put the emphasis on people and things of this world more than their spirit life understanding, condition and awareness of how 2 spiritual kingdoms are operating among us and what that really means. Prov. 27.23. 1Jn2.16. A strategy of hell is to hide their dark spirit kingdom operations in the earth. How've they been doing so far?

Even today, hell is still trying to keep folks in the flesh even by blinding them in their spirit life realities measured in Christ Jesus. 2Corin. 10.12. Tim 3.16. Jn 13.15. In this respect people will not be able to get out of the flesh and carnal spirit level until they receive spiritual cleansing and healing in their spirit life. Spiritual networking is being done (by dark spirit life activity) to create spiritual strongholds to keep people in the flesh. Isa 19.9. Eph 4.27.

Spirit life (or neglect of it) affects all levels of life and living.

Other human avenues that dark spirit life can gain entrance into your body, soul and/or spirit life

First, they (dark spirit life) seem to try to claim right to your body, soul and spirit life by any sins in your life. Past (ancestrally), present and/or future.

Second, then they try to lay claim to your life through principalic ancestral strongholds in community and/or through society (people, places and/or things) through familiar spirits, evil spirits and/or unclean spirits. Through associations……and/or through trying to develop dark spirit encouragement, friendships, alliances and/or connections through work, family, community, various religions or religious activities or church systems and/or secret societies or lodges, etc. Pet 5.8. Wherever the need or weak areas of your life. Darkness always will make an effort to make themselves available through either a victim or vessel of darkness (that also need healing, release and a greater understanding of spirit life activity) Prov. 4.5.7. All of life seems to be centered around spirit life activity and spiritual kingdom activity, whether we are aware or choose to be aware of it or not. There are only 2 spiritual kingdoms operating among us. Only 2! Every religion or non-religious person or spirit belief system will fit or be forced, or intruded upon, by dark spirit life into one or the other spiritual kingdoms. When and if this occurs we are admonished (biblically) to resist the darkness and/or praise. Is there a difference! James 4.7. Tim 6.12. James 5.13. Ps 22.3.

Some demonic spirit systems will use the following tools to draw, ensnare others by or through the following experiences:

Verbal abuse……………Physical abuse…………Emotional abuse….….…...Spiritual abuse
(Ultimately affecting children, love relationships, friendships, associations and one's life work and service to Christ).

*All of these abuses are to draw and pull you out of the will and purposes of the Lord for your life into deeper levels and arenas of dark spiritual levels of abuse, sooner or later bringing sex into the equation as your introduction to any deeper levels of satanic ritual abuse, giving the impression on the off-set that it could have been love. Not if the love is or has been satanically or darkly influence and/or initiated. Mt 7.18.

There are only 2 spiritual kingdom activities operating among us, no matter the denomination, religion, non-religious and/or spirit belief system. One of the concerns is that many people have been raised often under dark spirited traditions. The other concern is that many in society are in need of spiritual cleansing, release and healing from spirit impurities, defilement and/or seducing spirit violations (for one reason or another, when there is no resistance, along with a greater understanding of spirit life activity. Without which dark spirited traditions among men continue, giving the impression that their spirit or spiritual activities (independent of biblical and spiritual truth) are somehow appropriate. Mk 7.8. Col 2.8.

Any fear based methods and tactics to draw and/or pull you in enough (into dark spirit activities), beginning with some level of dark spirit penetration via. (trafficking and channeling) spirit methods to begin to process and spiritually spiral you into dark spirited professions, until demonic spirit personalities break through to appear in their dark spirited development of your life, life's work and career (or profession) has been affected. Sometimes our business name will reflect what principalic spirit life activity is influencing it and/or the owner. Example, the spirit that has been operating in one's life can begin to come through just like Jezebel, Laban and/or Jacob to a certain point. Because no matter what, the spirit level, spirit life will always:

1. Manifest to reveal their spirit kingdom's agenda. King 18.4. Gen, Chpt. 27. Gen. 31.41. Jn 6.63.

2. Always seek to reproduce itself. Gen. 1.

Therefore, if other spirit life without your permission manifest and/or begins to develop in or upon your life, seemingly without your permission…..spiritual release, cleansing and healing is needed because this usually means that someone is releasing the spirits into your life consistently. Time to make room, much room for the Lord. To learn how to resist dark spirit life activity, that is trying to establish its dark spirit kingdom activity in your body, soul, spirit life, relationships and/or profession.

This could literally mean that everyone in your circle of family and friends…..would need to gain the ability to learn how to spiritually cleanse and heal themselves in Christ Jesus (or designate one to help everyone), by the power of the cross or the enemy will attempt to use them to spiritually erode and/or weaken your spirit life and family life. Lk 12.53. In dark spirit activity, there is no such thing as respecting another's spiritual position and belief in Christ Jesus. In regards to dark spirit thinking, they are being spiritually programmed to kill, steal and destroy. There are no good devil spirit life. They reflect and those they infect are and become too spiritually affected. Release and healing is needed with a greater understanding of dark spirit life activity in light of Jesus Christ and Him crucified for our sake. Those in dark spirited operations are trained to attack, and or submit to the spirits operating in their lives, giving them the opportunity to "spirit attack-via.traffik or channel) into the life targeted by them. Dark spirited operations seem to be a use or be used system of no grace or mercy, continually opposing the mercy which the Lord's Throne is built upon. This is the operation of darkness. Rom 5.20. 2Corin. 8.7. Gal. 2.21. Eph 2.8. Heb 4.16. Like a spiritual virus of dark spirit life spreading among those who have yet to learn how to release their spirit life from spirit impurities and spiritual defilement is what's been happening among us. Because, when spirits manifest, they will always manifest, to reveal their spirit kingdom initiatives and agenda. Always.

Please note: With faith in God and His word, this root system is designed to help bring release and free us from being involuntarily used by dark angel spirit life and/or spirit seizes in certain environments (or dark spirit life within one's body, soul and spirit life). However, there is also a real need to learn how to openly resist dark spirit kingdom conflicts when you can't avoid them. Then you have those in dark spirit professions (sons and daughters of baal) that can literally cause and/or create spirit seizes to arise among men to cause conflict in any given environment. Wild, but true! Acts 19.16. 2Pet 2.20. Our independent flow chart on Christ's authority can help assist in this area.

We cannot afford to ignore dark spirit life influences and activity on our families, churches, culture and society….eventually, it exposes itself similar to a disease (developing, transcending and happening in one's spirit and natural life-if there is no release from it). Dark spirit life seeks to reproduce itself (because spirits never die), among mankind for harm, never for good will (there is always a ill-intent behind the scene waiting for the perfect time to reveal it's true intent). Jn 10.10. 2Corin 6.17. Gen 1.21,25. Gen 1.11.

Once a principalic stronghold breaks through the targeted person's mind and/or spirit life, without resistance (or sufficient resistance because help is needed, because spirits eventually gang up-like Jezebel or Laban's experience, etc.), they will begin to take over the person's character, their family, their occupation or career or one will be created for them (see the principalic sorcery group expression listings and professions of dark kingdom expressions) as the principality continues the demonic processing of spirit molding, forming and crowding the individual out by repetitiously eroding the individuals thought life and thinking patterns with continual dark spirited suggestions and/or ideas until the person can no longer discern and begins to accept the dark spirit remolding thinking and thought patterns as their own. It is part of the operation of darkness. It's what they do! Lk 6.44. Jn. 6.63. Rom 6.13-23. Then principalities will begin to erode other areas of the person's life by using the person as an instrument to spiritually connect to others to continue the spiritual reproduction of its kind and therefore, people need a greater understanding of spirit life activity, spiritual kingdoms and their purposes among us so that people do not continue to get spiritually sucked up and/or in the spiritual kingdom operation of darkness as they have so far been doing (from generation to generation). With seemingly little to no knowledge of how to spiritually recover from dark spirit intrusions and invasions going on now among us, as part of their process to spiritually pursue and over come, those who belong to Christ Jesus. This is how many of dark spirit captives are operating among us (dark spirit diseases are reproducing among us). They are literally "sprit targeting" the saints of Christ Jesus, singling them out and taking as much time as it takes to spiritually bring them into spiritual bondage and forcefully cause them to become servants of corruption. I hope the church can hear what is being said, some in dark spirited professions are taking 2 and or 3 years or more, if it takes that long persistently using dark spirited powers to bewitch and ritualistically spiritually penetrate to draw the saints into spiritual arenas of captivity. May this writing speak hope to those desiring to keep their body, soul and spirit life free in Christ Jesus, from dark spirit pursuits. And even though we have authority in Christ Jesus, many do not realize how to persistently stand in their authority in Christ and until they do are becoming spirit forced into being servants of darkness and corruption, by those in dark spirit professions (sons and daughters of baal) who believe that the "god" they serve (the god of this world) is powerful enough to pull the saints of God (out of Spirit and power of Christ) into dark spirited professions (by deceit, literally causing the saints to think they are one of the same in Christ until they weaken them to the point their error is realized by the saint) and by wearing the saints out, one at a time). Meaning, they befriend the saint, and then go home and release evil spirits into their lives and when they saint discusses it with them, they pretend they are concerned, then they go home and continue the demented spirit behavior because when spirits manifest they will always reveal their spirit kingdom initiatives and agenda, until they receive release and healing from dark spirit life activity. In actuality both are in need of healing, perhaps for different reasons. This is why dark spirit life activity need to be taught. Otherwise, our nation will continue to be spiritually sucked into this dark spirit vacuum system of ignorance, innocence, foolishness and spiritual blindness concerning spirit life activity.

ALL SPIRITUAL GIFTS SHOULD BE OPERATING AMONG US PROPERLY! THE BIBLE REVEAL THEY WILL PROFIT US! (Can I qualify this and say when one gains the spiritual ability to release, cleanse and heal themselves from spirit life impurities, defilement and seducing spirit violations, in Jesus name.

This is another reason why they are saying that Satanism is one of the fastest growing religions among us. However, from what we have seen, it's because many are being "spirit forced" into it? **This is serious!** Can anyone hear me? Spirit life activity must be taught and understood how to not be "spirit forced" into any dark spirit belief system working within or without religion and many need to learn how to recover from it in Jesus name! Help us Lord, to meet your people where they are at, not so much were we want them to be, in Jesus name. Gen, Chpt. 1. Rom 6.13.

Principalic spirit personality moldings are about dark spirit life activity trying to reproduce itself through people's spirit lives so that principalities can begin to reflect their spirit kingdom's agenda from community to community, city to city and family to family until it affects our nation, of those who have not yet learned how to resist them nor realize there is a reason to! Meaning dark spirits are finding coercive spirit ways to invite themselves (many are being forced and I hope the church can hear me (I candle hear me) and then stay in people's lives (like spiritual leeches or vipers) and once they do this, the dark spirit begin to cause the people to express their dark spirit kingdom agenda, especially if people do not know how to spiritually release themselves from these type of forced dark spirit life intrusions. If we would begin to observe, we would realize and begin to see that dark spirit activity and its operation is becoming like a second (silent) language (and spirit activity) among us within and without the church system. Excuse my language, but wonder if its due in part to no one seemingly teaching how to stay free and/or recover from the massive amount of questionable spirit life activity going on among us. And those trying to come forth and/or get through the seemingly spiritual confusion and/or religious nightmare for many, daily surmounts itself by those in dark spirit professions looking for those whom God is desiring to help to hinder them with the spirit vengeance of hell itself. Many of whom fell into spiritual captivity and never learned how to find release and healing have now become "spirit forced" into dark spirit life activity that continues to bring the saints of God, also into spiritual bondage because spirit life never dies, it reproduces itself. What a (spiritual) tragedy unfolding. Gen, Chpt.1. Jesus is saying, He is still the way, the truth and the life! Hallelujah! Bless the name of a risen Lord and Savior. Let the redeemed of the Lord say so!

What's in a name?

A good name means everything

Ps. 74.18. Ps 72.17-18.

Jeremiah said…..according to the number of thy cities are thy (spirit) gods……. Jere 2.28. Amos 5.26-27. Chr 4.33.2 Ki.10.25. Isa 1.27. Isa 33.20. Isa 35.10.

Ezekiel said….and the name of the city from that day shall be **"The Lord Is There"**. Ez 48.35.

Why did they call, "Tower of Baal, Tower of Baal"?

Gen 11.1-9 Jechrst Chairms

Jehovah-jireh……………… Gen 22.13-14.
…..is how God revealed Himself when He provided the sacrifice that replaced Abraham's son.

Isaac called the names of the wells after the names that His father had named them. Gen 22.13-14. Gen 26.18.

Abigail said of her husband's unkindness toward David: Let not my lord, I pray thee regard this man of Belial, even Nabal, for as for his name is, so is he. Nabal is his name and folly is with him………… Sam 24.25

Moses built an altar and called it Jehovah-nissi as a memorial unto the Lord, as a reminder of the Lord's war against Amalek from generation to generation. Exo 17.14-16.

A man during David's day was called Sheba, however he was also called or described as a man of belial. 2Sam 20.1.

Jezabel's fathers name was Ethbaal, King of the Zidonians….was it a coincidence that her father's name indicated who he served and how he raised and influenced his daughter, Jezebel's spirit belief system, which did also affect and influence her husband and their nation. Ahab. King 16.31.

Since there are only 2 spiritual kingdoms, there can only be a reflection of 2 spiritual type cities. One can reflect Zion so what would be left but Sodom and Gomorrah. Do we realize that Sodom and Gomorrah ultimately lost their ability to correctly (spiritually) discern, due to dark spirit infiltrations and infestations happening among them, because dark spirit life like to reproduce itself and will do so without appropriate resistance when they try to rise up and/or descend upon men. This is one of the dynamics of dark spirit life activity that also appeared true in Nineveh, as well as other individual, biblical situations or equations where dark spirit life activity was free to operate without appropriate resistance. Jude 7. 2Chr. 5.2.

Driving through PA into NY, I happened to catch the end of a radio ad that was letting its listeners know that a "Psychic Festival" is having its second annual "Psychic Festival", in 2008. Dear Lord, the businesses supporting this event are literally pulling themselves into the allegiance with dark spirit life activity and the operation of darkness …… supporting this event that can create demonic strongholds in the city and at the same time pull the people and the city into the judgment of God. Judges 2.16. Dt 5.7. Ecc 12.14. Some cities are known by their event(s) like Sodom & Gomorrah. What reward would there be in heaven anyone's city being known for having a "Psychic Festival"? Would this city fit best into a city of Zion or a Sodom and Gomorrah? Would you think that the people's gifts and talents operating behind those promoting and/or in this festival are operating properly, biblically speaking?

Then my heart broke when just 2 years later, as I was driving through Cleveland, Ohio, crossing West 130th and Brook park Rd. I saw a like sign advertising on a poster sign sitting on the grass that read "Psychic Festival". Another reflection, spiritual deterioration and condition of those among us and of those in our community and city in need of spiritual release, healing and a greater understanding of spirit life activity and how this type of spirit activity can transcend a city into deeper darkness and the judgments of God. Another reason people need to learn if their spiritual gifts are operating properly in light of the purposes of God. Corin. 7.7. Ecc. 12.14. Ps.105.1. Why? Because there are 2 spiritual kingdoms operating among us and contrary to what may appear, everyone is accountable to the Lord and King and He still visits sin!

…..every man has its proper gift from God. Corin 7.7. So then every one of us shall give account of himself to God. For none of us liveth to himself and no man dieth to himself. Rom. 14.7 & 12. How could one's gift operate properly within and/or without the church if spiritual release, cleansing and healing is needed? May this writing minister to those who need release so that their gift unto the Lord can be more properly and biblically operated, wherever you are, in Jesus name.

Scripture reveals that a good name is rather to be chosen than great riches and loving favor rather than silver and gold. Proverbs 22.1.

The following are some biblical and non-biblical spirit personalities and/or influences that dark spirit principalities have affected, violated, remolded, reshaped, encroached upon, crowded out, harassed and vexed….etc. It's what they (dark spirit life activity and those submitted to it do. It is how they operate) until they find the grace to be released from it, until the dark spirit's will and personality begin to express itself in and through the life desired.

Diana of the Ephesians, Acts 19.24-35 was a god lifted up in the city through the works of men.

Eve: Communed with satan's spirit influence and in dialog a little too long, by which the same influence affected Adam. Perhaps Eve, nor Adam understood the spiritual dynamics of "spirit" kingdoms.
2Cor 11.3. Eph 5.11. Eph 4.27

Principalic activity were able to use Herod to rise up against the church and kill boy children. Individually and territorially.
Acts 12.1-23.

Jezebel: Cut off the prophets of God.
King 18.4. 2Ki 19.

Solomon: Was spiritually influenced by the spirits who had affected his wives. Ki 11.1-9.

Adonijah: Exalted himself. Guess he thought it was him doing it. Ki 1.5. 2Cor 10.5.

Samson: Darkness operating in the city used 2 different occasions to bring Samson to his fall (who was a servant of the Lord). Judges 14.4.
Judges 14.15-18 & 16.5.

David: Did principalic influence cause David to be one of the the first peeping Tom?
Sam 11-2.

There are still, only 2 spirit kingdoms operating among us, as well as there was during OT times. One gives and promotes life, love, harmony, justice, good will and peace. The goal of dark spirit kingdom agendas is still to kill, seal and destroy, on whatever level it can find, has not changed. Jn 10.10. However, they have a variety of ways in which to do this. Besides continually seeking ways to find entrance into your life through people, family and incidences that may know nothing about the spiritual dynamics of the only 2 spiritual kingdoms there are, therefore, become easy access, vessels or victims for dark spirit activity and overall dark spirit kingdom agendas, initiations and over all operation among us.

These are other avenues that the enemy uses without to gain entry into your spirit and natural life. When this proves too difficult, dark spirit life will find ways to work overtime on the mind, will and emotions (the soul's chambers) or within the body, spirit and soul's system (to affect the mind subconscious and unconscious spirit realm, will and emotions and eventually one's life towards darkness-when there is no appropriate resistance and proper biblical understanding of what you are resisting, in Jesus name). James 4.7.

And then there is the name of:

What comes to mind?

<u>A name above all names!</u>

A.
Our Administrator
Corin. 12.5
Our **Authority**(in His name) Lk 9.1
Our **Avenger** 2Sam22.47

D.
Our **Defense** Ps 8.18.
Our **Dance** Ps149.3

G.
Great High Priest Heb 4.4.

J.
Judge of all the earth Gen 18.25
Just 2Sam23.3
M.
Most High Hosea 11.7
My **Mercy** 2Sam22.51
Mighty to save Isa 63.1

B.
Our **Baptizer** Jn 1.33
Our **Balm** Jere 8.22
Our **Balance** Prov 16.11
Our **Breath** Acts 17.28. Prov.18.24. Zec6.12

E.
The One who's **Eyes** are on the nations Ps 66.7
Exalted as Head above all. Chr. 29.11

H.
Horn of Salvation Lk 1.69
God of **Hope** Rom15.13

K.
King over all the earth Ps47.2 Rev15.3

N.
Name above all names Phil 2.9

C.
The **Consecrated One** Heb10.20. Heb7.28
The One **Crowned with Glory** Heb2.9 Rev.19
The One **Coming Back** Rev.1.7
Our **Confidence** Isa 30.15
F.
Faithful One Lam3.23. Rev19.11. Mk11.22
Fortress Ps 9.9
The One who Fights w/the sword of His mouth. Rev 2.16
I.
Incredible Acts 26.8

L.
Lord of Sabboth Mk2.28
Lord of Hosts Gen 32.1-2. Ps59.5. Lk48
Living God Gen 14.18.Mt.26.63

Mighty in battle Ps.24.8

Q.
The One whose word is **Quick** Heb4.12
The One to come **Quickly** Rev 3.11

T.
Our **Truth** Ps19.142. Lk4.4
Throne of Grace Rev20.11. Heb4.
True God 2Chr 15.3

W.
Our **Wisdom** Prov.2.6,7,Prov.3.13,21
Our **Witness** Rev.3.14
God of **Wonders** Ps77.14

Y.
Jesus Christ; the same **yesterday**
And today and forever. Heb 13.8
Yahweh

O.
Over-comer Jn.16.33
Omnipotent who reigns Rev 19.6

R.
Refuge in times of trouble Ps.9.2
Our **Redeemer** Jer 50.34. Isa60.16.Isa48.17
Our **Ransom** Jer 31.11. Prov21.18. Mt20.28
Our **Reconciliation** 2Corin. 5.18.

U.
Our **Unity in the faith** Eph4.13. Ps133.1.

X.
The One who **Xcelled** them all Corin.14.12

Z.
Founder of **Zion** Jere 50.5. Isa 34.8
The One who blesses us out of **Zion** Ps128.5

PP.
Prince of the Kings of the earth Rev1.5.Acts 5.
Present Truth
Praise ye the Lord Ps146.10Ps147.12

S.
Our **Savior** Jude 25.1 Jn4.14. Jn4.42. Hosea13.4:22.47
Our **Shelter** Ps 6.13
Stronghold in the day of trouble Nahum 1.7

V.
Our **Victory** Corin. 15.57
God that Visits Gen 50.25

Suicide

Suicide reveal yet another principalic ability to remold and reform the will and spirit life of men (voluntarily or involuntarily) a person's imagination (thinking and thought) processes with enough repetitious forced evil thought patterns of suicide until finally the negative repetitious patterns of remolding thought patterns convinces a person that suicide is the answer. Prov. 23.7.

The following list, from a suicide survey, that reveals non-biblical characters, but the same dark spirit life activity and operations of the kingdom of darkness that found (or spirit forced) a place into the spirit lives and minds of men to a point it became a mindset without the appropriate resistance, in Jesus name. Paul spoke of the warring within and without a soul. Jn 6.63. 2Cor 10.3&5. Rom 7.23. Pet 2.11.

The Wikipedia, on line encyclopedia revealed categories of suicide methods in how people were persuaded to kill themselves, as of September, 2008. http://en.wikipedia.org/wiki/list_of_suicides.

- Asphyxiation (suffocation) – 10
- Bomb – 1
- Burn – 3
- Drown – 18
- Euthanasia (assisted suicide) -1
- Grenade explosion – 1
- Gunshot – 198
- Hanging – 67
- Immolation (sacrificial meal) – 8
- Jumped – 54
- Overdose – 73
- Poison – 51
- Seppuku – 8 (A Japanese ritual suicide-usually a Sumari's way to die with honor. a type of stomach cutting)
- Slit throat (arm open, scissor, sword ,cut risk, razor or knife)=29 + 1 stabbed = 30)
- Strangulation – 2
- Starvation – 2
- Unknown – 105

Total suicides 632 (more suicides seemed forced)

Any type or kind of suicide is not natural or normal. One question that comes to mind is who did the dark angel spirits use to help influence this decision, was it a (working without, using others, or a working within)? If it was only or mostly an inside job, could consistent spiritual releases, from dark spirit life influencing this decision, have made the difference? Did the spirits work overtime within to produce the spirit fruit of suicide? Realizing that spirits never die and that there are only 2 spiritual kingdom operations in the earth and heavens; it is only when we can locate ourselves spiritually that we can begin to turn to God's spiritual kingdom life biblical expressions and solutions beginning with the cross for protection and to seek and find that special place appointed for us in Christ. Pet. 2.11. 2Tim2.26. Gal. 5.7-9.Acts 14.16-22. Acts 15.17. Lk 22.29.

Suicide is preventable. Suicide can be a choice or forced upon you by spirit life activity directly and/or dark spirit life working though men (aware or not) or with men in allegiance and/or devoted sons of baal who are able to assign evil spirits against its target (either way, both are in need of spiritual healing, release and understanding). Jn. 13.2. Our experiences and how we look at and interpret those experiences and even how we reflect is all a part of the evidences that help support or feed into the choices we make. The catch or possible snare is that spirit life (especially if it's on assignment) has the ability to play a part or role in our experiences. Only those in training to gain the mind of Christ can begin to gain the strength and desire to choose life. Jn. 6.63. Prov 4.13, 22. Realizing that the mind of Christ has to be developed in us through serious fellowship with God, the Father and with the Lord, His Son in His word. If not dark spirit life will locate you. Some of us are spiritually easier to take down than others. Eph 6. Some are more biblically and/or spiritually prepared to resist, dark spirit risings, some are not. Phil 2.5. 1.Jn 1.3.

There are only 2 spiritual kingdom systems operating in the earth. heaven and among us. One spiritual kingdom promotes life. One spiritual kingdom promotes death. Every religion, non-religion or spirit belief system will fit into one or the other spirit kingdom. Jn 10.10.

The reasons being is because spirits never die and whenever spirits manifest (or reveal itself)will always manifest to express its spirit kingdom agenda, whether we realize it or not and whatever spirit room is given to them to operate, will become their dark spirit position and strength to hold you and then advance in your life from that place you give (or that they are able to take) to the point then they can cause you to serve their dark spirit kingdom agenda, in ignorance, innocence, foolishness or weakness. But, I have found that even the weak can call upon the name of the Lord! And without faith, it is impossible to please Him. Heb 11.6. Ps 55.16. Rom 10.13. Ps 73.22. Acts 17.30. Pet. 2.15. Prov 1.11-15.

However or whenever one or the other spirit kingdom reveals or presents itself to us at any point in time, we will ultimately feed into one or engage the other by faith in Christ and Him crucified

Some of the professional categories who were convinced that they should commit suicide.

Actors	Obstetrician	Leader (of Nazi)
Writers	Officer Workers	
Air Marshal		
Businessmen	Painter	Sculptor
Baseball player	Parliament (member of)	Secretary of Defense (US)
Buddhist Monk	PhD Student	School Columbine Massacre
Boxing Referee	Philosopher	Songwriter Singers Social Worker
Comedian	Physician Photographer	Student (Tech Virginia)
A Nobel Prize winning Chemist	Physicist	Am. Software Developer
Child Actor	Psycho Analyst	Republican Statesman
Professional Catchers	Personality (TV)	Soccer player

College Student	Presidents (of another country)	Senator of (Kansas)
Congressman	Poet	
Composer	Pop Singer	
Cultural Theorist	Politician	
Chancellor	Prime Minister	
Chief of Staff	Publisher	
Deputy White House Counsel	Pulitzer Prize winner (Poet)	
Daughters of famous people	Radio Voice (person)	Union leaders
Diplomats	Race Car Driver	
Doctor	Religious Cult or Leader of Cult	
Drummer	Representative	
	Royal Family (British)	

Emperor
Engineer
Erotic Cancer

Feminist	General	Vice-President (Enron)
Fashion Model	Governor	Violinist-Composer
Farmer Activist	Guitarist	
Swiss Federal Counselor		
Field Marshal		
Financier, Entrepreneur		

Mathematician	High School Student	War Minister
Medal of Honor Recipient	Host (for TV)	War Criminal
Military Ruler		Wrestler
Military Commander		Writer
Musician		
Mistress (of Adolf Hitler)		

NBA Players	Inventor
NFL Players	Industrialist
Newsreader	
Novelist	

*Please check the website for the names that fit the above professions at: http://en.wikipedia.org/wik/list of suicides.

I should not forget to mention the recorded incidences of children who kill their parents. As someone said, no one in their right mind would kill their parent! That's exactly right. It is an expression of the un-addressed spirit life activity and influences operating in their life. There are only 2 spiritual kingdoms operating among us. Whenever a spirit manifest upon a person or in a child's life it will always express its spiritual kingdom agenda. Always! Our children are also in need of spiritual release, cleansing, understanding of spirit life activity and healing from spirit impurities, defilement and/or violations. Please share the "Spiritual Root System" with them and please join us in prayer to God for the spiritual security of our children and nation. The report on the rising number of children killing their parents was found at: www.FBI.com website.

Evil is considered anything morally bad, wrong, wicked, harmful, injurious, sinful or anything that causes harm, pain, iniquity, wickedness, or any unjust act. The people submitted (or spiritually captured) unto this spirit/spiritual system have no fear of God (because their god spirit) is of a evil spirit nature. It's in their spiritual DNA. Prov 21.10. The mind of the wicked are evil bent (towards evil ways influences). Therefore, since spirits never die, unless God grants anyone a heart to repent, they will forever begin to work evil into whatever work (family, church, community, neighbor, government/ police/security service) system or situation they belong to or are a part of. Their task or assignment is always to locate the undefiled (and therefore often attracted to the saint's spirit). They will take note of any people differences and distinctions and begin to find ways to spiritually defile and/or bring about (dark spirit) attitudes that cultivate division and strife within the people differences and distinctions. Sometimes the distinctions and differences are or could be the level of spirit holiness in ones life, which can be a reflection of ones relationship and/or service to Jesus Christ. Whether realized or not. It is a spirit nature thing, regardless of whether or not everyone understands spirit life activity or not.

This is why Jesus said, a good tree cannot bring forth evil fruit, nor can a evil tree bring forth good fruit. It's not in the spirit/spiritual DNA to do otherwise. Mt, Chpt. 12. Spirit life (good or evil) only live to exist to express and serve the spiritual kingdom they are from. We are all spirit beings journeying with other spirit beings who will try to make their way into your life through whatever "human experience" they can (or is being orchestrated, even those in dark spirit professions and/or sons of baal have gained this ability in the lives they target to take). Isa 5.12. Col. 2.12. Ps.28.5.

Any consistent confusion has always been with those operating in the kingdom of darkness trying to fit within the church system of God's kingdom of which they do not belong and so seeing they will not fit, they begin to change the spirit nature of the people of God in our church and many church systems and communities, until enough spiritual darkness is released and/or filtered into attitudes and behaviors, etc) that even God's people struggle with discerning the Spirit of God and His spiritual operation in their midst often unaware; and is another reason people need to spiritually locate their spirit life and spiritual allegiance and from there learn how to release themselves from spirit impurities, defilement and spiritual violations to the point they cannot receive God's biblical and spiritual operation again in their midst.

There is no spiritual confusion in the biblical and spiritual character of Christ Jesus. Only, righteousness, peace and joy in the Holy Ghost! Once understood, accepted and received. James 3.16. rom 14.17.

Some receive dark spirit natures from birth. Isa48.8. Ps36.1-4. Ps34.21. Pro11.21. Ps109.1-3. Prov12.5. Pro12.26. Ps37.17&20. Ps37.35-36. Ps38.18. Ps14.4-5. Prov29.7. Pro15.8-9. Pro15.28. Prov17.15. Ps119.110. Pro21.18. Prov10.2-5.

Evil as a correlation is also a work and spirit fruit of darkness and a "god" to those who consistently yield or can't or need to be broken free from its captivity, bondage and servant hood. 2Pet. 2.19.

I've come to see understand and perceive that every one under a evil system or rule are not all there by their permission. Some are being continually spiraled by deeper levels of dark spirit powers and, are even thrust into dark spirited professions and would desire top know how to break free. Beloved of the Lord, still, there is power in the cross. Lord, help us find the faith and the grace that your world declares is sufficient for us to be more than conquerors and over comers in Christ Jesus in these last days to help us rise up, in Jesus name.

EVIL

The spirit fruit sin nature work and/or activity most normally accepted & reflected by those operating in the kingdom of darkness in comparison

*When you go against your enemy keep from every wicked thing. Ps34.16. Dt 23.14. Jn 3.19. For the Lord weighs spirits. Pro 11.15. Prov 16.2. Jn7.7. Ecc12.14.

Kingdom of God spiritual activity, covenant, position & counsel

Sing for the Lord has delivered us from the hand of evil doers. Jere 20.13. Judges 9.57. Col 1.13.

The Lord shall deliver me from every evil work and will preserve me unto His Kingdom. 2Tim 4.18.

Evil bows before the good. Pro 14.19.

To those that listen to & dwell with God, no evil will befall them. Ps91.10. Prov1.33.

Through prayers God may grant recovery for those taken captive. 2Tim2.25-26. Sam 18.9.

Some need to be healed from evil spirits before they find recovery Lk7.21. Lk8.2.Pro2.10-15.Acts 19.12-19.

The righteous shall not be ashamed in an evil time. Ps40.14.Prov19.23.

Jesus makes a distinction between speaking well and speaking evil. Jn18.23.

Kingdom of God counsel Ps37.1-3.

Keep thy tongue from evil. Ps34.13-14.

Fear of the Lord. Depart from evil. Pro3.7. Ps37.27.

Turn ye every man from his evil way. Jere25.5. Rom8.6. Gal6.7-8. Ps119.11.

Abstain from all appearance of evil. Thess5.22. Remove thy foot from evil.

....neither will God help evildoers. Job 8.20.

The Lord will deliver me from every evil work. 2Tim4.18.

The highway of the upright is to depart from evil. Job 28.28.

He that keeps his way preserves his soul. Prov. 16.17.

Follow not that which is evil but that which is good. 3Jn.1.11.

To punish the just is **not good. Pro. 17.26

If ye have stood in my counsel ye should have turned the people from their evil way. Jere23.22.Rom13.4.Dt.30.15&19.

The part of the believer. To depart from evil is understanding. Job28.28.

My thoughts towards thee are good, not evil. Jere.29.11. Titus3.2.

Depart from evil and do good. Dwell forevermore. Ps37.27.

Wash you make you clean. Cease to do evil. Isa1.16.

Fret not to do evil. Ps 136.Ps15.1-4.Ps18.20.

Lord, we shall abide...who shall dwell in thy holy hill? He that walks uprightly and works righteousness, seeks truth... **nor does evil** to his neighbor. Prov.18.20.Ps.15.1-4.

The other kingdom allegiance & alliance dark spirit & sin nature activity

Some evil comes from within. Mt 6.23.Mt 7.22. Lk 6.45.Lk11.34. Mt 15.19.

Evil can come through thoughts...James 2.4. Jesus said why think evil....

Evil eyes can produce dark discernment. Mk7.22-23. Pro28.22. Dt 28.54

.....and thine eye be evil against thy poor brother & you give him nothing. Dt 15.19.

The wicked <u>watch</u> the righteous. Ps 37.32. Some are assigned to watch the righteous and help them fall. This is not only a figure of speech but a operation of darkness. Therefore, those with this spirit type personality are in need of spiritual cleansing, release from this spirit assignment & healing. But if thine evil servant say in his heart. (what one thinks is important). Mt 24.48. Mt 9.4.

The way of truth is evil spoken of. 2Pet2.2. Prov20.32. Acts14.2.

Go not in the way of evil men. Prov 4.14-15.

Do they not err that devise evil. Prov 14.22.

The ways of evil men. Prov 4.27.

They encourage themselves in a evil matter. Ps64.5.

They speak forwardly. Walk in darkness and rejoice to do evil.

Whose ways are crooked. Prov2.12-15.Ps50.19. Prov 21.7.

The wicked (evil) influenced person refuses to do judgment (due to their being more emotion or emotionalism) **They need spiritual release**.

Their soul (mind, will & emotion) of the wicked desire (is an emotion) is evil.

Where as there is among you envying & strife & division. Cor3.3.Prov21.10.

The law is weak through the **flesh**. Rom8.3.They that are after the **flesh** mind the things of the **flesh**. Rom8.5. For he that sows to the **flesh** shall of the **flesh** reap corruption. Gal6.7-8. Rom8.8. Gal5.19-21.

They that render evil for good are my adversaries. Ps38.20.

Evil seeks only rebellion therefore, a cruel messenger will be sent against him. Prov17.11. Ps52.3.

They are without natural affection, truth breakers, false accusers, fierce and despisers of those that are good. 2Tim3.3. Dt.24.12-15.

Evil shall slay the wicked. Evil shall hunt the violent man. Ps140.11.

Refrain thy feet from evil. Ps 119.101.

Speak evil of no man. Pro.24.13-14.Corin.15.33.

…know to refuse evil and choose good. Isa7.15.Heb5.14.

…to depart from evil is understanding. Job28.28.

Only those who fear the Lord depart form evil. Prov 3.7.

Our prayer: Ye that love the Lord hate evil. Ps 97.10.
Deliver us from evil men. Ps 140.1-2.Mt.6.13.

Let not an evil speaker be established. Ps 140.11.

I pray ye do no evil. 2Chr13.9. Joshua 24.23. Prov15.4.

*That you justify the righteous and condemn the wicked. Dt24.1.

Say not thou, I will recompense evil but wait….Prov 20.22.

Evil can affect our world elements

Evil provokes the Lord to anger (because it is a fallen spirit) Dt4.16-19:4-25.

The Lord can cause the land to become desolate because of evil. Jere44.22.

The Lord said behold, I will bring evil upon this city. Jere25.3-4.

Evil as judgment is only the Kings prerogative.
Joshua 23.15. Sam18.10.

The Lord hath made all things even the wicked for the day of evil. Pro 16.4.

Diminishing can be a part of judgment. Dt.4.27. Jere25.29:39.16:32:42,44 27-29. Amos 4,7-8.

I will render to Babylon all the evil they did in Zion. Jere51.24. Jere51.60. Dt 4.25-30. Dt31.16 & 29.

Their course, order of things or pattern/path is evil.
Their course, order of things or pattern/path is evil. Their force is not right Jere23.10.

Evil trees cannot bring forth good fruit. Mt7.17.They repay evil forgood. Sam25.21. The soul of the wicked desire evil. Pro2.10. Sam24.17.

These resist anything that has to do with the kingdom of God. They resist apostolic prophets or those sent by the Kingdom of God (vertically assigned). They are men of corrupt minds (undeveloped scripturally). 2Tim3.8-9,16.

Some like to pursue evil activity (naturally and spiritually so). Prov11.19.

Some will do you much evil (until they are released from the evil spirit in their life). 2Tim4.14. Mine enemies speak evil of me. They speak vanity. Ps41.5.

Whose rewards evil for good evil will not depart from their house. Prov17.

Evil men understand not judgment. Prov 28.5. Pro29.26.

The ungodly digs (like to find and/or uncover) evil. The intent is the concern. Prov11.27. Prov16.27. Ps35.7.

Evil men shall wax worse and worse. 2Tim3.13.

It is evil in the sight of the Lord to follow unfaithful prophets who lead you away from the Lord and his covenant. Dt. 13.1-5.Dt 13.12-14.

Evil Days All the days of the afflicted are evil. Prov 15.15.

Evil can be defined as, morally bad or wrong; wicked. Anything that causes corruption, pain or that is injurious. Naturally and/or spiritually so. The plowing of the wicked (of evil) is sin. Prov 21.14. So evil used as a tool to implement or used as a method to make ones way thru sin. Spiritual release and healing is needed.

Those who operate and help create dark spirited systems in the lives of others (in the workplace, church and/or community) know not the ways of peace. It is not in their spirit nature. It is not in their spiritual DNA. Non-peaceful ways (silent or verbal, I think of them as quiet storms because they are in need of spiritual healing. They seem to have an interest to learn enough of the ways of the Lord to entice and deceive a saint into believing they have something in common before they begin to attack. They are always attacking whether silent or verbal, it seems to be the policy of their dark spirited foundational structure and their spirit life is usually ruled by emotions as their base reasoning and is ultimately a type of dark spirited religion (created by dark spirit activity). Dark spirit life can create and help to formulate a person's belief system and ideology, when the light of the gospel is consistently absent in one's soul and spirit life.

Without spiritual, biblical guidance, principles and disciplines of Christ (as ones sense and level of soundness), how can one soundly cope and/or rule his spirit life without it. No matter the religion, non-religion or spirit belief system. My prayer is those that seem to fall into this spirit nature category consider learning how to spiritually release yourself as you begin to sincerely seek Christ and Him crucified with a repentant and grateful heart and allow Him to transform you and reveal to you, your appointed place in the Kingdom of God. Everyone needs a Savior but not many know or realize how to maintain their spirit lives in Christ Jesus. Rom 10.9. Jesus said these words I speak are spirit and life. Jn. 6.63.

Ministry Sheet. To help you in your business, church, family, community and/or area of influence, set the standard by not allowing evil works, methods and ways rule in your midst by those who are clearly in need of biblical and spiritual healing and hope. It's like a spiritual infection and/or virus that is able to spread in your midst that attaches by transfer and/or can be spirit channeled or trafficked into the lives of others. Because there are 2 spiritual kingdom activities operating among us spirits can act and behave independently of the other person once the person in question has collected enough spirits to affect one's environment; because someone did not know how, nor realize the need to release themselves from spirit impurities, defilement and spiritual violations found in families, ancestry, communities, cities and society at large. This tells me that everyone has a greater need to learn and understand the dynamics of spirit life activity if for no other reason, how it is able to encroach into our world. This is serious. This is curable. Only because of the sacrifice of Jesus! Part of the concern is than we have mostly seen and heard and been predominantly infiltrated by dark spirited system but there is another side (other than dark spirit activity). Jesus is Lord in the spirit realm also!

Creating cities of Babylon in our midst is a current activity of the operations of the kingdom of darkness. One city at a time.

Rev 18.2. Zechariah2.7. Obadiah1.17. Zephaniah 3.17.

Shall a trumpet be blown in the city and the people not be afraid? Shall there be evil in a city and the Lord hath not done it?

Surely the Lord God will do nothing but He revealeth His secrets unto His servants the prophets

A breach in the city…is where they enter the gate.
Jere.23.22. Jere51.24. Jere27.18. Ez26.10. Isa30.26. Jere2.28.

Isn't the church the gate to the city? Ez 44.11.

Breach is defined as a failure to observe a law, promise or a break in friendly relations. To violate a contract. Break, means to tear, break into. Force open. You can force a thing…by continual vexation ask Samson.

Iniquity: Is a wicked or unjust act. Wicked spirit fruit whose works can be expressed through evil. Micah 2.1. Jeremiah 11.10-13.

Example: Another person's spirit realm and life being affected, by someone deciding to use the spiritual method of "trance states" and "transmittal meditation to transfer and traffic and channel dark spirits into the life of another", by making a breach into someone else spirit realm and life seemingly breaks our civil laws and federal laws when the "spirit activity" to harm another crosses state lines. It defiles and violates another's spirit life (and create a breach or opening in their spirit realm that would not normally be their, except b the ill intent of a spiritual stalker and perpetrator) without their permission and opens up their life for "any" dark spirit activity illnesses and other social spirit diseases like idolatry and oppression which can then qualify the person for a mental institution if spiritual release is not found. Seemingly a new way to work iniquity, idolatry and spiritual defilement among us, methods perhaps more familiar to countries like Africa, have found their way into our nation. We need laws to protect the spirit life of the innocent.

Idols and idolatry have always seemed to get the Lord's undivided attention. Idols and idolatry continues to be a way…even a type of iniquitous system that hell uses as leaven to work in the lives of God's people until it provokes the Lord. In this way, hell continues to rise in an ongoing vie against the Lord, in a way that uses God's people as bait to provoke the Lord and at the same time cause the Lord to bring his people into judgment, if they take the bait. God's people would end up suffering in 2 distinct ways:

1. From the enticement or force of the sin of idolatry, the idol or idolatry begins to reproduce itself in the life and spirit activity of another. First he (or darkness) works the idea of the sin into our soul (mind thinking/thought processes will & emotions) until we actually carry out the sin. Ecc 12.14.

2. Then we could end up suffering judgment that comes from committing the sin, because the Lord judges every work.

There seems to be an continuing hate that satan likes to express in his constant uprising against the Lord. I think he's still trying to be like the Most High God, only he's using "ugly" ways to do it through those he can create breaches in our relationships to the Lord….. and eventually in the city, if it's not caught and/or corrected on the church level. And this is surely another reason the Lord would release a protocol as an initiate from the governing operation of His Kingdom and assign them to warn whatever church and/or situation that the Lord is desiring to protect to guard us from satan releasing his ugliness among us as a continuing rebel and retaliation against the Lord, whose Kingdom rules over all, regardless of Satan's continuing struggle with that truth. Rev 17.14.

> Thus saith the Lord: stand in the court of the Lord's house and speak unto all the cities of Judah, which come to worship in the Lord's house all the words that I command thee to speak unto them. Diminish not a word.
>
> If so be they will hearken and turn every man from his evil way that I may repent me of the evil which I purpose to do unto them because of the evil of their doings.
>
> And thou shall say unto them, thus sayeth the Lord. If ye will not hearken to me to walk in my law which I have set before you.
>
> To hearken to the words of my servants the prophets, whom I sent unto you both rising up early and sending them but ye have not hearkened thus will I make this house like Shiloh and will make this city a curse to all nations of the earth.
> Jere 26.1-19. Jere17.23. Ps.101.8. Ez 35.4. Ez36.17.

But they obeyed not nor inclined their ear but made their neck stiff that they might not hear, nor receive instruction.
Jere17.23. Prov.1.25. Ps 106.13. Isa 30.13. Prov 11.14. Ez 44.12. Ps 16.7. Prov. 12.15. Ez 44.23-24.

<u>Yet giving counsel and instruction is the way of the Lord and He does this by His initiate protocol and operation of His Kingdom</u>

Kingdom prophets are one of the protocols in the operation of the Kingdom of God

Kingdom prophets are to gain the ability to witness the righteousness of the King by their service to Him. Rom 3.21. Hosea 12.10.

Be wise now therefore, O ye kings. Be instructed ye judges of the earth. Ps 2.10. You will guide me with your counsel and afterwards you will receive me to glory. Ps 73.24. Ps 32.8. The counsel of the Lord stands forever. Ps 33.11.

Evil and/or wicked works (unless born and raised there) can enter a city through the operation of darkness working among the people with seemingly little and/or no restraint, spirit domination (prisoners of war) or evil could also come as released judgment due to God's people seemingly cooperating more with the operation of spiritual darkness than with God's Kingdom operation realized or not, for the Lord promises to judge every work, whether it be good or evil. This is His work. Judge is what He is. Judging is what He does. Gen 18.25. Isa 16.5. Rev 19 11. Ecc 12.14.

Certain men, the children of Belial are gone out from among you and have withdrawn the inhabitants of their city saying, lets go and serve other gods. Dt.13.13. Judges 19.22.29-30. Jere 51.60. Jn3. 19-20. Ez 11.12. Acts 13.50. Judges 20.2-8 & 12-13. Acts 13.50. Acts 14.2.

The Lord will reveal the fierceness of His anger, wrath and indignation and trouble by sending evil angels among His people…He gave their life over to the pestilence for the Lord's present concern, regarding the spirit activity of His people. Sam 12.9-12. Ps 78. 49-50.

Now the sons of Eli were sons of belial, they knew not the Lord yet they functioned in religious activity. Sam 2.12. Therefore, it appears that dark spirited activity and operations had the ability to divide families, ministry to the Lord and cities. Sam 2.3 & 23-27.

Some of the reasons the Lord would send in His Kingdom protocol and/or release judgment:

Idolatry is a worship of idols. An excessive reverence for, or devotion to a person or thing. The "idol" comes before the idolatry. Idol is a image (idea or thought) of a god, spirit, angel and or power…used as a object or worship (service to other spirits is also a form of worship). It is through this worship, conjuring attention or service that the power, spirit, angel, god or image of the idol begins to come into being…manifesting (or revealing itself first through thoughts – to the point of unrestrained imaginations, memories and visions) then stare gazing into another's soul unbroken, cold, hard distant type stares seemingly to help release strange spirit activity and seems to be a method by which spirit activity can work through people, like a conduit. Through much study, we find that excessive staring falls into the category of occult practice, according to the Christian counselor, Dr. Kurt E. Koch who wrote, "Demonology Past & Present and Hypnotism and Divine or Demonic, by Dr. Lester Sumerall.

Paul saw the city given to idolatry. Acts 17.16. Acts 19.26. Idols and idolatry need to be discovered and defined in each generation. Eph 3.5. If it is not caught on the church level, the activity will begin to infiltrate the city causing heaven to intervene.

The work of idolatry will get heaven's attention and will also cause the King to release the protocol (prophet) of the operation of His Kingdom. They are also simply known as His servants. Releasing and/or sending a prophet for service is a work of the Lord. This is another reason or still the reason that the Lord desires to build up Zion in every city because in the absence of Zion you will find Babylon, which will cause a city to more resemble and reflect the spiritual characteristics of Sodom and Gomorrah in the making. Mal 4.5-6. Sam 2.27-35. Sam 8.7.

After this 3rd writing, all initiated by the Lord, I am of the biblical opinion that unless our churches, our cities and it's inhabitants first learn how to release themselves from spirit impurities, defilement and spirit violations of others outside, as well as, within our churches they will not be able to receive God's spiritual kingdom operation and protocol in their midst whenever He sends them. Simply because there are 2 spiritual kingdoms operating among us and by process of time it becomes clear that the churches that will not receive God's Kingdom operation in their midst is because they really, spiritually can't. It is only the opposing infiltration of the spiritual kingdom of darkness and its influence that hinders a church from not receiving the spiritual operation of God's Kingdom in their midst. It's simply how the kingdom of darkness operates. Its what they do! Therefore, when the people of God learn how to spiritually release themselves from spirit impurities, defilement and spirit violations of others (this will also cause them to get out of agreement with what a spirit is or could be doing in this life), they will also gain the ability to biblically and spiritually see and understand in a different light (that is only found in Jesus Christ and Him crucified) and then they will be able to receive God's Kingdom grace in their midst again. Another miracle to unfold and behold. This is the work of the Lord in Zion. Thank you Jesus. Mal 4.5-6. Sam 8.7.

They also that erred in spirit shall come to understanding and they that murmured shall learn doctrine. Isa 29.24. Ez 39.23, 27-28.

Sometimes I think that the Lord would send a prophet as a kingdom protocol kindness. Sometimes people can get so caught up into what they are doing that they in fact may not realize that God is weighing their actions and/or activity, until He (the Lord) actually sends a kingdom protocol into the midst of a people, maybe as a gesture perhaps etiquette would be a better word. Had not Nineveh been warned, they would not have had the opportunity to repent. Which also did release God's mercy? Jonah 3.5. So then, you could say that the Lord would, could and in fact does, send a protocol prophet to a city He would desire to preserve. Sam 2.3. Sam 16.4. 2Sam12.1. Ecc 12.14. Hos 12.13. Ps 106.23. Isa 30.13. Isa 58.12. Prov. 15.4. Jere.32.31. Ps 55.9-13. Ez 9.9. Zeph 3.1. Acts 15.10. Job 33.27-28. Dt 32.5. Gen 19.15. Ps 101.8. Ps9.6. Mk 1.45. Johan 4.5.

Perhaps by this revealed dark spirit infiltration, we can better understand why the work of idolatry would get heaven's attention and would cause the King to release the protocol of the operations of His Kingdom. His Kingdom servants the prophets. This is His work. This is another reason or still the reason the Lord desires to build up Zion in every city. In the absence of Zion, you will find Babylon and it's cities of Sodom and Gomorrah in the making. In the midst of darkness all around us it might be easier in these days for people to fall into idolatry, perhaps unaware at first, and therefore using the spiritual root of the matter....manual and/or guides can help minister as a spiritual safe guard against the works and/or workers of idolatry. And help us to walk more upright and/or or effectivity for the cause of Jesus Christ and Him crucified. Bless the Lord with me. Mal 4.5-6. Sam 2.27-35. Sam 8.7.

MINISTRY SHEET

ALL

Souls are Mine!

And now what doth the Lord require of thee but to fear the Lord thy God to walk in His ways, to love him and serve the Lord thy God with all thy heart and with all thy soul. Dt. 10.12-13. Dt. 11. 16-22.

The law of the Lord is perfect converting the soul. Ps. 19.7. Ps 41.4.

He restores my soul…unto thee O Lord do I lift up my soul.

<u>Return unto they rest O my soul.</u>

In the day when I cried thou answered me and strengthened me in my soul. Ps 138.3.
God is my help. The Lord is with them that restores my soul. Ps 54.4. Isa 41.18
Say unto my soul, I am thy salvation. Ps35.3. Ps 94.17.

<u>**My soul waits for the Lord more than they that watch for the morning**</u> Ps 130.6. Ps 42.1. Dt. 30.

Let my soul live and it shall praise thee! Ps. 119.175. Lk146.

My Eye *is on Thee*……..

Ps. 141.8. Ps 84.2. Isa. 26.9.

The Root of the Matter is Found in Me.

Is for the individuals, families, cultures, neighbors, communities, educators, artists, business/marketplace, legal entertainers, and government agencies/police and security services, the body of Christ, ministers of our God, nations and/or society at large and our world communities can use this biblical system in the privacy of one's own home and/or used as a training manual in any of the above avenues to help maintain and/or restore spiritual and natural condition and soundness of one's body, soul, spirit lives, relationships and environment by faith in Jesus Christ and Him crucified.

We live in a society still looking for the answers to solve and resolve the growing inhuman people concerns-such as homelessness, child, sex and/or people trafficking and other social and relational ills and deterioration of (the soul, body and spirit life and other questionable behaviors), injustices, hate crimes, etc. All of these biblical and spiritual concerns no matter the religion, non-religion and/or spirit belief systems reveal and reflect a society still in need of Jesus Chris. Why? Because all of life is some level of spirit life happening. Some however only desire to address life and its conditions and/or situations only on the physical level of spirit life and in doing so, often do not desire to hear any "spirit" variables in any equations of life, yet it "spirit life activity" is a part of every equation of life and living. Jn 6.63. Some use "laws" as their reason to avoid the topic. Any verbalized "spirit" concerns are to kept to church matters and/or arenas, otherwise any spirit topics are viewed more as discrepancies(inconsistent), discriminate(partial), discredited(with doubt), always irrelevant, considered almost ignorant or bias topics and are treated always as out-of-context if the word is mentioned. Yet, all of life and level of living is either a by-product, experience and/or condition and reflection of one's spirit life activity (seemingly based on what one is or is not doing and/or what is being done to others-with or without another's permission and in this case is being done or presented often behind the scenes-it's like certain aspects of spirit life (which also need to be addressed) has a monkey see, monkey-do tattoo attached to it as something that is just done), but not talked about based on one's spirit belief system & or practice-same thing (played out regarding another person or oneself) often regardless of one's religion and/or non-religious association(s). It's like regardless of one's religion, non-religion and/or spirit belief system, spirit life and it's activity is just happening and happening all around us continually and some are seemingly getting caught up in it, others are seemingly being pulled into it no matter the culture and/or whenever "spirit life activity" rises, is found and/or is being presented and its just being allowed to run through out all levels of society's arenas (whether government, education, media, church, industry and/or religious or non-religious community, etc., without being much questioned or hindered. OK, but why? This seems to give and/or imply the notion that all spirit life is and should be acceptable, but how could that be true? And if it's not true, why is all "spirit life activity" being accepted? I'm not trying to be too deep it's just all of society (including religions) seem to be living under this notion. Meaning, ITS NOT SEEMINGLY BEING BIBLICALLY AND/OR SPIRITUALLY CHALLENGED FOR GREATER UNDERSTANDING! The question is, why is that, if this notion is affecting and impacting our society (to the degree it is).

To date; it is recorded that there are approximately 40 to 60,000 spiritual rituals abuses a year!
Which seems to reveal statistically, the growing need to gain the biblical and spiritual ability, to not only deal but recognize what and now spirit life and spiritual kingdom activities are operating among us with a greater understanding that could produce a greater resolve regarding human rights and humanity within and without religions, non-religious and our so-called secular society regarding spirit life activity as a common denominator. In light of the biblical belief that there are only 2 spiritual

kingdom activities operating among us, no matter the religion, non-religion and/or spirit belief systems and how spirit life seems to come into play on every level of life and living not just in matters of religion, non-religion and/or spirit belief system and therefore can be measured in light of any justice system and should be. Otherwise, there will always be this ongoing loophole in our society where spiritual behavior and/or experiences are not measured in light of the many spiritual crimes rising among us, not being addressed or accounted for their operating above and/or beneath our legal system and civil laws. I understand that it is said we have freedom of religious expression in our nation but why are we allowing some religions to use their spirit activities to operate above and/or beneath our laws in that whatever one labels religion, we simply consider it a freedom of religious expression. OK. But why are we not judging or should I say excusing wrong religious practices (just because someone labels it a religious category) yet challenges our civil laws that is incumbent to protect its citizens.

The National Institute of Mental Health has released the following growing alarming statistics:

A science update, in April, 2006, reveals that a estimated 4.4. percent of adults, ages 18 – 44 in the United States suffer from a prevalence of attention deficit/hyperactivity symptoms.

> A mental Health, Press Release, in June, 2005, revealed that mental illness is also exacting a heavy toll on our youth; that all lifetime cases of mental illness begins by age 14. A December 10, 2002, Press Release tells us that psychiatric disorders are common among detained youth. Among teens in juvenile detention, nearly two thirds of boys and three quarters of girls have at least one psychiatric disorder, noted by a federally funded study.

Researchers are still trying to solve the schizophrenia dilemma. One of medicine's still most perplexing unsolved mysteries. Statistics from the NIMH reveal that mental disorders are common in the United States and internationally. Estimating 26.2. percent of Americans ages 18 and older about one in four adults suffer from a diagnosable mental disorder in a given year. A 2004 U.S. census on residential population....estimate about 1 in 17 suffer from a serious mental illness. Mental disorders are the leading cause of disability in the U.S. and Canada for ages 15-44. Many people suffer from more than one mental disorders at a given time. Nearly half (45 percent) of those with any mental disorders meet criteria for 2 or more disorders with severity strongly related to co-morbidity.

A science update, in August, 2007, say that gene variants implicated in schizophrenia interact to degrade the brain's ability to process information. Discovered by NIMH researchers. They say these interactions impair working memory information moment to moment. The researchers reveal that such thinking problems are a hallmark of this severe mental illness that affects about one percent of the population.

However, certain ministries reveal that almost every person who comes to them for deliverance is found to have a varying degrees of the network of demon spirits which they say, actually cause schizophrenia. Sounds like many could be engaged (on some spiritual level) with trafficking and channeling (with spirit) activity but none (or not many) realize how to release themselves from this (spirit life) activity whether realized or not, it is a "spirit life" activity and can and does affect people on many mind levels and can affect and/or cause schizophrenia. Ministries have also found schizophrenia to be a disturbance, distortion and disintegration of personality, which I believe scripture reveals very clearly that it is a work or dark spirit activity of the operation of darkness. Which continues to be overlooked, and often looked down on, creating a place and tolerance in which they are free to work.

I believe the spiritual realm continues to paint a real clear picture that our growing society's ills on many levels including our mental institutions, jails, juvenile detention and children being given medicine (some too much) in treatment, for adult symptoms and/or disorder (like Bi-polar), etc… ,reveals the degree that we could be looking in the wrong direction in looking for remedy for spiritual hindrances that can be biblically met by spiritual application of biblical truth and faith in Christ Jesus and Him crucified.

Ministry study reveals that the spirit personalities of rejection and rebellion help to create the schizophrenic personality and that schizophrenia (a control spirit) always begin with rejection, which tells me that spirits need to work through other people, to produce enough rejection to help bring a person to a "state" of schizophrenia. This tells me that we need to take a closer look at the environments that those with schizophrenia are coming out of, simply because scripture reveals that trouble does not spring out of the ground. Job 5.6. Especially considering the up-rise and growing number of mental illness and disease. Seemingly, it would seem like those being used by spirits of rejection, need just as much release and healing as the schizophrenia spirit fruit, they help cause to produce. In short, spirits can't effectively make someone crazy, without someone (perhaps your) help.

One author states that schizophrenia can be demonically inherited sins in the spirit realm that were not reconciled ancestrally before the relatives natural death. However the hereditary disease is not in the blood, nor is it in the genes. **It's in the demons.** Meaning, demons seek to perpetuate their like kind. Gen. 1. It is easier for demons to perpetuate themselves within a family (or in other consistent common meeting or gathering places). For example, the author says, suppose the schizophrenic mother feels rejection…the rejection within herself can possibly create problems in her relationship with the child. This then reveals that the child is opened for rejection by the mother's instability.

The point of rejection, like any other behavioral conditions, should be considered spiritual concerns or issues first. One biblical analysis for this reason that comes to mind regarding this statement is, can the body live without the spirit or can the spirit live without the body? James 2.26. Why wait till one's symptoms get to the schizophrenic level where study reveals that rejection and rebellion help to produce it. There is a need for people to learn soul, body and spirit maintenance (in Christ), with the understanding that everything in life needs to be maintained at some level (of effectiveness). Something to help lift the soul and spirit life without taking a drink or use drugs as a stimulant. Why not Jesus! There are only 2 spiritual kingdoms and spirit life activity happening among us. One can revive for good. The other spirit life activity is in need of healing and needs to be more spiritually healthily maintained and a more healthier spirit life condition could be found in Christ Jesus because of His sacrifice at Calvary. And usually everything else in the world worth anything, is maintained. Why should our spiritual lives be any different?

As a people of God, we must make room in our lives daily to allow the Lord to help us sustain, preserve and recover (if necessary) our spirit lives from many in our midst who may allow themselves to be used or have been snared by dark aggressive angel spirit activity (and of those in dark spirit professions) literally seizing the souls of men to bring them into spiritual bondage. Trafficking and/

or channeling spirits into a life could also cause and produce this spiritual bondage, and is biblically considered, a dark spirit life activity and part of the operation of darkness, which will eventually affect the mental, emotional and/or the body without continual and/or consistent release from dark spirit activity. Why? Because, dark spirits seek to perpetuate their kind. Why? Because there are 2 spiritual kingdom operations and activity, that have risen in our midst. <u>"The Spiritual Root of the Matter is Found in Me"</u>, is a biblical, godly method to help off-set dark spirit aggressive "power influences and/or defilement"; trafficking, channeling and trance seizes into the lives and souls of men. Mental disorders and illness is a real biblical work of dark angel spirit/demon activity and the operation of darkness . The condition of our society and statistics are proving it every day. We must deal with the spiritual, root of the matter, because spirits never die. If allowed to work with no resistance, dark spirits work consistently and endlessly to spiritually corrupt and degenerate the spiritual lives, souls of men and society itself. 2 Pet 2.19.

Demons and Deliverance, by H.A. Maxwell Whyte. Chpt. 7, pg.95; reveal that schizophrenia can be caused by demonic interference.

BOOKS

The following books are listed here more so, for their excellent content. Perhaps general remarks were used from some of the book references but not all listed here were used per se in this writing.

Dealing with Demons, by Selwyn Stevens, Ph.D. Published by Jubilee Resources, 2006.

Demonology Past & Present and Occult Bondage & Deliverance: both by Kurt E. Koch, A Christian Counselor.

Destroying the Works of Witchcraft through Fasting and Praying, By Ruth Brown, Copyright, 1994. Published by Impact Christian Books, Inc.

End Time Control, by Win Worley. Booklet #25. WRW Publications.

Evicting Demonic Intruders, by Noel & Phyl Gibson. Published by New Wine Press.

Hunted Houses, Ghosts & Demons by Roberts Liardon, Laguna Hills, CA 92654. Published by Albury Publishing, Tulsa OK, 74137.

Nelson's New Illustrated Bible Dictionary, Copyright, 1995, 1986, by Thomas Nelson Publisher.

Portals to Cleansing, by Dr. Henry Malone. 4th printing, 2006. Vision Life Publications, Box 153691. Irving, TX 75015.

Shadow Boxing, by Dr. Henry Malone, 2004. Vision Life Publications, Box 153691. Irving, TX 75015

Strongsman's Name, by Dr. Jerry & Carol Robeson. Publisher, by Whitaker House. New Kinsington, PA 15068.

Suggested Bible:

The Expositor's Study Bible, by Jimmy Swaggart. Published by Jimmy Swaggart Ministries, Baton Rouge, LA. 9th printing. 1-800-288-8350.

Suggested DVD movie and CD teaching:

"Fallen" and "The Hurricane", with Denzel Washington and John Goodman. Both can be ordered on line at www.amazon.com.

Suggested Teaching CD:

Seven Secret Snares, by Dr. Erwin W. Lutzer (On getting free from the devil's grip); reveals that there are approximately 40-60,000; Satanic spiritual ritual abuses a year!

Suggested Readings:

All of Rebecca Brown's books.

Katie Souza: Teachings on how the glory and light bring healing www.expected end ministries – get connected!

**Those need further assistance and/or a greater understanding of Multiple Personality Disorder (MPD/DID) Satanic Ritual Abuse (SRA) or Bi-Polar can be found at Righteous Acts Ministries website: www.ramministry.org. 1850.390.4104.

Those under a doctor's care should check with their physician first before proceeding by faith in this manual and, or use this manual in conjunction with medical care.

The Spiritual

Root of the Matter is Found in Me.

Daily or Weekly Journal Worksheet.
Things to remember or consider. Reminders or thoughts from the Lord. Ps 139.17-18.

Week 1

___

Week 2

___

Week 3

___

Week 4

___

Week 5 (or extra lines)

___

Copies can be made up as needed. Also, you could make a copy for each stronghold category or just use one form to make general notes.
Lord Ministry Services

Helping to turn spiritual tragedies into triumph.
2 Corin 2.14

Restore your people, one person at a time. One family at a time.

Once church at a time. One community at a time. One city at a time. One state at a time. Lord, restore our nation! Lord, restore our world communities. Lord, restore our land! In Jesus name we pray, as one in Christ and Him crucified for our sake, for the earth is the Lords and the fullness there of! Ps 24.1.

The revelation from this writing reveals that if we as a people, collectively, and individually learn how to release ourselves from spirit impurities, defilement and spirit violations of others that have been spiritually affected (including occult attacks against humanity); which is inclusive of our learning how to maintain our spirit lives and activity in Christ alone, then we would gain the ability to extend (our historically short-lived efforts towards) reformation and/or seasons of revival, in Jesus name. Eph 2.20. Eph 3.5.

We all have a creator. We all need a Savior.

Let us honor the King! Let us bless His holy name. Thank you Lord , again, for being mindful of us. We bless You! We thank You. We truly love You, Jesus!

GRACE FOR THE NATIONS. GRACE FOR SOCIETY. GRACE FOR YOU. Rev 1.4-6

Notes

Notes

Notes

CPSIA information can be obtained at www.ICGtesting.com
Printed in the USA
BVOW11s1826090715

408158BV00001B/3/P